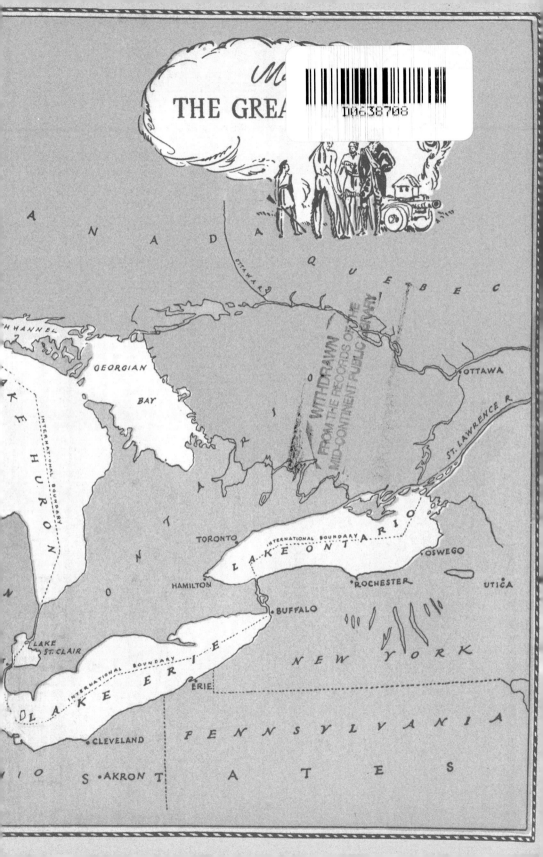

THE GREA[T]

A   N   A   D   A
Q   U   E   B   E   C

OTTAWA R.

OTTAWA

ST. LAWRENCE R.

GEORGIAN

BAY

NORTH HANNEL

LAKE HURON

INTERNATIONAL BOUNDARY

L   A   K   E   O   N   T   A   R   I   O

O   N   T   A   R   I   O

TORONTO

INTERNATIONAL BOUNDARY

OSWEGO

HAMILTON

ROCHESTER

UTICA

BUFFALO

LAKE
ST. CLAIR

N   E   W   Y   O   R   K

L   A   K   E   E   R   I   E

INTERNATIONAL BOUNDARY

ERIE

P   E   N   N   S   Y   L   V   A   N   I   A

CLEVELAND

IO   S   •AKRON T   A   T   E   S

The Third Coast

The Third Coast

Sailors, Strippers, Fishermen,
Folksingers, Long-Haired Ojibway Painters,
and God-Save-the-Queen Monarchists
of the **GREAT LAKES**

TED MCCLELLAND

CHICAGO
REVIEW
PRESS

Library of Congress Cataloging-in-Publication Data

McClelland, Ted.
  The Third coast : sailors, strippers, fishermen, folksingers, long-haired Ojibway painters, and God-save-the-Queen monarchists of the Great Lakes / Ted McClelland. — 1st ed.
      p. cm.
  ISBN-13: 978-1-55652-721-0
  ISBN-10: 1-55652-721-7
  1. Great Lakes Region (North America)—Description and travel. 2. McClelland, Ted—Travel—Great Lakes Region. 3. Great Lakes Region (North America)—Social life and customs. 4. Great Lakes Region (North America)—Biography—Anecdotes. 5. Great Lakes Region (North America)—History, Local. 6. Lake States—History, Local. 7. Ontario—History, Local. I. Title.

  F551.M38 2008
  917.704—dc22

                                        2007027101

www.tedmcclelland.com

Some of the material in this book was originally published in *Gapers Block*, the *Chicago Reader*, *True North*, and *Stop Smiling*.

Interior design: Jonathan Hahn
Interior images courtesy of the author
Great Lakes map on page x and endpapers from *Lake Michigan* by Milo M. Quaife (The Bobbs-Merrill Company, 1944)

© 2008 Edward McClelland
All rights reserved
First edition
Published by Chicago Review Press, Incorporated
814 North Franklin Street
Chicago, Illinois 60610
ISBN: 978-1-55652-721-0
Printed in the United States of America
5 4 3 2 1

To my parents, Robert J. and Gail A. Kleine

Contents

Acknowledgments

First and foremost, I want to thank Bill and Bonnie Rossberger, owners of 7726 North Eastlake Terrace, the Chicago six-flat where I wrote this book. Bill grew up near Lake Michigan, building his first (unseaworthy) boat at age ten. As a young man, he dreamed of living on Eastlake Terrace, which is closer to the lake than any street in Chicago, and owning a sailboat. He did both, even becoming commodore of the Chicago Corinthian Yacht Club. Bill also had a successful career as a salesman for Ryerson Steel, a subsidiary of Inland Steel, which built the *Joseph L. Block*. Our living room windows overlooked the water. I set up a table in front of mine, so I could look at the lake as I wrote. Bill set up a telescope in front of his, to watch passing freighters. "I look out on that lake every day," he told me. "It gets into your spirit." Living in Bill's building, I absorbed his love of the lake. It's one of the reasons I wrote *The Third Coast*.

Also in Chicago, I want to thank Rod Sellers, my guide to the East Side, and Ben Joravsky, who gave me a primer on "lakefront liberals" and the history of Lake View. Andrew Huff, publisher of the Web site Gapers Block, ran monthly installments from this book when it was a work in progress. Alison True of the *Chicago Reader*, J. C. Gabel of *Stop Smiling*, and Keith Gave of *True North* also ran excerpts.

It's not easy to leave home for three and a half months. David R. Kazak and his wife, Kristin, looked after my dog when I was on the road. Kathleen Schmidt took in my cat, and Eric Bremer sublet my apartment. Jennifer Leslie let me borrow her tent.

Cynthia Sherry at Chicago Review Press gave me the quickest green light in the history of publishing. I hadn't even finished the first sentence of my pitch when she said, "That's a great idea."

Most of those who helped me with this journey are mentioned in the book, but I'd like to give special thanks to Mitch Gerber,

Buffalonian-in-exile, who provided me with several introductions there, and proofread the upstate New York chapters.

For their early confidence, I'd like to thank the late Professor Stephen Dunning of the University of Michigan, as well as three editors: Kathryn Olney and David Beers of *Mother Jones*, who encouraged me to write about the Midwest, and Richard L. Manugian, who told me, simply, "You'll write books." This is one.

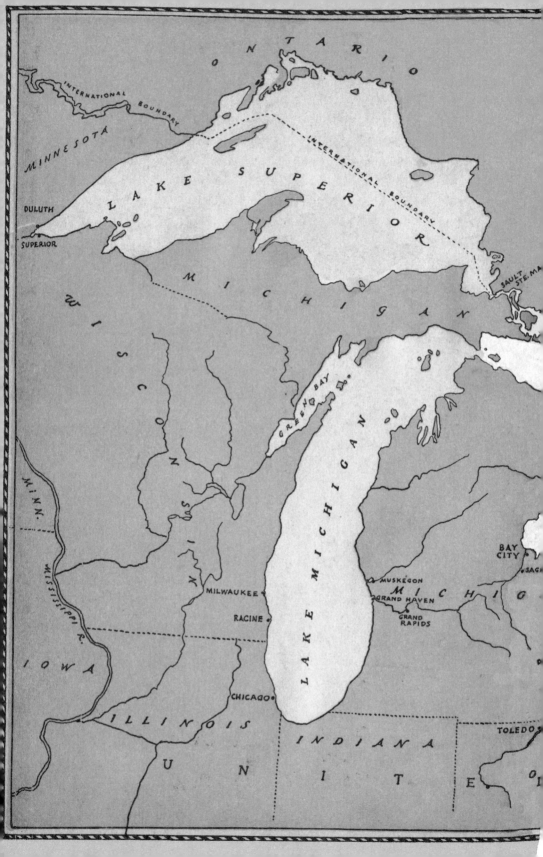

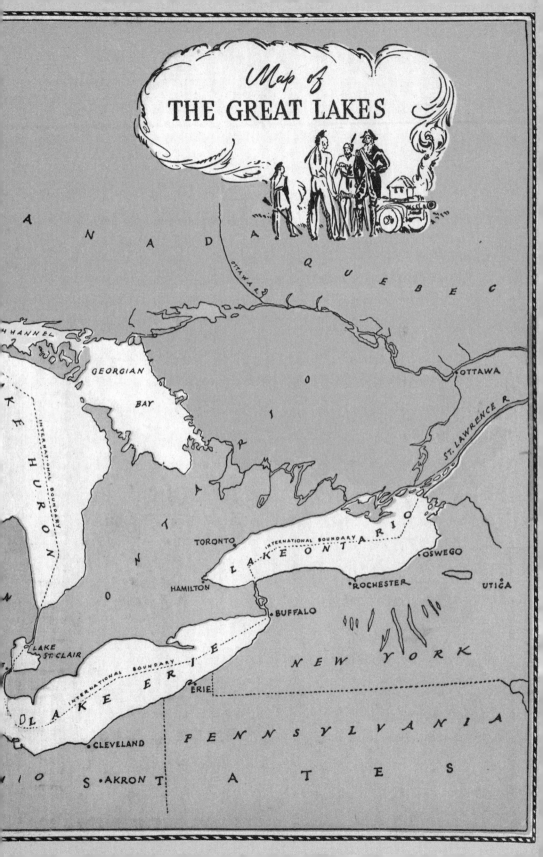

Introduction

first got the idea for this book over fifteen years ago. I was living in San Francisco, interning for *Mother Jones* magazine, but I'd left my heart on the Great Lakes. One day I was browsing in the City Lights bookstore when I came across *North Star Country*, by Meridel LeSueur. It was a history of the Upper Midwest, told through the stories of common people. Not long after, a book called *The Encyclopedia of Southern Culture* appeared in the magazine's office. As I paged through it, I wondered, "Why doesn't someone write an encyclopedia of *Northern* culture?" A book about hockey, and deer hunting, and *paczki*, the lardy doughnuts served in Polish bakeries the day before Lent. That summer I moved back to Michigan and tried to do it myself. I didn't get very far. I think I finished a chapter about ice fishing, and that was it.

In 2004, I decided to try again, because I was getting the feeling that the South was taking over the country. Wal-Mart was invading the city of Chicago, NASCAR had displaced hockey as America's fourth sport, and we hadn't had a genuine Northern president since Gerald R. Ford. A newspaper columnist, commenting on the spread of the word "y'all," wrote, "The North won the war, but is losing the peace." That was unacceptable. The pride that united Dixie into a nation-within-a-nation had to be countered with Northern pride.

The problem was that the North, as I saw it, is really divided between two countries: the United States and Canada. Growing up in Michigan, I'd always felt more in common with the people across the water in Ontario than with the people in, say, Alabama, or New Mexico. The first concert I ever attended was Rush, at Joe Louis Arena, a hockey rink in Detroit, right across the river from Windsor, Ontario. So many strands of Northern culture came together that night, as Americans and Canadians grooved on arena rock.

The Great Lakes are the North's most remarkable natural feature. In fact, they're one of the most remarkable natural features in the world. Only the polar ice caps hold more freshwater. Drained, they would cover the continental United States to a depth of nine-and-a-half feet. They generate their own weather, cooling the summers and sealing their port cities in snow each winter. Because they're as deep and broad as seas, they allow saltwater ships to sail a third of the way across North America. Since they contain a fifth of the world's drinking water, they'd be much harder to live without than the Himalayas, or the Sahara Desert, or even the Amazon rainforest. They also comprise a nation within North America, as surely as the South. I call it the Freshwater Nation.

My circle tour around the Great Lakes provided the framework for this book. In June 2005, I loaded the trunk of my Dodge Neon with a borrowed tent and an assortment of camping equipment: a backpack, a propane stove, an aluminum pot, heavy boots, an air mattress. I threw a bag of clothes on the backseat, and hung a safari blazer in the window, in case I had to meet anyone important. I had two cell phones, a sports watch, and a box of granola bars. There was a Great Lakes library on the floor—Ernest Hemingway and Francis Parkman made good campsite reading. I had sublet my apartment, and sent my dog to spend the summer with a friend in the suburbs. I had just quit my newspaper job. It was a kinda-sorta job: I never had to go into the office, and I was getting tired of working out of an empty house. Anyway, I had never considered myself the employee type.

Most other thirty-eight-year-olds had a job, and a marriage. If I couldn't settle down, like my peers, I could do something else, something open only to the wealthy, the indigent, and the restless: I could hit the road, for a season and then some. At 8:15 on a Wednesday morning, I drove out of Chicago. I wouldn't be back for 106 days. On my 9,600-mile journey, I drove clockwise around the five lakes, always keeping the water on my right. My route took me as far west as Duluth, Minnesota, as far east as Kingston, Ontario, as far north as an Ojibway reserve on Lake Superior. I never lost sight of the Great Lakes, or of the ways in which they shape the people who live along their shores.

1

East Side Stories

ILLINOIS—CHICAGO'S EAST SIDE; INDIANA—HOBART

The Great Lakes begin in Chicago, in a neighborhood known as the East Side, because it lies on the east bank of the Calumet River. The Calumet is an oily channel with concrete banks, running at ruled angles between pyramids of coal and snarls of scrap metal. The river sulks alongside the weedy ruins of steel mills. It oozes past monstrous Hulett shovels, whose iron jaws dip into ship holds, scarfing up seventeen tons of ore with one bite. It flows beneath the collapsible bridge the Blues Brothers jumped in their 1974 Dodge Monaco. This is as far as thousand-foot lake freighters and oceangoing "salties" can travel. A few miles upstream, next to a garbage heap punctured with natural gas wells, is a lock connecting the Calumet to a network of canals and rivers that drift down to the Mississippi. Only barges and pleasure boats can thread that needle.

The East Side is a remnant of the Rust Belt, populated by Croatians, Poles, and Mexicans. When the steel mills were still burning coal and melting ore, the nights glowed red and the mornings

1

A freighter steaming up the Calumet River.

sparkled with a metallic confetti of steel and graphite. In the after-noons, the soot was so heavy that steelworkers needed three shots of whiskey to wash it from their throats. Then, the Calumet was busy with freighters from Minnesota's Iron Range. Sailors roamed the neighborhood, passing out in bars and waking up in rooming hous-es. Peckerhead Kate ran a tavern where she greeted all her customers with that eponymous insult. The long-jawed Horseface Mary owned a flop where merchant seamen wintered over while the lakes were locked in ice.

Chicago always stowed its industry on the East Side, so the wealthier neighborhoods wouldn't have to smell the smoke. Now, Chicago hides its industrial decay there. The East Side is, literally, the city's flyover. It is bypassed by the Skyway, a toll road that walks across the neighborhood on hundred-foot-tall iron legs, hurrying motorists from northwest Indiana to the Loop. If they look down, they see blocks of brown bungalows, punctuated by steeples marking the loca-tion of St. Francis de Sales or Our Lady of Guadalupe—"OLG" to the Mexicans who began settling here in the 1920s.

The neighborhood's last foundry was extinguished in the early 1990s. Now, most days, you can see a ship flying a foreign flag, docked across from a cornmeal-colored wall that is all that remains of U.S. Steel. The East Side was once nicknamed "the Ruhr of America," but today, it's cheaper to import steel than to forge it here. That was why the *Neva Trader*, a Norwegian freighter with a Latvian crew, was docked in the Calumet, with fifty-nine-hundred tons of plate in its hold.

★ ★ ★

I first became fascinated with the East Side in 1996, when a newspaper hired me to help compile a database of Chicago's restaurants and nightclubs. Down on the East Side, I didn't find many nightclubs in the neighborhood, but as I walked the prosaically named streets—106th, Avenue O—I was taken home to Lansing, Michigan, the factory city where I'd grown up and gone to high school in the shadow of an auto plant.

I saw my first Great Lakes freighter near the mouth of the Calumet River. I'd led a friend on a biking expedition to this secret neighborhood. We were lounging on the beach when I caught sight of a dreadnought, looming offshore. Seven hundred feet long, it seemed ludicrously out of proportion on Lake Michigan—so dark, so angular, so Teutonically modernistic that it looked like a rusting sculpture on a public square.

"I'd love to get on one of those things," I said to my friend.

I pedaled to the river to watch it sail upstream, heard the gull-scattering horn blast that signaled the tender to unfold the bridge, watched the boat slide between banks, as snugly as a bolt in a lock, and waved to the sailors on deck. Jaded by quayside gawkers, they ignored me. As the bridge subsided, the ship displayed its stern, where its name and port were painted: *Fred R. White*, Wilmington, Del. Not exactly romantic. But I was hooked.

For a year afterward, I bugged a manager at the Illinois International Port. Most Chicagoans didn't even know we had a port, I argued, and if they did, they saw the fleet only as long, faded silhouettes, skating along the horizon. Finally, he relented. If it was OK with the captain of the *Neva Trader*, I could go aboard.

The *Neva Trader* is a salty, sturdy enough to cross the Atlantic, narrow enough to pass through the Saint Lawrence Seaway. Ever since the Seaway, connecting Lake Ontario to the Atlantic, opened in 1957, the Great Lakes have been the eighth sea, a blue-leaved branch of the ocean reaching into Middle America. There is no other place on Earth a vessel so vast can infiltrate a continent so deeply. The *Neva Trader* is shorter than a lake freighter, but taller, and more stylish: with a white apartment block in its stern, it looks like a barge hauling a piece of Bauhaus architecture.

Unloading a ship is a longshoreman's job, not a captain's, so Oleg Mitirevs had two free hours to show me the *Neva Trader*. Oleg was thirty-eight, but had the slender figure of a man ten years younger, and the bald pate of a man ten years older. These clashing characteristics gave him the spry authority you expect in naval officers. He also wore a blue military sweater, although it was late spring.

"Would you like to see the bridge?" he asked.

The bridge was five stories above the deck. Oleg ascended the steep metal steps at a lanky jog.

The *Neva Trader* had been commissioned in 1977, so its lime-and-chrome control panel looks like a Sears oven. On the desk were a chart of Calumet Harbor and a sextant, the instrument that guided Magellan around the world. If the global positioning system breaks down, sailors navigate by the stars.

It's common to see Eastern Europeans on salties. Sailing was an attractive career for men living under communism. You had to be away from home four months at a time, but at least you got to see the world beyond the Iron Curtain.

"Those times in Russia, nobody could go abroad, but seamen had this privilege," Mitirevs said. "A lot of people join just for this reason. When I was growing up, I read books about the sea, about pirates, sailing vessels of the eighteenth and nineteenth century. I'm never thinking about how much money I could make. I could see the world, go to different countries. The position here as master is pretty much what I imagined as a child. It's still pretty romantic."

I told the captain I'd be glad to take the crew downtown in my car. I wanted to see how sailors spent their shore leave. Perhaps they would go shopping tomorrow, Oleg said. Could I come back then? But when I returned the next afternoon, the captain had bad news.

"We went yesterday to downtown," he said. "We will have to leave that part out."

I was already back on the dock when I saw a sailor at the top of the stairway. He was wearing a loud tropical shirt, narrow sunglasses with a rubber strap dangling down his neck, baggy chinos, and a knapsack. Without a word, he descended the steps.

Fjodorov Jurijs wanted to go shopping.

Fjodorov, known to his shipmates as Yuri, left no port unvisited, anywhere in the world. Older, jaded sailors spent their evenings watching videos, or reading in their cabins, but Yuri's motto was "five day port, five day city." On the *Neva Trader's* first day in Chicago, he'd taken the train downtown (after wandering for two hours in search of a station) and found the Gap.

Yuri saw America as a giant mall. Video cameras, cell phones, athletic shoes, PlayStations, jewelry, perfume—they all cost half as much in Chicago as they would in Riga. He wanted to take home bags of gifts for his family. In the post-Communist world, *this* was the greatest perk of life at sea.

"Very small price, shirt, jeans," proclaimed Yuri as we walked to my car. He was a pink, robust man with a thinning crew cut. "My country, very big price."

Yuri asked me to take him to the closest shopping strip. That was Commercial Avenue, fifteen miles south of Macy's, and a hundred times more ghetto. Our first stop was Foot Locker. Yuri wanted to buy shoes for his wife, Ludmilla, and his sons, Dennis and Karoll.

"New Nike," he declared, pronouncing the name as one syllable. Striding into the street, he began telling me what he knew about

Chicago. He'd seen a lot of movies. On the ride down Lake Michigan, the captain had shown the crew *No Mercy*, a Richard Gere cop film. And back in Riga, Yuri had once run a video store.

As soon as we stepped out of the car, Yuri pointed at the emblem on the side of a police cruiser—four red stars between blue bands.

"Flag for Illinois?" he asked.

"Chicago," I said.

"Chee-cago!"

Yuri raised his arms, cocking his thumbs and forefingers. It's universal sign language for Chicago: the tommy gun. He pretended to spray the street with bullets as his lips vibrated at hummingbird speed.

"Russian movie, *Brothers Two*. Downtown Chee-cago, Mafia, gangsters!"

Yuri's English was limited, but he knew enough to discuss the important topics: food, women, movies, and brand-name products.

Yuri went into Foot Locker, where he began admiring a pair of workout pants. He wanted to buy them for his wife, but first he wanted to be sure they were the right size. He summoned a clerk.

"I want 103 centimeters," he explained. "How many centimeters is this?"

"I don't know centimeters," said the clerk, who was dressed like a basketball referee. "It's thirty-two inches."

Yuri didn't know inches, so he pulled an electronic Russian-English dictionary out of his knapsack. It had a metric conversion function. As Yuri calculated, a security guard appeared.

"They want to know what is the purpose of measuring this," the guard said flatly. "This is the women's section."

"Is for my wife."

"How *tall* is your wife?" the clerk asked.

In her exasperation, she did not speak slowly, as most people do with foreigners, but forcefully, as you would with a shy child.

Yuri held his hand up to his eyebrows.

"Why don't you try a medium?"

Yuri folded the pants over his arm. Now he needed some shoes for Ludmilla. He grabbed a cross trainer, and held it out to the clerk.

"You have European size 39?"

The clerk sagged. Her forehead dropped to her arm.

"I'm gonna be here all day measuring shoes. Hold on, let me go in the back and see if I can find out. Shirley, help me out here!"

Yuri settled on the pants and a shirt. He paid for them from a sheaf of twenty-dollar bills, and left the store distressed by the bad American service.

"Latvia, no problem shop," he concluded, heading out the door. "Very quick. Here, very slow. No size."

Yuri had to get back for his afternoon shift—as a member of the deck crew, he worked in port. While the ship's cranes swung steel coil onto the dock, Yuri inspected the rubber packing on the hatches, to make sure it was airtight. Sailors work four hours on, eight hours off, and Yuri wanted to hit Commercial Avenue again before closing time. So I killed the time chatting with an elderly longshoreman. He was a wiry black man, sixty-two, with a lightly salted moustache. This was the world's second-deadliest job, he boasted as a steel plate rappelled through the air, descending on us from eight stories up. Only miners had it worse.

"Everything's overhead," he said. "There's nowhere to go but down, and that's where you are. Just like when the mine caves in, there's nowhere to go."

★ ★ ★

Yuri had shucked his coveralls and showered, and was again pounding down the metal stairs in full resort casual. We had less than an hour before the prowler grates were drawn on Commercial.

Yuri finally found his "Nikes" in a hip-hop shoe boutique where the sneakers were heaped in chalky piles. I'm not using those quotation marks to mock his pronunciation. The uppers were stamped with backward swooshes. "Made in China" was printed inside the tongues.

They were twenty-five dollars a pair. After checking the lengths with a tape measure, Yuri bought shoes for his entire family. In Latvia, people might think they were the real thing, at least for the month they lasted.

Yuri could shop so ardently because, for a Latvian, he belongs to an elite profession. The average Latvian laborer earns two hundred dollars a month. The average Latvian sailor earns fifteen hundred. That's enough for Yuri to house his family in a fashionable Riga neighborhood. He explained this to me as we walked down Commercial in the graying evening, looking for a Mexican restaurant. He pulled out his Russian-English translator, so he could locate the right words for a sailor's story.

"My country, sailor, seaman—big money," he said.

The restaurant was nearly empty. A neon Tecate sign glowed in the window. A serape was pinned behind the counter. Sailing, Yuri said, after we'd ordered burritos, was not a life he wanted to lead forever. The long stretches at sea were lonely for a family man. But they were a family man's duty.

"Men work," he said, his shrug filling in the missing words of that spare sentence.

Besides the months away from home, there was the danger of shipwreck. A vessel as small as the *Neva Trader* was a toy to the North Atlantic. On its last voyage, a storm had swamped the decks. "This not cargo ship," Yuri thought. "This submarine."

Unlike his captain, he did not sail for love of the sea. He wanted money to start a business on land.

"I work, work, work, open a bar. My wife barmaid, experienced."

I know three Slavic words, all Polish. One I learned from a Kielbasa ad on Detroit TV. When the burritos came, I tried it out on Yuri.

"*Smaczna,*" I crooned, pressing a thumb and forefinger to my lips.

"*Smaczna!*" Yuri slapped the table. His face flushed pink to the peak of his crown, where the razor-stubbled hair began. It meant "tasty" in Latvian, too.

"You coming tomorrow?" Yuri asked.

The ship was sailing then, half-an-hour after the last plate settled on the dock. I told him I'd be there to see it off.

"You bring mug?"

Yuri bought a mug in every port he visited, but he'd been unable to find his souvenir on Commercial Avenue. So I'd promised to buy him one myself. The next day, just before his ship sailed, I presented him a mug with a wraparound Chicago skyline. In exchange, he gave me a postcard of Riga.

When the *Neva Trader* arrived in Chicago, it had wallowed in the river. Now, after losing twelve million pounds in three days, it balanced on its winnowed hull.

The captain paced the deck in Bermuda shorts. On the dock, forklifts loaded steel into a semitrailer. A minivan with Wisconsin plates arrived, and a bald, burly man emerged. This was the Great Lakes pilot, who would guide the *Neva Trader* to Duluth, where the ship was loading grain bound for Scotland. As he ascended to the bridge, the red-and-white "pilot on board" flag slid up the pole. The diesel engines sounded an underwater note, fathoms below the scale. The ship quivered like an idling truck, the smokestack exhaled rags of exhaust, a pipe vomited ballast.

Once the *Neva Trader* had coughed and hacked and cleared its innards, Yuri and his bosun climbed down the metal staircase to gather its rope railings. They coiled it, and lashed the stairs to the hull. The propeller, spun by fifty-six-hundred snorting horses, whipped the river to lather. One by one, the mooring lines slackened. The longshoremen slipped the nooses off their stays, and the lines were spooled on board, flopping and spraying like trophy fish. The ship sidled to mid-channel, then floated into the lake, as though freedom alone propelled it away from Chicago. The stern said "Neva Trader—Oslo," but ships don't really have homes, I thought. As restless as terns, or dolphins, or any other creature not bound to terra firma, they migrate from port to port. I looked up from the lettering, and there was Yuri, holding up the mug. I waved back, and turned toward land.

★ ★ ★

I met Oil Can Eddie at the Southeast Side Historical Museum in Calumet Park, a few blocks from the *Neva Trader*'s anchorage. If I wanted to know what had happened to the East Side's steel industry, the museum director said, Eddie's the man to talk to. That afternoon, he was sitting at the bullshitters' table, drinking coffee with a pair of retired steelworkers. White-haired, blunt-featured, his head looked as though it had been chipped off a statue and grafted to a 260-pound man. Eddie couldn't sit around and drink coffee all afternoon, so he gave me his card. That Saturday, he was going out to Indiana to teach some wet-behind-the-ears ironworkers about their blue-collar heritage. I was welcome to come along.

"But you're gonna have to be there at seven," he growled. "I can't wait around. If you fuck up, you fuck up. I'm not trying to be a drill sergeant. . . ."

Ed Sadlowski was a steel worker without a mill, a sloganeering, hymn-singing, street-marching, banner-waving, boss-hating labor captain without a union. Had he been born a generation earlier, he might have been a glowering counterpart to George Meany or John L. Lewis, exhorting the picket lines with his bullhorn, cussing out the Yale men across the negotiating table, condescending to bended-knee Machine pols who needed his legions on Election Day.

Eddie had made a bid for that power. In 1956, after the Army was through with him, he followed his father into Inland Steel. That was the heyday of factory life in the clanking industrial belt that girded the southern fringe of the Great Lakes, from Milwaukee, Wisconsin, to Hamilton, Ontario. He got the nickname "Oil Can Eddie" because, as a machine repairman, he walked around the mill all day, squirting oil, and talking union politics. At twenty-five, he was elected president of the ten-thousand-member Steelworkers Local 65. Ten years later, he ran for international president, as a reformer. Eddie was a charismatic figure, a young proletarian rebel with a Bobby Kennedy forelock and a leather jacket. *The Washington Post* called him "a new labor star," and *60 Minutes* filmed his rallies. Jane Fonda endorsed his campaign. Of course, he lost. Young Turks always lose. The old guys vote, and they don't like to be told it's the new generation's turn.

Chicago's steel mills have been torn down, so Oil Can Eddie was spending the twenty-first century as a member of the Illinois Labor Relations Board, caged behind a desk, stuffed inside a suit.

The next time I saw Eddie, it was 6:45 on a Saturday morning, and I was knocking on the door of his bungalow.

He answered the door in his underwear. "You're early," he muttered. The dining table was stacked with literature—union pamphlets, printouts from a left-wing Web site.

"Excuse the mess," Eddie said. He pulled on a pair of faded jeans with a grass stain on the knee, a windbreaker, and a Cubs cap. Swallowing a handful of pills with his unsweetened tea, he moaned about the state of his head and his belly.

"Ahh, I'm tired. I went to a fish fry in Northern Indiana. I was there half the night. That fish is still with me. That's always been a big thing—East Chicago, Northwest Indiana. For one hundred years, the staple was lake perch. Now it's so expensive, I don't know what they use."

In my Dodge Neon, we vaulted onto the Skyway. At U.S. Steel, in Gary, a flame wavered on a chimney's tip, and battle smoke swept into downtown, obscuring the dome of City Hall in a grainy haze. Indiana's Calumet Region—"Da Region" in the local urban patois—is linked to the East Side culturally, historically, and geographically. People cross the state line for church services, union meetings, fish fries, and Catholic schools.

"The common bond was the mills," Eddie said. "You went to high school, and they would have a recruiter from the mills, have a big assembly. Damn near everybody lived in South Chicago worked in that fuckin' mill. This used to be the biggest steel-making area in the world. From South Works in Chicago to Burns Harbor, Indiana, there were a hundred thousand steelworkers—now, there's maybe twenty thousand. It's horseshit. They took all the money they could out of it, and left nothing. That's what all industries do."

A school bus was parked in the lot of the Ironworkers Hall in Hobart. The apprentices were young men lanky in blue jeans and work boots, eating bleary breakfasts out of fast-food bags. When Eddie boarded the bus, they came to life.

"Today, we're going to go on a labor heritage tour." He stood in the aisle, and you could hear the union-hall orator who'd drawn in thousands of steelworkers, thirty years before. "That's the heritage that belongs to the working man in this country, and the working woman. That's an important part of your identity."

The bus took us back to Chicago, into the parking lot of a one-story brick building on Avenue O. It was a day care center, belonging to a local church, but it had once been a union hall. The new owners rented a meeting room to the aged remnants of Local 1033. This was a sacred site. Out on the sidewalk stood a monument shaped like a ten-horned menorah. Eddie told his students why it was there.

"Back in 1936, on May 26, there was a strike vote at Republic Steel"—he gestured across the street. You had to imagine the brick mill, the black sky. The land was back to prairie now, guarded by a snow fence hung with NO TRESPASSING warnings. "The company locked the gates. Four hundred workers were locked in, a couple thousand locked out. A rally was called for the thirtieth. Two thousand people marched to the gates, and fifty yards away, the police opened fire. They murdered ten men. The cops were saying a lot of them were communists, because they kept chanting 'CIO, CIO.'"

The names of the dead were cast on a brass plaque, as polyglot as a platoon in a World War II movie: Anderson, Causey, Francisco, Popovich, Handley, Jones, Reed, Tagliori, Tisdale, Rothmund.

Eddie led his gaggle inside, to the low-slung auditorium with the flag-flanked stage at the distant end. This was where the Christmas parties were held, where the sixteen-inch softball teams returned with their trophies, where tickets were sold for the big once-a-year night at Sox Park. As Eddie stood on the tile floor that had been crowded with a thousand steel-shank boots, his eyes focused on something in 1965.

"This was a booming hall when the mills were going," he said. "It was really an integral part of the community, more than just a sterile hall. You can raise your voice in a union hall. You can't argue in a bank, you can't argue in a church. Union hall, you have differences of opinion. It's OK. They used to serve great bakala here during the meetings."

"What's bakala?"

Eddie glared at the questioner.

"You never ate bakala? Some of youse are Polish and don't even know how to pronounce your name."

There was a stop in Pullman, the company town where, in 1894, striking workers rebelled against railcar builder George Pullman's paternalism. Then the bus dropped Eddie in front of a bakery, a block from his house.

"Get that associate's degree," he told the apprentices, before he stepped off. "There's a lot better things in life than being a carpenter or a millwright. There's a lot worse things, too. You are the salt of the earth. The smartest people I ever met were guys who ran cranes in the mill."

And then Oil Can Eddie was stamping down the sidewalk, broad shoulders clenched inside his bulging windbreaker.

2

Suburbia's Waiting Room

ILLINOIS — CHICAGO'S NORTH SIDE

I f the East Side is the museum of Chicago's past, Lake View is the chrysalis of its future. Lake View sits on a gentle curve of Lake Michigan, three miles north of downtown, but it is separated from the water by the green buffer of Lincoln Park, which has a marina, a golf course, and a crushed limestone running path burdened by the tread of aspiring marathoners. Inland are Lake Shore Drive, always congested at its Lake View exits, and a battlement of doorman apartment buildings that have hogged the good maritime views and charge their tenants a two-hundred-dollar premium for looking out the window.

On a spring evening, a group of fresh-faced ward heelers held their annual membership drive in a Lake View bar. Young Chicago Lakefront was the youth auxiliary of the local Democratic machine.

At your typical Chicago political meeting, burly truck drivers and asphalt rollers, who owe their jobs to party loyalty, sit on folding chairs in the back room of a ward office, eating Dunkin' Donuts while the alderman tells them who they'll be voting for in November. The machine is modeled on the Catholic Church—the mayor is the pope, the aldermen are bishops, the precinct captains are priests—and there is the same religious reverence for authority.

Not in Lake View. The president intercepted me at the door, slipping a fragile hand into my grip.

"Welcome," she said. "No, you don't have to pay the ten dollars. I've got you on the list. Why don't you come over here and sit down? Ted, this is Greg Holcomb. He works in the state senator's office. Can I get you anything to drink?"

I had wandered into a professional mixer. Everyone was wearing a glossy button-down Oxford; everyone gripped a beer bottle as though it were the handle that would keep them from tumbling out the door. They had political jobs, but they were *West Wing* types, all angling to be the next George Stephanopolous, or the next Rahm Emanuel, who had his own congressional seat, right here in Lake View.

A long arm waved from the bar. Matt Kooistra was a young man from a pious Dutch Reformed community in Iowa who'd moved to Chicago, announced he was gay, and then broken his family's heart by becoming a Democrat.

Matt handed me a business card. He was a spokesman for the governor now. In Lake View, coming out is good for your political career. It contains the city's gay ghetto, known as Boys Town. Boys Town throws a Pride Parade every summer. The mayor has marched. The mayor loves gays. They keep up their houses and never move to the suburbs "for the schools." Even the alderman, Tom Tunney, was gay. He was sitting a few stools over. I sidled down and asked him for an interview. The alderman stared at me evenly as I made my pitch—he had fifty-five-thousand constituents calling his office, all the time.

"Call my scheduler," he said, turning back to his beer.

Greg, the senatorial aide, was waving a sheaf of tickets.

"The state senator is in Springfield next Tuesday, so he's donated his Cubs tickets." The whole bar was paying attention now. In Lake View seeing the Cubs is a social coup akin to going to the opera in

Gilded Age New York. "I've got four tickets for anyone who can tell me what the 24th Amendment says."

All around me, the bidding was desperate.

"Prohibition!" "Women's suffrage!"

I decided to rattle off every amendment I could think of. As a high school quiz bowl dork, I'd once read the entire Constitution.

"Poll tax!" I stabbed.

That was it. Greg came down from the bar and handed me the tickets. I felt guilty about winning, so I passed out the spares to the people standing closest.

"See you next Tuesday," I told them. "Meet me at the Harry Caray statue."

★ ★ ★

Only one Young Democrat showed up. Joe Lambert had gotten the afternoon off from his job at a consulting company that installs sales tax software for businesses. He walked off the "L," shouldering the same backpack he'd worn as a Michigan State business major less than a year before.

A sudden cloudburst chased us into the stadium. By the time it cleared, the groundskeepers were dragging their huge plastic handkerchief across the sodden infield. "We'll just come back next week," I said.

Joe and I lined up at the information booth for our rain checks. A tired clerk glared at our presumption.

"We can't give out rain checks," he said.

"You can't give out rain checks?" I said. "The game was rained out."

"We're sold out all season. If you want a refund, you'll have to mail the ticket to the address on the back."

Since there wasn't going to be a ballgame, Joe and I walked to a bar around the corner from his apartment. It was the University of Iowa bar. The Big Ten rivalries have contracted into these five blocks of Chicago. We ordered pints of microbrew, and Joe told me about his hometown, Houghton Lake, Michigan, a blue-collar resort for autoworkers who want to spend a weekend Up North, but can't afford a Lake Michigan cottage. Lake View has been colonized by so many Michiganders it's sometimes called "Michago." The ambitious migrants have driven the working-class Chicago natives off the lakefront.

"I think there's a lot of people around here who are kind of small-town, small-town Iowa and Michigan and Indiana," Joe said. "This is their big break."

In the big city, it is possible to live on a block more homogenous than any small town. That's Lake View. Not only is it segregated by race—almost everyone is white—it is segregated by age, too. Rarely do you see anyone younger than twenty-two or older than thirty-five. If Florida is God's Waiting Room, Lake View is suburbia's.

"I know a lot of kids who are just passing through," Joe said. "There's a lot of people I've met who kind of have the attitude, 'You're not going to live in the city forever. What if you have kids?' Honestly, there are not many families here. Most of the people in my building are young single people like me. Some as old as twenty-seven. I know one guy who moved to Denver, he was twenty-six, twenty-seven, he was starting to think about the next phase of his life. This area, it's intensely individualistic, and everyone's moving on to the next thing."

Joe shared a twenty-three-hundred-dollar apartment with a project manager for a credit card company and a woman who had just finished graduate work at Harvard. They were both twenty-seven, at the venerable end of the Lake View lifespan. The living room's centerpiece was a forty-seven-inch high definition television. Netflix sleeves flopped over the top. An Xbox was umbilically linked to the control panel. The shelves were crammed with DVDs, as glossily colored as the spines of anime comics.

"I busted my ass all summer to buy a TV," Joe said. "I worked two jobs in East Lansing."

The books were in the bedroom. He'd been reading *America: The Book*, *Bill Clinton: My Life*, the *Che Guevara Reader*, *Animal Farm*, and a few novels by Chuck Palahniuk. Dangling from a nail next to the bookcase was a VIP pass to a John Kerry rally. I asked why there were so many Young Democrats in Lake View, when everyone here was white, well educated, and rich.

"I think there are two things," he said. "Gay rights and abortion. I think they would be the two things that would get people off their ass, especially with Boys Town, and with the young women culture, they're intensely pro-choice. They're not ready to settle down."

★ ★ ★

The alderman would see me at one o'clock. I waited in his lobby, feeling starched in my best blazer and slacks. That was how politicians dressed. My own alderman was paunchy and jowly, always parted his hair, and never wore anything racier than chinos. Tom Tunney elbowed into the office five minutes late, wearing a blue sport shirt with a garish orange stripe, jeans, and zippy running shoes. His unkempt hair had receded far up his carroty Irish face. He represented a prosperous ward. He didn't need to impress City Hall with a suit.

Before he became an alderman, Tunney had owned a chain of Swedish restaurants. He ran his office like a Saturday-night kitchen. It was the only way to operate the most crowded corner of the city. As he walked back to his sanctuary, paper coffee cup in the fore, he was intercepted by frantic aides.

"I got a call from the elementary school. They say they need a pickup zone in the morning and the afternoon."

"We need to work on a date for the Jimmy Buffet concert in Wrigley Field."

"OK. We'll do that this afternoon. I'm going to be in a *meeting here!*"

I'm afraid my questions for Tunney would have been better posed to a senator than an alderman. As the first gay alderman, he was a civil rights symbol. As Lake View's alderman, he was preoccupied with street parking and baseball. In Chicago, the Lakefront Liberal is a well-known political creature. I had a theory about port cities. Anyone could wash ashore, so you learned to accept all sorts of people. Tunney shrugged.

"Sure. Places on water attract industry, they attract immigrants. That leads to big cities, and big cities are more open to different people."

He did have a smaller theory, about his own ward. When he was a young man, in the early 1980s, everyone wanted to move to New York or San Francisco. Chicago was a stolid Midwestern burg, about as lively as Kansas City. Then AIDS struck the saltwater coasts, and Chicago didn't look so bad. Tunney took a job in a hotel and settled into the gay enclave by the lake. Back then, when urban America was at its ebb, nobody with money wanted to live in Lake View. Gays are always the outriders of a bourgeois white invasion. When gays move onto a block, black folks look at each other and say "Uh-oh, here comes the neighborhood." If the pink canary doesn't die or get mugged, artsy kids edge in, then young professionals, then families, who stay at least until the kids are ready for kindergarten. A sociologist once found a correlation between a city's gay population and its high-tech industry. The white-collar kids, in league with the gays, had gentrified Lake View from a funky enclave of hippies, actors, Mexicans, and old German immigrants to what it is today: the most tolerant, least diverse neighborhood on the Third Coast.

"In twenty-five years," Tunney predicted, "the entire city is going to look like this. It's going to be Manhattanized. There's nothing anyone can do about it. There's too much demand for land in the city."

"Then where will the poor people live?" I asked.

"In the suburbs," he said.

★ ★ ★

Lake View's land may belong to the rich, but the poor still come for its water. Every warm day, they fish in Montrose Harbor. They buy their worms from Willie Greene.

Nearing eighty, Willie is still hale enough, and crusty enough, to putter around the bait shop he's owned since the 1950s. His daughter runs the store now, but all the fishermen want to see Willie. On a sunny day, the lakefront melange of Bosnians, Mexicans, metrosexuals, and old retired farts lines up at the counter for minnows. Willie doesn't have time to talk then. You had to catch him when it rained.

Willie was in his wood-paneled office, a room with handwritten records of old pheasant hunts tacked to the walls. A pinkish man in a sagging Norwegian sweater and a nylon vest, he was cutting up a plateful of bacon and waffles. He'd answer questions between mouthfuls. When you've owned a fishing shack for fifty years, you get used to doing things on your own time.

Willie had caught the fishing bug early. When he was in grade school, he spent his mornings on the horseshoe pier. "I knew there wasn't gonna be anything special until one or two in the afternoon, so I slipped out."

The Depression was still on then. What's bad for business is good for angling. The harbor was crowded with men fishing for their supper. The regulars had nicknames out of a Nelson Algren novel: Harry the Jap, Diversey Shorty, Coffee George, Uncle Henry. They adopted Willie as a mascot, and warned him when his mother was looking for her truant son.

"This Uncle Henry, he sort of took me under his wing," Willie said. "He was kind of a character. He used to say 'Willie live or Willie die?' Before the Depression set in, he had been an executive of a food chain on the East Coast. He ended up out here with the other guys. Didn't give a shit whether he worked or not."

After he got out of the Navy, in 1949, Willie sold bait on Montrose Avenue, when the street was still the Great White Way for night crawlers and maggots. Eight years later, he bought the park bait shop. It was just a concession stand then, but Willie built the shed with the five-thousand-gallon minnow tank in the back, and the come-on "Nightcrawlers, Redworms, Minnows, Coho Bait Tackle, Coffee" on the front entrance.

It was an era when Chicagoans were still in touch with their rural or Old World traditions. They'd grown up fishing in Mississippi, or in Poland, and they were looking for a honey hole they could reach by streetcar. Back then, the spring smelt run was televised, and "the whole lakefront was lit up with Coleman lanterns." Those bait shops are all gone. Only Willie is left, and he isn't doing nearly as much business as he'd used to. In an irony of Chicago life, the people who lived by Montrose Harbor were the people least likely to fish in it.

"A guy, if he doesn't have a job, he can spend a day fishing and not spend any money," Willie said. "It's a Depression business. This neighborhood don't do me any good for that reason. In the '90s, I was starving to death. Marine Drive, Lake Shore Drive, big buildings like that, they don't produce the people who fish. They don't have the time. They have the money and resources to do other things. They may own a place at Lake Geneva. But they're not the ones that do the fishing."

There's no longer a beach bus, either, so the fishermen can't park for all the soccer players and rollerbladers crowding the lakefront.

"They're trying to put ten pounds of shit in a five-pound bag," Willie grumbled. "There's more people involved with the park than the lake, because the people that want to do the fishing, they can't park."

Willie walked me to the door. On one side was a photo of a crowded pier, taken in the 1950s. It looks like a fishing derby, so many men are dipping their bamboo poles into the lake. On the other side is Willie's motto: "The Time Man Takes Off To Go Fishing Is Not Charged Against His Allotted Time On Earth." If that's true, Willie should last another fifty years.

"It's a good thing you came on a rainy day," he told me, as I was dismissed. "If you'd come when it was sunny out, I wouldn't have had time to talk to you."

★ ★ ★

The next time I stopped in, it was a clear day for fishing. I am a hapless angler. When I discovered the Park Bait Shop, it had been nearly twenty years since I'd caught a fish without professional help. Fishing wasn't part of my upbringing. My father had given up the sport as soon as I graduated from Indian Guides, and let his tackle—ovoid sinkers, snarled yellowish line—molder in a cupboard of our garage. Since coming of age, I've fished the Grand River, the Looking Glass, the Sangamon, the Vermilion, Lake Michigan, and Busse Lake. For all that effort, I've caught a six-inch-long sunfish.

Willie tried to complete my education. He tied a pink thread around my line, to regulate the height of my bobber, and told me where the fish might be biting.

"The fishing hasn't been good since that storm last Friday," he said. "That storm whipped everything up. There's dirt all over the place. Go to the south side of the harbor. They're catching perch over there."

The Park Bait Shop faces toward the lake, away from the highrises. Willie sees no reason why a Chicagoan can't lead a complete outdoor life. This isn't New York City. The door was open to the spring, and as we were talking, something out there caught Willie's eye. He led me to the threshold and pointed out a flock of geese, black punctuation marks against the sky.

"Look at that," he said. "The first geese of the year. Are they settling down there?"

The geese dipped out of sight, below the land line.

"They're gonna settle in," Willie said with satisfaction, "and start pairing off."

★ ★ ★

"You catching anything?" I asked two Mexicans as I walked around the horseshoe pier, carrying my pole and my night crawlers to a spot near the harbor entrance.

"Just gobies," one said. "We caught about a dozen gobies. We threw them all back."

"You can't eat gobies," I agreed.

"There's a guy out here who does. He makes goby soup."

Pheh. The goby is a blunt, chubby fish native to the Baltic Sea. An invasive species, gobies have as much business in the Great Lakes as white people have in North America. They arrived here in the ballast holds of oceangoing ships around 1990, and are ruining the harbor for decent, hardworking fish, like perch and salmon.

Overhead, the jets flying into O'Hare looked like Northern pike. The harbor was pebbled green glass. On my third or fourth cast, my line began to quiver like a banjo string. Something was noshing on my worm. This had happened before, but every time I reeled in my line, there was an empty hook at the end. This time, I was patient. I walked back and forth along the breakwater, letting whatever was down there swim after my hook. The line never stopped pulsing. I cranked my reel. As the sinker broke the water, I looked down and saw a fish. My first fish in twenty years.

It was a goby. Catching a goby doesn't even count as catching a fish. It's like winning a free ticket in the Instant Lottery. Some wildlife biologists urge fishermen to stomp gobies to death. I was not that bitter. I unhooked him and threw him back. I've heard gobies eat zebra mussels—another invasive species—so they're not all bad.

A while later, a pair of nuns stopped to watch me fish. Sister Alba and Sister Maria Joseph belonged to the Little Sisters of the Poor. In their white habits, they looked like cloistered Muslim wives.

"Jesus's first disciples were fishermen, weren't they?" I asked Sister Maria Joseph.

"They certainly were," she said. "Thomas and Peter."

"Why do you think he chose fishermen?"

"Well, they were docile. They were open to the word of God. Fishermen were poor, common people."

"That's the way it is here. A lot of immigrants come and fish for their supper. Did the apostles go back to fishing after Jesus died?"

"No, they became preachers. Fishers of men."

"How did they support themselves?"

"Well," Sister Maria Joseph said. "When you do God's work, God always provides."

My score for that afternoon was one goby, one religious lesson. As I made my way back to the bait shop, to replace the snagged hook that ended my day on the water, I saw a man fishing with a line wound around a Coca-Cola can.

"Do you catch anything with that?" I asked.

"Just . . . " He held his fingers a few inches apart.

"Gobies?"

"Yeah, gobies."

3

The Drunkest City in America

WISCONSIN—MILWAUKEE

When I think of Milwaukee, I think of beer, bowling, hot ham and rolls, and Polish barmaids. So really, there's no reason to go anywhere else but the Holler House. It has all four.

The Holler House is decaying along with the rest of Milwaukee's south side, a neighborhood of working-class frame houses and graveyards. A tavern is an essential adornment to any Milwaukee street corner. In classic urban fashion, Holler House's facade advertises a far less friendly welcome than its inhabitants provide. It's in a weathered old wooden building. The final *e* is missing from the word "House," and a hand-lettered placard warns strangers that there's "No Public Restroom." Push open the windowless door, and you'll find a barroom with brassieres dangling from the ceiling fans. A sinkless men's room, labeled *Chlop* in Polish. But what's in the basement makes Holler House a living museum of all things white, ethnic, and urban: a bowling alley. Two sloping lanes, built of planks laid down in 1908, carrying balls toward a cage where a pin boy gathers up whatever the beery, smoky bowlers knock down.

There used to be a Holler House in every German or Slavic ghetto on the Third Coast. Its alley is the oldest certified bowling lane in the United States. After World War II, everyone in south Milwaukee bought a car and started driving out of the neighborhood to multiplex alleys with twenty-four lanes and automatic scoring. But the Holler House hung on, thanks to the stubborness of its owner, Marcy Skoronski. Marcy moved into the apartment behind the bar in 1952, when she was a twenty-six-year-old bride sharing the space with her husband, Gene. He is dead now, but Marcy is still behind the bar, even though eighty years have squashed her to four-foot-ten, and she can barely see over the bottles.

I went to Holler House on a Sunday afternoon. The second-shift bowling league was clattering downstairs. Marcy and her daughter Cathy were in the kitchen between the bar and the apartment, fixing a turkey dinner for the patrons. During Marcy's break, she told me the bar's history.

"I gotta sit down, 'cause I got a hangover," she said, flumfing into a chair next to the out-of-tune piano. "We were open till 2:30 last night."

Holler House started life as Skoronski's. Its founder, "Iron Mike" Skoronski, was Marcy's father-in-law. A short but powerful man, Iron Mike possessed a handshake that squeezed thirty-year-olds into submission. After Mike died, the tavern was called Gene and Marcy's, a name that still lights up the window in green neon. But it was dubbed Holler House by a German woman who couldn't believe the racket inside.

Marcy has had more than one offer to leave Milwaukee. After Gene died, she bought a condo in Arizona, but decided "that's for old people." A man from Ohio courted her, "but he lived in the boonies, with the trees and the squirrels. I didn't want none of that."

She has made only one concession to age: she stopped drinking beer.

"I can't drink beer," she said. "I drink wine. Years ago, I drank gin rickeys. I used to carry my own lime, 'cause not all the bars had fresh limes. I'd carry a lime and a knife."

I told Marcy I'd tried to order a lime rickey at Gibson's Steak House, a Chicago restaurant famous for its celebrity clientele. The waiter had looked startled. "No one's asked for that in twenty years," he'd said.

"Oh, for God's sake!" Marcy sputtered. "It's nothing but gin and lime and seltzer!"

Marcy slid off her chair and shouted at her son-in-law, who was tending bar.

"Todd! Make this guy a gin rickey!"

I carried the cocktail down to the basement, to watch the bowling. Earl Anthony once bowled at Holler House. He didn't come here to pump up his average. The lanes slope inward. The planks are real wood, not synthetic. They're oiled with a spray can, not a computerized roller. There hasn't been a 300 game here since the New Deal was still a new deal. Weekend bowlers lose twenty pins off their average. It's also hard to find a pair of shoes that fit. The Florsheim disaster area under the stairs is assembled of castoffs from dead bowlers and moving sales.

"A common expression here is 'Only at the Holler House,'" a bowler said. "You'll have one or two pins here where every other place has a strike. I've seen a lot of 200 bowlers on their hands and knees here. It's real. Nothing sterile. The other day, the pin boy had to wipe up water because the roof was leaking."

To see the pin boy in action, I walked along the rubber mats in the gutters, then slithered under the pinsetting machine on my belly. Twelve-year-old Alex Frank was jumping from lane to lane, scooping up fallen pins, restocking the racks, yanking a wire that lowered them into place, and rolling the ball back to the bowlers on a wooden track. For this, he got thirty dollars a day, plus tips. After knocking over the pins, the balls plumped against a leather pad at twelve miles an hour, but Alex professed not to be afraid, even though he was once nailed in the ankle with a flying pin. In his frantic dance, he sometimes lost track of whether a bowler was on his first or second ball, but when he made a mistake, he always heard about it from the other end of the basement.

"They tell me which pin to put down," Alex said. "I like it when it's a strike. It's easy to figure out where it all goes."

Up in the bar, Marcy was serving dinner—a Thanksgiving buffet of turkey, mashed potatoes, creamed corn, stuffing, and cranberries, even though this was the first Sunday in April. After everyone had sopped up the last puddle of gravy, Marcy and Cathy reminisced about the celebrities who'd visited Holler House.

"Joe Walsh from the Eagles came here," Cathy said proudly. "Lazer 103, the rock station in town, they wanted to do a party for him here. I called my mom and I said, 'Who's down there?' She said 'Some scuzzy guy in a pink limousine.' 'What's his name?' 'Joe Walsh.' 'Joe Walsh from the Eagles?' 'I don't know.' I took off from work to come see him."

Cathy turned to her mother.

"Who was the porn star that was here?" she asked.

"Traci Lords," Marcy said.

"Traci Lords is a nice girl."

"Oh, yeah," Marcy agreed, remembering her visit during the filming of an indie comedy called *Chump Change*. "Very pretty girl. She started when she was fifteen. If I'd known then what I know now, I'd'a' become a porn queen. I wouldn't have become a slut, but a, what do you call it?"

"Woman of the world?" I offered.

"Yes. That's it."

And then there was Frank Deford, the dapper *Sports Illustrated* writer who stopped by Holler House on a nationwide bowling alley tour. He interviewed Marcy for an hour, then used the quotes she gave him during the two hours of drinking afterward. But she wasn't bitter about that reporter's trick. She still keeps a softening copy of the magazine behind the bar.

"It was the Super Bowl issue," she said. "John Elway was on the cover. I got more ink than he did, and I don't even play football."

★ ★ ★

The Germans failed to conquer Britain, Russia, and Africa, but they did get Milwaukee. It was once nicknamed "the German Athens," and a journalist remarked that "Germany seems to have lost all its foreign possessions with the exception of Milwaukee, St. Louis, and Cincinnati." Wisconsin's German settlers were either farmers who found the state's climate and soil similar to the Fatherland's or they were radicals fleeing the revolution of 1848. As a result, Milwaukee became the largest city with a socialist mayor. I once asked a political science professor how Wisconsin could elect both the enlightened progressive Robert La Follette Sr. and the troglodyte red-baiter Joseph McCarthy. Germans, he explained. They loved good government as passionately as they hated Russians.

Milwaukee's German identity survived both World War I and Prohibition. Its most historic restaurant is Mader's—here you can sit at the table where Gerald Ford dined during his presidential campaign. Milwaukee is an ethnic neighborhood inhabiting the body of a metropolis. Downtown is as lifeless as Grand Rapids, or South Bend, but beyond, there's a tavern every other block. Ninety miles up the shore from Chicago, Milwaukee will always be the Second City's second city. Lew Alcindor began his professional basketball career here. After winning a championship with the Bucks, he changed his name to Kareem Abdul-Jabbar and demanded a trade. The city did not meet his "cultural needs" as a jazz fan, a history buff, and a Muslim. On the other hand, Henry Aaron, a more homespun personality, remembered the Braves' years in Milwaukee as the happiest of his career.

★ ★ ★

Milwaukee is not for sophisticates; it's for beer drinkers. In a recent survey, it was named "the Drunkest City in America." Most of that thirst is satisfied by the Miller Brewing Company, which has its headquarters on the west side of town, in the same industrial area as the

Harley-Davidson plant. Only in Wisconsin do beer and motorcycles make good neighbors. Miller High Life competes with milk for the title of state beverage. Down at the beach, you can buy a cold one from the ice cream stand. Wisconsin was the last state to raise its drinking age to twenty-one, doing so only after Washington threatened to cut off its highway money. When *The Onion* was still published in Madison, its page 3 pinup was a "Drunk of the Week."

The Miller tour is rightly renowned as the most entertaining in North America. Not because the brewery is so fascinating, but because the one-hour walk ends in a tavern, where free samples are dispensed. Only the U.S. Mint could offer an equal enticement, and I'm told its parting gift is a bag of shredded singles. Miller's is one of the few tours where you get carded at the gate. Children are welcome—it's important to whet their appetite for this pleasure of adulthood, so they can get puke-drunk on their twenty-first birthdays—but they can't wear the coveted wristband.

The tour began with a movie. I got in line behind a man with a T-shirt from the Spam factory, in Minnesota. He took a lot of pop-culture food tours.

"They were giving out free samples after that one," he said. "Spam with pretzels. Nobody wanted it."

Jonathan, our tour guide, was young and blonde. He exuded a John Denver wholesomeness.

"Good afternoon," Jonathan burbled.

We weren't ready to raise our voices yet. Class had just started. Our refreshments hadn't arrived. We mumbled "good afternoon."

"C'mon, let me hear some more enthusiasm," Jonathan shouted. He was a male cheerleader for *b-e-e-r*.

From the film, I learned one memorable fact: Milwaukee became a fountain of beer not just because of its German émigrés—they'd settled the entire Midwest—but because it is located next to a Great Lake. Put Germans next to source of fresh water, and they'll start growing hops and barley to ferment in it. When you drink a Miller, you're not just drinking the champagne of beers, you're drinking Lake

Michigan, too. The Great Lakes are also the number one ingredient in Stroh's Beer, from Detroit, and Molson, brewed near Toronto.

The lights went up.

"OK, what time is it?" Jonathan prodded.

"Miller Time!" we shouted, like a game show audience ready to be wowed by the big prize.

Before we could drink the beer, we had to look at it. The Milwaukee plant generates 500,000 cases a day. Its warehouse was a golden metropolis of beer. We stood on a balcony, looking down on pallets of Lite, MGD, High Life, Leinenkugel's, and Milwaukee's Best, stacked as high as the tines of a forklift could reach, and laid out like city blocks. It was ephemeral: within twenty-four hours, all the beer before us would be trucked away to groceries and party stores from Fargo, North Dakota, to Columbus, Ohio. This was a day's drinking for the Great Lakes region. Everyone had to pitch in. At a conservative rate of consumption—one six pack per day—it would take a lone tippler four thousand years to drink all this beer. And once he got that old, and that drunk, he'd probably be getting up a dozen times a night.

Next, we had to smell the beer. The climb to the fermenting room was forty-six steps, the weather inside eighty-five and humid. That was enough to make anyone thirsty. Inside, pressurized vats exuded a cereal odor of mashed hops and barley. It was a heartland aroma, one I recognized from the Kellogg's plant, in Battle Creek, Michigan, and the Staley mill, in Decatur, Illinois. Beer is a classic Midwestern staple, like corn, or Wheatana.

Finally, it was time to drink. In the tavern, Miller's beermaids seated us at round tables. They set out airplane-size packets of pretzels to soak up the alcohol. We'd been promised three samples. I was expecting shot glasses—small tumblers, at the most. But instead the barmaids came bearing hefty mugs laced between their fingers. Free. Mugs. Of. Beer. Tom T. Hall would have driven all the way from Nashville for this.

It was 2:00 in the afternoon. I hadn't eaten lunch, so I would have to drink my way through the free samples on an empty stomach. A real brauhaus would have provided sausages and smoked meats to absorb the alcohol and inspire a thirst for more. The first course was Miller Lite. That goes through a real beer drinker like ginger ale, but I'm a two-drink-maximum lightweight. A Miller Genuine Draft followed. Once I chugged the third course—a Leinenkugel's—I was quite buzzed. At that point, all the beer was gone, and there was nowhere to go but my car.

Stepping onto the sidewalk, I felt as though gravity had been turned down a notch. On a viaduct, the words "Miller Time" appeared at a skewed, plunging angle, as though filmed by an unsteady video camera. I got into my car, intending to drive only a few blocks in this out-of-body state—just until I found a diner or an authentic German restaurant. But the West Side offers nothing except U-Haul rentals, neon dry cleaners, and cottage-industry sweatshops with chrome lettering over the doors. Before I knew it, I'd been swept onto Interstate 43. Above the first exit was an Iron Skillet Truck Stop. There is nothing Wisconsin about an Iron Skillet. It does not serve potato pancakes, or hot ham and rolls. It is designed to make big-rig drivers from Alabama feel at home, with steak and egg platters and Earl Thomas Conley CDs in the gift shop. There is something very Wisconsin about driving drunk, but I'd had enough of that local folkway. I pulled over, and lowered my blood-alcohol content with a Denver omelet.

4

Ya Hey!

WISCONSIN—ELKHART LAKE, HOWARDS GROVE, HAVEN, TWO RIVERS

Many years ago, I had a job interview in La Crosse, Wisconsin. The G. Heileman Company brews Old Style beer in LaCrosse, storing it in tanks painted to look like a giant six-pack.

"You know," my prospective boss warned me, "we have a lot of eccentrics up here. It may be the cold weather."

We have cold weather in Chicago, too, and we have eccentrics, but none of them are as locally famous as David Gumieny, proprietor of the World's Largest Barber Pole, the signature monument of Elkhart Lake, Wisconsin. In the big city, deviants are celebrated, but eccentrics never leave their apartments. In a small town, deviants are driven out, but eccentrics are harmless, amusing characters. They give everyone something to talk about. They may even be good for tourism.

The World's Largest Barber Pole is a silo, striped red, white, and blue, with a working barber shop in the bottom floor. Dave gives all the haircuts himself. I'd first heard of him when I was writing a

35

The world's largest barber pole.

"World's Largest" feature for the *Chicago Tribune*. Wisconsin has a lot of those: the world's largest grandfather clock, the world's largest penny, the world's largest Trojan horse, the world's largest talking cow. The *Tribune* likes its travel writers to do their stories by phone, so I never got to meet Dave, but I'd always remembered the career advice he offered me at the end of our interview: "Have you ever thought of starting a magazine for people who collect old tractors? I've got a lot of them here in the yard."

I would be passing through Elkhart Lake on my way to the Door Peninsula, and I needed a good, trim Boy Scout haircut for camping, so I called Dave for an appointment.

I had no trouble finding his shop. The international symbol for "barber" is visible a section away. It's a red, white, and blue rocket ready to launch from the farmyard, a Bullet popsicle cast in concrete. If you're going to cut hair this far from town, it's good to have an eight-story silo wrapped in patriotic stripes to snare passers-by. Out front were a dozen John Deere tractors, chained together in a caravan.

The waiting room is inside the old milkhouse. It's a little Northern lodge: nailed to the dark paneling are a bluegill thrashing on a chunk of driftwood, a saw painted with a pretty winter scene, a *Hee-Haw* cast photo, signed "Best Wishes." I sat down, picked up a copy of *Men's Journal*, and pretended not to listen as Dave cut a local farmer's hair.

"Sid," he said. "There's a lot of people living on this Earth that are . . ."

". . . very naive."

"So why should I be the one to try to save 'em? The last guy that tried it, they nailed him to a piece of wood."

"Oh, I sold the motor home," Sid related.

"You did! You are one lucky man! Did you get what you wanted for it?"

"Oh, yeah. Sold it to a dealer friend in Texas. They wired the money to me, and sent a couple to pick it up."

"Doesn't get any better than that! You must be living right."

"How's your golf game?" Sid inquired.

"Oh, it's getting better."

This is why old men wear their hair so short: they have a lot to tell their barbers.

When it was my turn, I settled into the bright arena of the barber's chair, and told Gumieny to buzz me to the nub.

"I'm going to be doing a lot of camping on this trip," I said. "I don't want to have to worry about combing my hair out in the woods."

"Camping?" He clicked on his clippers. "I never liked to do that. You know what you should do? A lot of universities rent out dorm rooms in the summer. That'd be a lot more comfortable."

A fine powder of brown hair sifted to the floor. Dave asked me about Chicago ("Now why wouldja wanna live in a big crowded place like that?"), offered a political opinion ("You know, people say the casualties are so bad in Iraq, but it's a lot safer over dere den in somea da big cities here"), then told me the story of the Barber Pole. It was an immigrant's saga. He'd been a big wheel in Greendale, a suburb of Milwaukee: owner of his own barber shop, village trustee. Then, at age forty-four, he abruptly moved his family to this farm, so his children could grow up in the country, just as he'd done. Dave had spent his childhood on a farm near New Berlin, with a dozen brothers and sisters.

At first, the Gumienys' new rural life was a disaster. Elkhart Lake didn't need another barber. Dave sold off thirty-five of his forty acres to a deer hunter. Then he got stomach cancer. He went on welfare; the bank threatened to foreclose. As he was cutting a wealthy man's hair, he mentioned his plight. The man offered to pay off the entire mortgage, all twenty-four thousand dollars.

After that came another intervention. Dave thought a barber pole outside the house would draw more business, but he didn't know where to put it. One morning, he was staring at his tiny homestead.

"I looked up at the silo, and I just saw a barber pole light up, like the Lord had given it to me."

This was in 1976, so there was a bicentennial angle, too. It took three men and a cherry picker to paint the silo. Once the job was done, Gumieny became even better known here than he'd been in Greendale. You couldn't build something like this in the suburbs. The neighbors would complain. In the country, you can paint your barn any damn color you want. That's why none of Wisconsin's "World's Largest" attractions is in Milwaukee or Madison. Dave made it all the way to retirement by cutting hair during the day and working as a prison guard at night.

"It's been on television so damn many times," he said. "Every one of the local stations had it on. The History Channel had it on. They showed Pepsi's big sign, they showed Microsoft's, and then here comes the barber pole."

All the credit belonged to the Lord, who had given him that divine vision, thirty years before.

"Have you ever read that book, *The Magic of Believing* by Claude Bristol?" Dave asked me. "I read that book, and I took off like a rocket."

My hair was now sprinkled across the shoulders of my plastic bib. I was swiveled to confront the mirror. Dave had shorn me to bristles, leaving a tuft of forelock. With my round, wire-framed glasses on my ovoid face, I looked like Jiminy Cricket's military ID card.

"Now, I didn't cut it too short," Dave said. "If you meet somebody who wants to take your picture or put you on TV, it won't shine through to your scalp."

I made for my wallet, but he waved me off.

"No, no. Save that for one of the universities. I hate to think of a guy sleepin' on the ground."

"I already made a reservation tonight. For the state park near Sheboygan."

My wallet was snug in its pocket by then. I'm not the kind of guy who insists on paying for anything. I just wanted him to know I was man enough—and cheap enough—to sleep in a tent. John Steinbeck traveled with his poodle Charley in Rocinante, a heavy-springed Ford pickup with an apartment on its back, fit for a Nobel Prize winner. William Least Heat-Moon drove the blue highways in a van he called Ghost Dancing. I had a nylon tent, stuffed into the trunk of a Dodge Neon that was missing a hubcap. But those guys were out to Discover America. You need heavier equipment for a project like that. I was only driving around the Great Lakes. And I would be spending half my trip in Canada, where modest living and northern hardiness are appreciated.

"Well, if you've got any time, you've got to meet my son, Jeffrey," Dave said. "He owns a butcher shop in Howards Grove. It's a real landmark."

* * *

I could understand why a butcher would be a celebrity in Sheboygan County. Sheboygan County is the bratwurst capital of Wisconsin, which is, in turn, the bratwurst capital of the United States. Supermarket entrances are papered with flyers announcing benefit Brat (pronounced "brot") Frys for the Kiwanis Club, or an ailing local child. Brats are also *the* culinary accessory for watching a Green Bay Packers game. Southern Wisconsin is the heartland of a Deutsch-Amerika that spreads west into Minnesota and the Dakotas, importing every hearty delicacy that can be culled from pig or cow: bratwurst, knockwurst, cheese curds, butter, ice cream, pork chops, ring bologna, all washed down with whole milk or Milwaukee's Best.

We climbed into Dave's twenty-year-old Jaguar and roller-coast-ered over the country roads, all lettered A, B, or C. Dave forced a cas-sette into the dashboard.

"Now, Ted, here is something that's big in Wisconsin," he said.

A jaunty accordion bounced out of the speakers, anchored by a stolid, huffing tuba.

"It's our state song, the polka."

I was being feted like a foreign guest. Maybe that was appropri-ate. There is a remarkable change in customs, foodways, and language at the Illinois-Wisconsin state line. Drinking fountains become bub-blers. Pop becomes soda. ATMs turn into Tyme machines (for "Take Your Money Everywhere"). Wisconsinites even have a nickname for their southern visitors: FIBs. It's the short, polite acronym for "Fucking Illinois Bastards."

The Howards Grove Meat Market, established 1891, sits in a two-story brick house on a main street that had locked up and gone home for supper by the time we arrived. Only Jeff Gumieny was still at work. Dave let himself in the side door and led me into the kitchen, where Jeff was filling hog intestines with bratwurst. The marbled gray sausage extruded from the mixer's mouth, as loose as concrete from a truck. Every six inches, Jeff tied a link in the ballooning sleeve. He wasn't built like a German butcher. There was a lean intensity to the compact figure wrapped in a white apron. Jeff was a teetotaler, a divorcé, a young man who devoted fourteen hours a day to his meat. Making brats in Sheboygan County is a public trust. The people are German, so the sausage has to taste like Thuringia. When out-of-towners visit Howards Grove, their hosts serve Jeff's brats. And there is always a run on autumn Sundays, the most sacred days on Wisconsin's calendar.

"The Germans were known for great sausage, meats, and bacon," Jeff said. "Sheboygan County is the bratwurst capital of the world because of all the sausage makers that emigrated here. This meat market was established in 1891, by Frederick Nordholz. I learned from the late Ted Toepfel and Nelson Kuhn."

Jeff delivered this history in a rapid, deadpan voice, biting off sentences at every full stop. He spoke with a rounded Northern accent, a contrast to his father's sharp urban voice.

"To me, it's an art," he said. "It's like painting a picture. Sausage making and meat cutting is an art. I told my Mom when I was a kid, she said, 'Jeffrey, stop playing with those pork chops.' I said, 'Mom, I'm gonna cut pork chops someday.'"

At first, I thought he was riffing on this standard scene from an artist's biography ("Ludwig, quit banging that piano!" "Miles, cut it out with that horn!"), but his face never wavered from its stare. I decided to test his sense of humor with another cliche.

"Do you agree that without meat, it's not a meal?"

"Absolutely," Jeff shot back, with military rapidness. "We have a wide variety of meats here: braunschweiger, homemade summer sausage, brats, wieners, ring bologna, straight bologna, ham, bacon, dried beef, liver sausage, Italian sausage, Polish sausage. We make all the Old World sausage. It's all homemade."

Jeff shut down his machine, tied off the last brat, and led us out to his two-story brick smokehouse. It stood on the last rise before the land sloped eastward to Lake Michigan, four miles away. It was just the right spot for a smokehouse, Jeff explained. The immigrant butchers came to this corner of the Third Coast because they knew the lake would cool their curing meats. But it was getting harder to do this the traditional way. The weather was changing. The summers were more humid. And Jeff didn't believe in refrigeration. It wasn't Old World. Old World meant heat from hardwoods and fruit trees, tempered by lake winds. He opened the door to a room whose smudged black walls radiated the fresh, ashy smell of a wooden house the morning after a fire. Jeff reached in and lifted out a chunk of dried beef, twisting on a string.

"You won't find that in a grocery store," he boasted, gazing at the cut like a woodcarver regarding a perfectly shaped doll. "I'd never be able to keep up with the demand."

He could hardly keep up with it now. Apparently, the Meat Market was even better known than the World's Largest Barber Pole. Jeff had standing orders from two celebrities: a black-hatted country singer and a gun-mad rock guitarist from a nearby state. He told me their names, then told me not to print them.

"That's the way it has to be," he said flatly. "Otherwise, this place'll be flooded with paparazzi people. It's gettin' worse. There've been lawsuits against 'em."

Already, television had discovered Jeff Gumieny—the Food Network had featured his brats in a spot about tailgating. And *The Daily Show* had come to Howards Grove.

"Stewart was here," Jeff tossed out. "I know him good. I got the tape at home. My Mom's dubbing it."

I could understand why Jon Stewart had wanted to interview Jeff Gumieny: the earnest, deadpan butcher made a perfect foil for the TV host's big-city smirkiness. And meat's Middle American associations makes it an easy joke for New York comedians. David Letterman used to give away a canned ham before every broadcast. Now he has an audience quiz called "Know Your Cuts of Meat." But Jeff didn't see the irony. He is a master butcher, not just feeding the world, but bringing taste, color, and enlightenment to its palate. To his mind, that makes him as worthy of fame as Jack Nicholson.

"I was told that if I put one of these in Beverly Hills, 'You'd be more famous than the TV and movie stars, with all you've done. You wouldn't be watchin' them, they'd be watchin' you.'"

I never got to taste Jeff's bratwurst—my pocket campstove wasn't powerful enough to fry it. Dave and I left Jeff to finish his bachelor-long day, and we went to a German-American restaurant in Howards Grove. I ordered a pork chop with a side of potato pancakes.

I am not much of a carnivore—I'm not a trencherman, period— but since I was in Sheboygan County, I figured I ought to have my daily helping of meat. When I was a boy, the Department of Agriculture published a food pyramid. A good day's eating, it declared, consisted of four servings of fruits and vegetables, four of bread, three of dairy, and two of meat. I was already behind in the last two categories, even though I'd been in Wisconsin all day.

While we ate, Dave fretted about his son.

"He's so intense," he said. "When he was getting divorced, I told him, 'Ya know, maybe you wanna stop drinking.' And he hasn't had a drop since. He sure works hard at that meat market. You know, he didn't even finish high school. He dropped out so he could go to vocational school and become a butcher. That's all he ever wanted to do."

★ ★ ★

There are two rules for driving clockwise around the Great Lakes: always keep the water on your right, and stick to the road closest to the beach. This plan led me to the Haven Hi Guy. I was headed out of Sheboygan on County Road LS (for "Lake Shore"). A mile or two south of Haven, I began seeing signs for "Whistling Straits." It sound- ed like a picturesque lake scene for my digital camera, so I followed along. I was still looking for the straits when I puttered through

Haven, a T intersection consisting of two or three houses and a shut-
tered filling station. As I drove by an old barn, a soft-bellied man in a
lawn chair raised his arm to hail my passing. He wore a golf cap and
a patchy white beard that blended into his Nordic face. Great Lakers
are reserved folk. We don't wave at strangers, even on roads where the
cars are spaced like numbers on a clock. Encouraged, I stopped to ask
for directions.

"I'm looking for Whistling Straits."

"Whistling Straits? It's just at the end of this road."

There were two signs nailed to the barn behind him. The top read
SMILIN' RAY. The bottom was his rural street number, W1043, and
the word WELCOME, with dot eyes and a crescent grin making a
face of the O. I peered through the screen door. Dimly, I could see
posters, picture frames, and long magazine bins, shaped like the lower
halves of pinball machines.

"What's in your building?" I asked.

"Oh . . . " He seemed bashful about the enterprise, even though
it was advertised to the road. "Comic books. Movie stuff. I've got a
golf museum, too."

Whistling Straits is a golf course. The Kohler Company, famous
for its sinks and toilets, hired a renowned landscaper to gouge and
plump the Lake Michigan shoreline into a replica of a Scottish link.
(That's not so farfetched. *Link* comes from a Scots word for coastal
dunes.) Then they built a tony spa, the American Club, "the Midwest's
only AAA Five Diamond Resort Hotel." At $275 a round, Whistling
Straits is exclusive. Every day, Haven is buzzed by private planes, carrying corporate peers who can't stand to be excluded from anything.
It's a big-game golf course. The PGA Championship was held there
in 2004. That's when Ray Olbrantz, the shy man who'd waved at my
car, became the Haven Hi Guy.

Ray led me into his barn. There wasn't much light, and every step
echoed on the planks underfoot. It felt like the inside of an old farm
museum. But *Star Wars* action figures posed on the shelves, and banks
of old comics were sealed in plastic sleeves. A poster for the Shaquille

The Haven Hi Guy.

O'Neal movie *Kazaam* adorned a wooden wall. All this had been imported from Milwaukee. After retiring as a printer, Ray opened a comic book store there. One day, he was mowing his lawn when a man walked up and offered to buy his house. Ray had always wanted to live Up North, so he accepted the offer, using the money to move his family—and his comics—to Haven.

The room's centerpiece was the golf museum. Balanced on a plastic grid, like eggs in their trays, were twelve hundred balls Ray had collected during his walks on the course. They were painted with the logos of the world's wealthiest corporations—ING, Bank of America, Aon—and its grandest golf courses—Medinah, Troon North. Ray couldn't afford the greens fees at Whistling Straits, but sometimes, he hit duplicate balls around his yard.

There is only one road in and out of Whistling Straits, and it runs past Smilin' Ray's. When Ray heard the PGA Championship was coming to his hamlet, he had a dream.

"I had dreamed about six months before that I would meet Tiger Woods," he said. "I figured, 'How's a little guy like me going to meet Tiger Woods?' I couldn't even afford to go to the course."

The tournament began on a Thursday. Early that morning, Ray set up his lawn chair, and waited for the caravan. Limos drove past, and glossy Cadillac Escalades. Ray waved at every one. At first, only a few of the passengers waved back. But by the weekend, the guy in the lawn chair had become a tournament celebrity. Japanese champion Kadayama Shingo pulled up in an SUV filled with golfers to give Ray an autographed program. Ben Crane proffered a ticket to the Wanamaker Club, the course's VIP lounge.

"Almost every member of the PGA stopped here and shook my hand, from the president on down," Ray said. "Some old guy came up on Sunday and said, 'Put this in your collection.'"

Ray handed me a PGA Past President's badge, mounted on a metal clip that clapped over a breast pocket.

"How could you sell something like *that*?" he wondered. "I wouldn't sell it, unless things got critical. He saw something in me that made him want to give it to me."

That same morning, a Buick SUV rolled up the dirt driveway. Tiger Woods's caddy stepped out and handed Ray a practice round map, signed by Tiger himself. Through the truck's open window, Ray saw the man he'd dreamed about. He wasn't going to miss his chance. He reached inside, and shook the hand of Tiger Woods.

The map was preserved in a glass frame, hung on a pillar. So was this letter from the PGA president: "The memories we all have of the beautiful setting near Lake Michigan, the excellent golf course and the wonderful fans will never fade," he wrote. "You know what also won't be forgotten? Your enthusiasm for the thousands of strangers that passed by your doorstep on the way to the Championship."

Beneath it was a proclamation from the governor of Wisconsin, declaring Ray the "Haven Hi Guy."

"Oh, that was something they came up with," Ray protested, as I read the governor's thanks to the man who "smiled and waved at every car, bus, service vehicle, limousine, motorcycle, and skateboard that passed by."

"*I* never called myself that," he said.

I can't imagine Ray Olbrantz sells many comic books or action figures in Haven. Certainly not as many as he had in Milwaukee. Anyone who can afford to golf at Whistling Straits doesn't need a fantasy life. But Ray had distinguished himself on his rural road in a way that would have been impossible in the city. If he had waved at the traffic from the sidewalk of a Milwaukee store, he would have looked like a street person. In Haven, he looked folksy.

"It's the only thing that gets people to stop once in awhile," he said.

After I left Smilin' Ray's, I followed his road to Whistling Straits. Beyond the gates was a long, manorial driveway that knotted itself into a loop in front of a stone clubhouse. SUVs idled at the curb, and caddies in white jumpsuits waited for bags. The lake was nearby. The air smelled as fresh as snapping laundry, and the blue-screen sky was chalked with jet-trail clouds. From where I was parked, I couldn't see the water. You have to pay admission for that.

★ ★ ★

My last stop before Door County was Two Rivers, birthplace of the ice cream sundae. Unlike Danish kringle and fried cheese curds, the sundae is a Wisconsin delicacy that went national. You can eat one anywhere, any day of the week. Ordinarily, I advise readers to avoid small towns that bill themselves as "historic." That usually means nothing's going on there. But the nativity scene of the sundae is re-created at a parlor in the Washington House Hotel, on a side street a block from the town square.

Two Rivers isn't the only town that calls itself "Birthplace of the Ice Cream Sundae." Ithaca, New York, and Evanston, Illinois, make the same claim. All three creation legends are similar, but Two Rivers' is the oldest. In the nineteenth century, the story goes, puritanical town elders across the North banned soda pop on Sundays. The fizzy drink was considered too racy for the Sabbath. One Sunday afternoon in 1881, a man named George Hallauer walked into a soda fountain owned by Edward C. Berner and asked him to top a dish of ice cream with that sauce he used for chocolate sodas. It tasted so good Berner started selling the dish for a nickel, but only on Sundays. Then, according to the plaque that occupies a space on the wall next to the soda jerk's old derby, "a ten-year-old girl insisted she have a dish of ice cream 'with that stuff on top,' saying they could 'pretend it was Sunday.'"

The parlor evokes the decade we used to call the Gay Nineties, before another, gayer Nineties intervened. The chairs are backed with dainty wires twisted into butterfly wings, and against the pinkish wallpaper is a photo of Berner, a spruce young buck sporting a topcoat and smoking a stogie. In the corner, a white-haired man in a peppermint-striped apron was scooping ice cream.

"What's the most popular topping?" I asked.

"Hot fudge."

"OK. I'll have hot fudge."

"Do you want nuts?"

"Of course. Can I get a cherry, too?"

"It wouldn't be a sundae without a cherry."

He handed me my ice cream, already melting in its long-stemmed dish.

"Tuna quarter," he said.

That's not another Wisconsin treat. That's Ya Hey pricing. I paid him $2.25.

5

Door to the North

The Door Peninsula, which is separated from the rest of Wisconsin by the wedge of Green Bay, looks like a long arm hailing the state of Michigan across the lake. Its northern half, where the tourists cluster, is actually an island, joined to the mainland by a bridge.

On the Great Lakes, the sun rises over cheap motels and sets on expensive cottages. Door County has the only sunsets in Wisconsin. It has been a resort for rich Chicagoans since the 1890s, when steamers dropped North Shore wives and children at grand summer hotels. Highways have made the 250-mile trip from Chicago a weekender, but a weekend isn't long enough to shed the acquisitiveness that scores you a place in Door County. You'll probably need it again on Monday morning. Fish Creek, the toniest village on the Green Bay side, is crowded with boutiques. There's the Harbor Shop, which has sister stores across the lake in Charlevoix and Petoskey, Michigan. The C&C Supper Club boasts wireless Internet. At Hide Side, you can buy a $250 globe, with each country carved from a semiprecious stone.

The Fish Creek Market sells gourmet sauces, spices from San Francisco, and voluminous racks of wine.

It was suppertime as I cruised Highway 42, so I looked for a fish boil. A fish boil is as essential to Door County as a beignet is to New Orleans, or a crab to Baltimore. But it's even more particular to its native soil. You can't enjoy a fish boil on your patio back home. There's too much fire involved.

In Ellison Bay, I found the Viking Restaurant. The Viking sat across the road from L. Johnson's Swedish Restaurant, which was capped with a steep grass roof, kept in trim by grazing goats. The Viking was humbler. Its aluminum siding shed paint like psoriasis. Its tar roof was swollen with lumps from a half-century of snowfalls and thaws. I walked past picnic tables wrapped in blue plastic, and life-size carvings of Ole and Lena, the proverbial butts of every Norskie joke. Dan Peterson, master boiler, was standing beside his kettle—a Speed Queen washing machine tub. A Speed Queen held twenty gallons of water, plenty for the forty or fifty trays he filled each half hour. Scrap metal plates formed a legionary's skirt around the bottom, to hold in heat from the flames.

An evening at the Viking is like a cookout in your old man's backyard. Dan was gray and shaggy, his jeans hung loosely, and he listened to country music on a portable radio while he cooked. He can afford to relax. The Viking Restaurant Fish Boil is the longest-running show in the United States, after Old Faithful. It dates back to the earliest days of mass tourism, when four-lane highways grew like vines into the North Country, making a path for middle-class Chevys. The restaurant hasn't aged a month since then, even as the rest of Door County changed with the century.

Dan is a second-generation fish boiler. The meal was invented by Scandinavian fishermen who poached their catch on potbellied stoves aboard gill-netters. It was brought on shore for church suppers and community picnics. The American Legion threw boils at its flag-burning ceremonies. In the 1940s, Dan's grandfather, Amandus "Mandy" Peterson, started serving fish boil at his hotel, hiring a

Boil on!

farmer as master boiler. A decade later, the Viking put it on the menu, making Dan custodian of the oldest commercial boil in Door County.

At his father's hotel, fish boil was made with trout and cost fifty cents a plate. Dan had gone along with the switch to whitefish, but any more advances would be an abomination.

"What I like about the fish boil is the simplicity," he said, watching his roiling kettle. "Water, salt, onions, potatoes, fish. You go out of Door County, they start changing it. In Sturgeon Bay"—which is still in Door County, but perilously close to Green Bay—"they add corn. Down in Milwaukee, shrimp seasoning. There's even people here that do it with *gas*. That's sick."

Dan's son, Matt, ran a boil at Pelletier's, a white-tablecloth restaurant down the peninsula in "Fish Crick." It was a generation ahead: Pelletier's served margarine, which was once *illegal* in Wisconsin, and hosted corporate tour groups.

"We're not quite as busy as Matt's," Dan allowed. "He's in a high populous area. I'm very proud of him. He didn't have it easy. He was an English major."

When Dan was growing up, "we didn't have a lot of tourism. A lot of the homes that people grew up in, they're all gift shops or restaurants. There's no farming anymore. Even on Washington Island there's no milking cows."

Some locals call the tourists "turkeys," because their heads swivel back and forth as they take in the view through their car windows. They blame a 1969 *National Geographic* article for ruining the idyll. Natives carp that Door County is "going to become another Wisconsin Dells," an overdeveloped tourist trap of water slides and go-kart tracks. Dan didn't disdain the visitors—they kept his restaurant open. He was resigned to the forces drawing Door County closer to the urban world.

"The ways of Chicago are the ways of Door County," he said. "We never had inspectors inspecting electrical, but they're here now."

As the water bubbled and steamed, two sidekicks dropped in a perforated vat of red potatoes and onions. They flipped fish into the kettle, chasing it with mugs of salt.

Dan excused himself to clang the dinner bell. The sound drew the cameras closer.

"You can step back now or run later," he warned the tourists playfully, edging up to the kettle with a tin cup of cooking oil.

"Boil over!" he bellowed.

He splashed oil onto the flames. For a roaring instant, they blossomed into an orange bonfire, with a sinister exhaust of black smoke. Flames rippled over the kettle. As the flash subsided, his assistants raced for the kettle, and hauled up the streaming vat. (The fireball isn't just for show. It burns off the water's oily glaze.)

After the fireball, we diners picked up aqua cafeteria trays, scuffed from a thousand scaldings, and lined up at a steam table. Women in lunch-lady smocks dished a course into each compartment—cole slaw, rye bread, onions, potatoes. Dan stood at the end of the line, serving whitefish with tongs. There was even a helpful souvenir placemat, with three-step instructions on "How to De-Bone Your Whitefish." I worked out this puzzle with a couple from suburban

Milwaukee. It's not easy to make whitefish taste like something, but Dan's oozed lemon. It wasn't exactly an old-fashioned Door County fish boil—a real native would condemn it as a plastic abomination, and tell stories of church suppers run by fishermen boiling their catch. But it wasn't hectically modern, either. It fell into that tween-er era called "retro." It was a half-step into the past, when people went Up North to get away from the city, instead of seeking its conveniences in a rural setting.

★ ★ ★

My campsite in Peninsula State Park, a few miles above Fish Creek, gave me an inkling of what had drawn the Midwest to Door County. The state has claimed the high ground, so the park sits on a bluff jutting into Green Bay. My first morning there, I ran the Eagle Trail. It was too rocky for rubber shoes, so I dodged the stones like a football player doing the tire drill. A ruffed grouse jogged beside me for a dozen yards, fanning his turkey tail to warn me I shouldn't veer too close.

At the top of the trail was Eagle Point, a vista made even loftier by a seventy-five-foot tower. I climbed to the viewing platform. Standing on its stilts, I could see across the bay, to the hazy coast of Michigan's Upper Peninsula. In the foreground, uninhabited Horseshoe Island was a green patty on the wind-scored water. Up the peninsula, white cottages, hidden in forest niches, edged to the waterline.

That evening, I took my camera down to the bay and captured one of the five best sunsets of my fourteen thousand evenings on Earth. I caught it at the very moment it was exchanging evening for night. Lake and sky mirrored each other. A fluorescent orange stripe lit the horizon, glowing weakly on the water. There was just enough wind to announce the air, so the ripples on the water were the same shape as the long faint clouds.

After the sunset, I went to the bonfire that opens Fyr Bog, a Scandinavian festival. It took me fifteen minutes to find a parking space, and another fifteen minutes to walk three-quarters of a mile up Highway 42, counting Illinois and Wisconsin plates as I went. The Door Peninsula was too crowded. So the next day I drove to Gills Rock, at its northern tip, and took the ferry across the Porte des Mortes, to Washington Island.

★ ★ ★

Washington Island is Door County's Door County. It's the dot on the inverted exclamation point. It's where you go for rural silences, because only thirty-five hundred people live there in the summer, and most tourists won't pay the twenty-eight-dollar fee to bring their cars. I didn't. As soon as the ferry tied up, I rented a one-speed bicycle and began pedaling the flat roads. It was a mile through the pines that conceal the waterfront cottages, but then the landscape opened up into wood-fenced fields, scattered with spools of hay and incurious cows. I watched an inning of the Brewers game over a brat and a beer in a tavern, bought a laminated guide to Great Lakes trees and wildflowers in a bookstore, and thought that was it for my Washington Island mini-break. Until I heard about Hannes Andersen.

I was waiting for the ferry in the Detroit Harbor gift shop, browsing Norwegian joke books and Winter on Washington Island plates, when I confessed to the clerk that I was writing a book. She was a native Islander—her grandfather had been a lighthouse keeper, and she'd graduated from high school with eight students, the same size as the class pictured in that week's *Washington Island Observer*. A year-round life on Washington Island was an idyll few could afford—the winter count was seven hundred humans—so seven months of the year, she worked at a maternity shop in a Chicago suburb.

"You've got to talk to Hannes," the clerk insisted. "He grew up here, and he knows *everything*."

If talking to Hannes meant spending more hours on Washington Island, I wanted to talk to Hannes. The clerk raised him on the phone, then drove me to his house.

Eighty-nine years had pared away every bit of spare flesh on Hannes Andersen's body, and it looked as though the ninetieth might burrow all the way to his core. But Hannes was determined not to let death in. If he were gone, who would tell stories about Washington Island when it was a snowbound rock peopled by dairy farmers and fishermen who seldom visited the mainland? Hannes was the *Observer's* history columnist, and every week he extended his long life with a tale from its beginnings.

Hannes stood in his doorway, holding every thin limb parallel to his gaunt body. He led me into his office, where a half-written column was spooled in an electric typewriter. His head was bald, and his yellowed skin was speckled with liver spots, like stained wallpaper. Putty-colored hearing aids nestled in each ear. I didn't have to ask him questions. He simply began telling me stories of his boyhood, in the adolescent years of the twentieth century, on a farm of which this house was the only remnant.

They had plowed with horses, growing produce for the tourists who visited even then. "It was very rare that we got a day off, or even a half-day." Only the postal service reminded them that the United States lay beyond Porte des Morts. In the winter, the postman walked across the ice. Later, he carried the letters in a horse-drawn sleigh.

"The first time I was off the island was in the sixth grade," he said. "The teacher was from Sebastopol, and she was going home for the weekend. It was a great experience, you can imagine. Some students grew up without ever leaving."

At the age of seventeen, Hannes rode a railcar all the way to Chicago, for the 1933 World's Fair, where he encountered the modern world for the first time.

"That fair was a real eye-opener," he said, his voice still full of marvel after threescore and twelve. "The things that you could see! They had White Castle hamburgers. They had square gears working. My brother and I couldn't believe it!"

After that, Washington Island was too small for Hannes Andersen. He went away to the state teachers' college in Platteville, and taught on the Peninsula until World War II erupted. That cataclysm carried

Hannes Andersen.

him away from Door County entirely: after serving with the Merchant Marine in the Pacific, he spent thirty years with the Oakland Fire Department. He didn't make it back to his native island until 1977. It was a life course repeated by every generation of islanders. Most of the young went away to college. Few came home. There wasn't enough work. The island supported a fair amount of carpenters, but there were only two fishermen.

Hannes's father was a Dane from Milwaukee, but on his mother's side, he belonged to one of America's tiniest ethnic groups, so small they are barely more than an extended family. The Icelanders must have been attracted to this obscure northern island because it reminded them of their Atlantic fastness. There are more of them here than anywhere else in the United States. Hannes's mother was the first Icelandic child born in Wisconsin, and spoke the language fluently until she died in 1970. Icelandic is close to Old Norse, the mother tongue of Scandinavia, so she could also talk to the Danes, Norwegians, and Swedes who made the island a pan-Nordic colony. In the 1980s, a professor from Reykjavik visited to invite the sons and daughters of Iceland home. Eighty-five islanders took him up on it. Hannes showed me a button commemorating the journey: "Washington Island— Iceland Homecoming Trip. April 16, 1987."

Even at eighty-nine, Hannes was too vigorous to leave this visit as an interview with an oracle. His office was not a place to prepare for the tomb. We were going to lunch, he announced, snapping on a windbreaker, since Washington Island rarely feels eighty degrees.

The restaurant, K. K. Fiske, was owned by a local fisherman who stocked the kitchen from his own nets. Before we went inside, Hannes had something to show me. He rolled aside the cargo door and lifted out a hip-high contraption, composed of three panels, like a cricket wicket. The middle was grooved, and shorter than the others.

"Do you know what this is for?" he asked.

I couldn't imagine.

He held it against his legs and flipped up the middle panel.

"So you don't get any on your shoes!"

His face thawed into a wry smile, as he savored this perk of seniority.

In the restaurant, he had another good one for me.

"They serve a fish here called 'lawyers,'" he said, opening the menu. "Their official name is burbot. Kenny, the owner, says they're called lawyers because the heart is so close to the bunghole. Burbot can't be iced and shipped. The flesh is delicate and loses flavor. They have to be served on the day they are caught."

I took this hint, and ordered a basket of burbot with French fries. Frying makes all fish taste alike, but I can report that burbot are chewier and fleshier than the whitefish at mainland boils.

Washington Island is only thirty-five square miles, but because it is so flat, Lake Michigan is seldom part of the landscape. In Hannes's mini-van, we drove string-straight gray roads, alongside dairy farms that could have been patches from any county in Wisconsin. We passed a wild meadow, hazy with the crowns of a golden flower.

"What is that?" It looked like a page from a "Mountain Vistas" calendar.

"Mustard grass."

"Pull over. I want to take a picture."

Hannes pulled over. Then he stopped in the parking lot of the Lutheran Church, and led me across the road, to a tall, weathered structure that looked like a pagoda built by trolls. Gray-shingled, bark-skinned, it seemed a sinister gatehouse to the forest. It was a *stavkirke*, a replica of an old Scandinavian church, and it was just as rough-hewn inside. The unfinished walls, posts and benches were freckled with brown knots, and in the nave was a triptych, with the cross in the middle panel, painted directly on the wood.

There, at the edge of a copse of spindly birches, the *stavkirke* could have been the setting for one of those frightening Teutonic fairy tales, with their forests menaced by wolves and witches. No Episcopal church could look so ominous. The English, blessed with gentle hills and temperate weather, had never imagined such horrors hidden in their land. The Upper Midwest is a harsh country of blizzards, cracking freezes, boat-swallowing storms, and thick, hardy forests. This chapel seemed almost indigenous, as do the wintry-complexioned Scandinavians who have transplanted themselves here.

Hannes had one last place to show me: a farm museum. The organizers had interviewed him for a video on rural life during the Depression, so he got in free. The yard was full of skeletal tractors; the barn held broken-down churns and rusty sickles, collected from farmers who'd sold out to the summer people. Hannes led me to the loft, where he pointed at a photograph.

"That's my father," he said, pointing at a man with a beard like a surrender flag, staring grimly into the lens as he posed behind his plow. Hannes was standing in front of the machine, with his brothers and sisters. "He died when I was ten, and the next year, I was behind the plow."

Before I boarded the ferry, I got Hannes to pose for a photo. His arms gangled at his sides, and his ball cap was tilted like an old fire captain's hat. He grasped my arm as we shook hands.

"Thank you for coming to Washington Island," he said. "And I envy you all the things you're going to see."

We were at opposite ends of our journeys, then, because I envied Hannes Andersen all the things he had seen. The doctor had ridden to his cradle on a horse; his birth had been of no notice to anyone beyond Washington Island. He will go out in a hearse, with his obituary posted on the Internet.

★ ★ ★

Washington Island is twenty-three miles from Escanaba, Michigan, if you have a boat. I didn't, and the steamers that once called at both ports are long gone to scrap, so I had to drive two hundred miles, back down the peninsula, and around Green Bay.

Green Bay entered history in 1634, when French explorer Jean Nicolet, the first white man on Lake Michigan, stepped out of his bateau in Mandarin robes, believing he had landed in China. He didn't find the Forbidden City in Wisconsin, only a tribe of baffled Fox Indians. Green Bay remains in history as the smallest city with a professional sports team. The Third Coast was the cradle of the National Football League back in the early 1920s, and the Packers are the lone survivor of those industrial teams from broken-nose blue-collar towns: the Hammond Pros, the Muncie Flyers, the Decatur Staleys, the Rock Island Independents. They're still here because the Packers are held in a community trust. For years, the bylaws dictated that if the team were ever sold, the proceeds would go to a local American Legion Post. Today, you could never put an NFL franchise in Green Bay, but after eighty-some years, the Packers have become so inseparable from the city's identity that *every game* sells out. They're the biggest high school football team in America.

Lambeau Field, the home of the Packers, is actually in the suburb of Ashwaubenon. As you drive north on Onieda Street, you expect to see the Barnes & Noble bookstore. You expect to see Applebee's. You expect to see Old Navy. You do not expect to see a modern Colosseum. Those soaring ovals fit so well into downtown Nashville and Pittsburgh. But across the street from a suburban mall, Lambeau Field looks like the mothership from an alien invasion movie.

Most Wisconsinites consider Wausau the Gateway to the North, but Green Bay can claim the title, too. Interstate 43 ends there. The country north and east of the right angle formed by Duluth, Minneapolis, and Green Bay is the largest area without a highway on this side of the Mississippi. Green Bay is also your last chance to participate in American consumer culture. If you can't find something you don't need here, it's going to be awhile before you see it again. I went into Old Navy, looking to replace a pair of whisked blue jeans my dog had chewed. The store didn't have my size.

"Do you have an Old Navy in Escanaba?" I asked.

The clerk checked her computer.

"No."

"How about Sault Ste. Marie?"

"No."

"Anywhere in the UP?"

"No."

"Duluth?"

"I think there's one in Duluth."

I couldn't wait that long. I settled for plain old denim.

★ ★ ★

Wisconsin greets its visitors with cheese shops. The Mars Cheese Castle, on Interstate 94, is a few miles north of the Illinois state line. At the other end of the state, just outside the border village of Marinette, is Seguin's Cheese. Its sign is subtitled "T-shirts, Moccasins, Western Boots."

As the last chance for Wisconsin cheese, Seguin's has a counter offering wedges and wheels in every variety—mozzarella, cheddar, gouda, Swiss—alongside deluxe models speckled with bacon and roasted vegetables. I plucked a cube of cheddar with bacon off the sample tray, sucked it off the party stick, and let that pellet of animal fat melt all over my tongue and the soft lining of my cheeks. Mmmmm. It tasted like an entire fast-food meal, in pill form.

But I hadn't stopped here for gourmet cheese. I'd come for the most elemental cheese of all: the cheese curd. You can't get cheese curds outside of the Dairy State. I picked up a bag—they looked like orange dice, mashed into a wad. At the counter, I learned why the cheese curd cannot travel.

"The curds are the separation of solids from liquids during the cheese-making process," said the owner, Ron Seguin, trying to give me the story in the five minutes before he had to leave for a wedding reception. "The liquid is whey. In this area, they feed that to the pigs. Probably through the years, when they were making it in the factory, people would try it, and that's how it became something to eat. In this immediate area, or anywhere close to a factory, you'll find it in convenience stores and grocery stores. We get ours from Springside, in Suring, Wisconsin. They only taste good when they are fresh. They mold very quickly. As far as traveling out west, it wouldn't taste very good."

Like American cheese, curds had no bite, but they don't have that artificial, Cheez Whiz flavor, either. They taste as fresh as cold milk. I snacked on curds until I saw a sign for the next Wisconsin delicacy: "Culver's—Home of the Butterburger." The Butterburger is a beef patty, fried with a dollop of butter inside. Cheese with bacon. Beef with butter. Wisconsinites know how to cram meat and dairy into a single serving. I can't say the Butterburger tastes different than any other hamburger, but maybe the symbolism is more important than the flavor. Just knowing there is butter in your meat makes you feel like a cheesehead. It helps the dairy industry. It clogs your arteries just that much more than a standard hamburger. It helps build a Wisconsin physique. I crossed the Menominee River with a heavy gut, looking forward to the hardy outdoor life—the tenting, the hiking, the fishing, the all-terrain vehicles overturning on snowmobile trails—of Michigan's Upper Peninsula.

6

Yoopers and Trolls

MICHIGAN—ESCANABA, THE GARDEN PENINSULA,
MANISTIQUE, WHITEFISH POINT, PARADISE

Escanaba is regionally renowned as the setting for *Escanaba in da Moonlight*, actor Jeff Daniels's play about a hapless deer hunter known to his neighbors as "the Buckless Yooper." Its sad-sack protagonist, Ruben Soady, is forty-three years old, and has never killed a deer. In the UP, that's worse than being a virgin, but Ruben thinks he can change his luck by drinking a potion prepared by his Ojibway wife. *Escanaba in da Moonlight* takes place in a hunting cabin, and with its jokes about pasties, outhouses, UFOs, flatulence, and the Michigan Department of Natural Resources, it does not travel well. The movie was a flop, but the play is in constant production at summer stock theaters around the Upper Midwest. Back in Door County, the Peninsula Players were putting it on, and it was the biggest smash in the history of Daniels's Purple Rose Theater, located in his Downstate hometown of Chelsea.

Escanaba—"Esky," as the locals call it—is 430 miles from Detroit, but it is unmistakably Michigan, exuding the blue-collar weariness I feel whenever I visit Flint or Muskegon. On 12th Street, Escanaba's share of U.S. 2, the Burger King sign read "New Careers Start Here." The city is a working port, shipping iron ore from the North Country mines to the Indiana steel mills, but the *L. E. Block*, a freighter that last sailed in 1981, rusts in Little Bay de Noc, waiting for its masters to call it home from an exile longer than Odysseus's. Its twin, the *Joseph L. Block*, still picks up iron ore at Escanaba, and carries it to the Mittal Steel Works in East Chicago, Indiana. Escanaba and East Chicago are hundreds of miles apart; but, as I'd learn much later, to the sailors on the *Joe Block*, they're the two most important towns in the world.

The most overused adjective for the Upper Peninsula is "unspoiled." Most people apply it to the county-sized forests, but it's true of the cities, too. A French explorer once called this corner of America "the fag end of creation." Franchise Nation hasn't bothered with it. Escanaba's Ludington Street, which runs from the highway to the bay, is a train-set diorama of downtown shopping before the depredations of malls and interstates. Gust Asp tobacconists (the neon sign blinks intermittently to "Just Ask") sells cigarettes, fishing licenses, and the Detroit papers. The Michigan Theatre no longer shows movies, but it still stands, advertising "Silver Winds Church" on the marquee. When I peered into a taxidermist's shop, a stuffed wolverine snarled at me, hysterically defending his window.

When the UP was lumber country, Ludington Street was the rowdiest honky-tonk in the wild North. Every spring, after the logs rushed down the swollen rivers, Escanaba was swarmed with lumberjacks swollen with pent-up paychecks and libidos.

"Like the logs they drove down-river, they jammed the broad straight streets from sidewalk to sidewalk, a surging flood of bearded men, fighting, drinking, swearing, whoring, on down to the red-light district by the railroad yards," wrote John Bartlow Martin in *They Call It North Country*, his lively history of the UP. "Here the girls were waiting, and twenty-four hours a day the drab buildings bulged with ribald song and brawling. The whorehouses stayed open until 1942, when the police closed them because the Government moved into town to build a big ore dock."

I checked into the Hiawatha Inn, a forty-dollars-a-night motel across the highway, and asked the Ojibway clerk to recommend a sports bar. That night, the Detroit Pistons were playing the San Antonio Spurs for the NBA championship.

"Go to Tailgators, on Washington. They'll have it on."

They more than had it on. Escanaba is farther from Detroit than is Buffalo, or Louisville, or Pittsburgh, or Toronto, but Tailgators was decorated like the basement man-cave of a Motown sports nut. There was a mural of old Tiger Stadium, a poster for the Michael Spinks–Larry Holmes title fight at Joe Louis Arena, pennants for the Tigers, Red Wings, and Pistons, a program from the 1953 NFL Title Game between the Lions and the Cleveland Browns. (The UP is not unanimous on the Lions. Many Yoopers consider the Packers the local football team. When Steve Mariucci coached the Lions, Escanaba was torn: "Mooch" is from Iron Mountain, the next city west on U.S. 2. After he was sacked, the town became even more devoted to Green Bay.) In the back room, I found a record sleeve for *Denny McLain at the Organ*, an album of mellow hits recorded by the thirty-game winner of the 1968 World Champion Tigers, whose career was as brief and as brilliant as a pop star's.

The basketball game was on every television in the bar. I sat down to watch next to Troy, a young man wearing a Pistons jersey that fitted him like a smock.

"I got this one here in town," he said. "It's 2XL. Goes all the way down to my knees, but it was the only one left. So I took it. I want to get a Tayshaun Prince jersey, too. I'm gonna have to go to pistons.com and order it, eh. Do you know if you need a Visa card?"

Troy was crippled by a limp—his left calf turned away from his knee at a twenty-degree angle, and his foot dragged as he walked, but he could imagine himself on the TV screen as easily as he could inside Tailgators. He had played basketball for his high school team, the

Escanaba Eskymos, and "I could have played in the NBA if I hadn't messed up my knee."

The Finals were tied, 2–2, and the game was tied 89–89 at the end of regulation. No one was more absorbed than Troy. Cries of "Dee-troit bas-ket-ball" went up in the bar, but Troy gnawed the cuticle of his thumb, even as the Pistons took a five-point lead.

"Go San Antonio!" shouted a hockey fan, bitter about the NHL strike. "If I can't have my Red Wings, you can't have your Pistons."

With nine seconds left, the Pistons led by two. But they left Spurs forward Robert Horry unguarded. The man the sportswriters call "Big Shot Bob" hit a three-pointer. The Pistons failed to score on the riposte, as Tayshaun Prince's flailing shot missed the basket.

"And the air has gone out of the Palace," the announcer narrated, over a pan shot of glum faces.

The air had gone out of the entire state, from Detroit to Escanaba. Troy looked crestfallen.

"Well, that's why they call him Big Shot Bob," I commiserated. "I think he just punched his ticket to the Hall of Fame. Now they're going to have to win two games on the road. That's tough to do."

"I know what the coach is saying," Troy said, before naming his heroes: "Get it to Chauncey Billups, or Ben Wallace, or Rasheed Wallace."

Then he left the bar, with the word "Wallace" glowing in a white arc on his shirt, probably imagining himself taking the final shot.

★ ★ ★

The Eighth Street Coffeehouse ("Yup, We're Open") was the only wi-fi hotspot in Escanaba. I read my e-mail there before heading east. Behind me, a circle of unemployed men killed the mid-morning with a game of euchre, and an old woman praised the weather to the counter girl.

"Nice day, eh?" she said, exaggerating the Northern interjection. "It's going to be hot today, eh?"

I didn't see a bank clock on Ludington Street, but sweat prickled under my T-shirt, so I guessed eighty degrees. According to an old Yooper joke, the peninsula has two seasons: ten months of winter and two months of bad sledding. This was bad sledding. The midsummer heat was another reminder that I was in Michigan. In the Lower Peninsula, the days also begin with cool, damp mornings, which ripen and spoil into bright, listless noons. Eighty degrees is more than a Michigander should have to endure: an Edenic summer is the reward for the gray purgatories of fall, winter, and spring.

* * *

I was due in Sault Ste. Marie on Thursday, for the Boat Nerd Convention, a gathering of shipwatchers celebrating the 150th birthday of the Soo Locks. That gave me two days to drift across the Upper Peninsula. Beyond Little Bay de Noc is a broader body of water, Big Bay de Noc. At its mouth, I found a ghost town. Fayette's gray wooden buildings, their last chips of paint scoured away by 135 winters, tell the story of the entire Upper Peninsula in just a few blocks. The town had been built around a deep, aquamarine cove, shortly after the Civil War. A tall limestone cliff blocked the winds off Lake Michigan, making Fayette a placid haven for schooners. And it was perfect for smelting pig iron. The mines were nearby, the thick forests fueled the furnaces, and the limestone purified the ore. Now the mines were tapped out, the bright-burning hardwoods were logged off, the cliff was stripped of limestone, and the government had taken over. Fayette, which shipped out 229,288 tons of iron during its twenty-four-year life, is a state park. A few carpenters tapped away at the two-story hotel. They were transforming Fayette into the last-ditch incarnation of a dead town: a historic village, with a restored blacksmith shop, a kiln, a boarding house, and a livery stable.

Fayette is out of the way even for the UP. It was built for ships, so it sits in the cul-de-sac of the Garden Peninsula, a knuckle of land reaching toward Door County. The two peninsulas are separated by stepping-stone islands, of which Washington is the largest. As I drove back toward U.S. 2, the northern highway that runs from the Straits of Mackinac to Puget Sound, I passed a low-roofed brick school-house advertising USED BOOKS. This was hardly out of place: long winters make avid readers. Plus, the UP attracts a lot of idiosyncratic cranks from Downstate. When I was at the University of Michigan, I met a girl whose stepfather quit his job as the Cleveland police chief to open a used bookstore in Ishpeming. It lasted nearly twenty years.

The school was in the midst of a repainting. A roller leaned against the wall, and the floor was two different shades of gray. The hallway was full of junked desks. I slipped into an old classroom where books were bursting from packing boxes. I was browsing through a paper-back when the proprietor appeared. A strongly built old man, he'd obviously been hard at work in this stuffy schoolhouse: his face was flushed, his thin gray hair was matted to his scalp, and his wire-frame glasses had slid down the sweat-greased slope of his bulbous nose. His arms and hands were streaked pink, where he'd skinned himself.

"I've got ten thousand books in here," he announced. "I've got another thirty thousand I haven't even looked at. My daughter got me to buy 'em all. She's a reading addict. She went to Hawaii, and I asked her what the best part of the trip was. You know what she said? 'Uninterrupted reading.'"

John Thill was the grandson of a plasterer from Luxembourg who came across in 1870 to work in the Fayette Hotel. That was big money for a nineteenth-century immigrant: he earned $2.50 a day, making him the highest-paid tradesman on the grounds. Fayette struggled on for decades after the smelter went cold. A few people still lived there when John was a boy, and he explored the abandoned buildings with his playmates, finding beds and desks that hadn't been moved for decades.

The Garden Peninsula is the only corner of the UP that grows crops, hence the name. John pointed to an orchard across the road. Those were his apple trees—five thousand of them. If he'd lived on the other side of U.S. 2, forget it. He'd be cracking ice off his fruit.

"It's really an extension of Door County," he declared. "You go twenty miles north in the winter, and the temperature drops six degrees. Half the time we don't have a white Christmas here."

As a native Yooper, John had an inborn suspicion of Trolls—the UP epithet for a Downstater. Like the mythological monster, the Trolls of the Lower Peninsula live under a bridge—the Mackinac Bridge, in this case. He believed his peninsula was in the wrong state. It should have been part of Wisconsin. It almost happened that way. In the 1830s, when Michigan was preparing for statehood, it coveted the Toledo Strip, a 468-square-mile rectangle of land on its southern border. After a skirmish between farmers on the state line, Congress awarded Toledo to Ohio. As compensation, Michigan was offered the UP.

At first, the new state felt cheated. "By now the song they sing to us / Is trade away that land, / For that poor, frozen country, / Beyond Lake Michigan" ran an acrimonious ballad. Now, most Michiganders agree they got the better end of the deal. Not John. He still hadn't gotten over the Mackinac Bridge, which was about to celebrate its Golden Anniversary. It brought in the wrong element. Back in the 1950s, there were no summer people. Now, the Garden Peninsula was overrun with retired auto workers who couldn't afford a home in Traverse City or Door County. And they'd just cut the bridge toll in half, from five dollars to two fifty! If people weren't willing to pay five bucks to get into the UP, then who the hell needed 'em?

"What is it they say about the bicyclists?" I prodded him.

Thill grinned. His lower jaw looked like a weathered fence with half the pickets busted off.

"They come up here with twenty dollars and a pair of underwear, and they don't change either."

The UP is a state within a state, remote enough to have its own dialect—"Say Yah to da UP" is the Yoopanese bumper sticker—and its own State Fair, in Escanaba. Only 300,000 people live here, down from half a million in 1900. There was once talk of seceding from Michigan, but the UP could never stand on its own economically. Stripped of its richest natural resources, this land of second-growth forests and empty mine pits depends on summering Trolls—even the bicyclists.

I noticed another book-lined room and asked if I could look inside. Hesitantly, John let me. It housed the UP collection. I found *Anatomy of a Murder*, which was written by a state supreme court justice from Ishpeming, then became a Jimmy Stewart movie, and *Soo Canal!*, a historical potboiler about digging the Soo Locks.

"How much for these?" I asked.

"Well, I really wasn't planning on selling 'em," he began, then decided on a dollar for *Soo Canal!*

"The other one you can have." The glue on the paperback had rotted. Whole chapters were slipping out.

★ ★ ★

Northern summers may be short, but each day is endless. Michigan has the longest summer evenings in the Lower 48. The UP is at the sunset end of the Eastern Time Zone, and it's closer to the North Pole than it is to the Equator. On Midsummer's Night, I camped in a state park near Manistique. My tent flap looked westward, over Indian Lake. As I watched the sun decline, leaking evening rays over the water, I fiddled with a headphone radio, trying to pick up the basketball game in San Antonio. The dial was white noise and theremin squiggles. Once in a while a voice broke through—"Lindsay Hunter," "three pointer," "down the stretch"—but then a country music band or a right-wing talk show host butted into the game. Finally, I tuned in WWJ, from Detroit. A newsman was watching the game on TV and relaying the score to his listeners. I timed the sunset—the first star pricked the darkness at 10:20, during the third quarter, when the game was tied. On the horizon, an orange-pink backdrop silhouetted a picket of evergreens. A father and son walked along the shore, living shadows in the dusk. The last crescent of day faded to black at 11:20. By then, the Pistons had a twelve-point lead with seven seconds to go. There would be a game seven.

★ ★ ★

I got my first look at Lake Superior when I pulled into the parking lot of the Great Lakes Shipwreck Museum, at Whitefish Point. To get to the beach, you have to walk past the Whitefish Point Lighthouse, which was placed here to guide ships through the narrowing bay that empties into the Saint Marys River. Like most Great Lakes beacons, it's built in the shape of a wooden schoolhouse, but the skeletal antenna tower that supports the lamp is distinctive.

The beach beyond was the emptiest strand I'd seen on the Third Coast. Whitefish Point thrusts into the Big Lake, so when you stand on that long, bleached boulevard of sand, you face a half-compass of blue water, filling the curve of the Earth. Lake Superior is so vast, the moon lifts and lowers it three inches a day. Lacy whitecaps ride in from the north on waves that fold gently over one another when they expire on the beach.

I went inside the museum. The ninety-one miles between Whitefish Point and Munising are known as the Shipwreck Coast. Over three hundred vessels have foundered here since the *Invincible*, a British warship on a mission to squelch an uprising at Fort William, went down here in November 1816. To the west, the shoreline is rocky, the narrow passage is heavily traveled, and the nor'westers blow unchecked for four hundred miles before bursting against this corner of the lake. But the museum is here because of one wreck: the *Edmund Fitzgerald*, which sank in 1975, fifteen miles off the point. The ship's brass bell is the first thing you see when you walk in the door. It was salvaged at the insistence of the crew's families, and now hangs here, as the only grave marker for the twenty-nine drowned sailors. The first thing you'll *hear* is Gordon Lightfoot's "The Wreck of the Edmund Fitzgerald," which is in heavy, heavy rotation on the sound system. Herman Melville once wrote that the Great Lakes "have drowned many a midnight ship with all her shrieking crew." Because of that song, the *Edmund Fitzgerald* stands for every one of them. Lightfoot has sung it at the annual November 10 memorial service, his CDs are on sale in the gift shop, and his signature is on one of the museum's four *Fitzgerald* paintings, a storm scene titled "Every Man Knew." He's the reason the museum draws so many visitors.

"That's a living legend here," said the site director, Maria Zielinski, when I found her in the gift shop. "If it hadn't been for that song, the interest would have been zip. It would have been the locals here on the lakes. He was just doodling one night. He wrote it with no intention of singing it."

(He probably wouldn't have sung about the *Edwin H. Gott* or the *Stewart J. Cort*, if one of those boats had sunk. Their names aren't lyrical enough for a ballad.)

Even without Gordon Lightfoot, the wreck of the *Edmund Fitzgerald* would still be talked about in sailing towns. It didn't kill as many sailors as its unsung predecessor, the *Carl D. Bradley*, but it was the *Titanic* of the Great Lakes. The *Fitz* wasn't supposed to sink. When it was launched, in 1958, the 729-foot *Fitz* was the largest freshwater vessel in the world. Bulkier ships soon surpassed it, but boatwatchers admired its sleek, elongated-tugboat profile, and it never lost the nickname "Queen of the Inland Seas."

The "gales of November" in Lightfoot's song are not a poetic device. The second week of November is the most treacherous season for sailing Lake Superior. The water is still warm, but Arctic winds are creeping down from Canada, and the jarring temperatures whip up storms. "The Big Blow," November 9–11, 1913, sank ten ships, drowning 235 sailors. The Armistice Day storm of 1940 took down five boats. On November 10, 1975, the winds blew as hard as they ever had in the twentieth century. A truck overturned on the Mackinac Bridge. Across northern Michigan, trees snapped and windows shattered. On Washington Island, Wisconsin, waves swept a beacon off a twenty-three-foot tower. A sailor on board the *Joseph H. Frantz*, bound from Toledo to Ashland, watched the most ominous sunset of his career: "The sky was an odd, strange, peculiar color, and the water was a glassy slate gray, as if brooding. By midnight watch, the wind had reached hurricane strength and the waves looked like mountains." The *Frantz* reached safety in the lee of Madeleine Island. Even with two anchors to hold it fast, the ship rolled wildly. The Whitefish Point lighthouse was swamped, too, forcing ships to navigate the bay by radar.

When the *Edmund Fitzgerald* left Superior on November 9, loaded with twenty-six thousand tons of taconite, bound for a steel mill in Detroit, the skies were clear. But a low-pressure system was inching northeast from Kansas. The *Fitz's* captain, Ernest McSorley, conferred with the *Arthur M. Anderson*, another downbound ship. They decided to take the North Shore route, which would keep them close to the harbors on the Ontario coast. It was the last run of the season, and they wanted to come home safely.

That evening, squalls of rain, mixed with snow, needled Lake Superior. At midnight, as the ship passed Nipigon, the northernmost point on the lake, McSorley radioed the National Weather Service in Cleveland. The *Fitz* was struggling through "heavy rain, snow flurries, and forty-two-knot winds."

The fatal hours began at three o'clock the next afternoon, as the ship passed Michipicoten Island, seventy miles north of Whitefish Point. By then, sixty-knot winds were rocking the *Fitz*. The seas were "tremendous," McSorley radioed the *Anderson*. "The worst I have ever seen."

The storm had knocked out the radio beacon on nearby Caribou Island. Unable to take bearings, the *Fitz* wandered close to a thirty-six-foot-deep shoal north of Caribou. As it roller-coastered on thirty-foot waves, its hull may have struck bottom. At 3:30, McSorley told the *Anderson* that water was pouring into the vent pipes, and his ship was listing.

"Will you stay with me until we get down?" he asked calmly.

To the very end, Captain McSorley's messages carried his confidence that his ship would power home through this rainstorm. On the museum's walls, there is a black-and-white photo of McSorley, trim in his nautical uniform, his hair full and dark after four decades on the lakes. Beside it is a transcript of his last known words.

"How are you making out?" asked the *Anderson*.

"We are holding our own."

By then, the *Fitz* had lost its radar and needed bearings from the *Anderson*. At 7:10, the *Edmund Fitzgerald* disappeared from screens all over eastern Lake Superior. The next morning the *Roger Blough* spotted an oil slick where the *Fitz* had last been seen. In three days of searching, the Coast Guard found a lifeboat, two self-inflating rafts, and two life jackets. The ship wasn't seen again until the following May, when an underwater camera sent back photos of its broken hull, the stern resting upside down, taconite pellets scattered across the lake bed.

There hasn't been a shipwreck in over thirty years, a record on the Great Lakes. There are fewer boats, and they're more cautious. Toward the end of the year, "our gale time," Zielinski sees them anchored in Whitefish Bay, waiting for the seas to calm.

"In November, I've seen four freighters in the harbor, lit up like a city," says Sandy Thomann, who works the gift shop register.

The *Fitzgerald*, which lies five hundred feet deep in Canadian waters, is off-limits to divers, although the team that brought the bell back was given an exemption on "humanitarian" grounds. Their diving suit, which looks like a puffy yellow movie robot, with claws, is on exhibit in the *Fitzgerald* corner.

The rest of the wrecks are fair game. The sailors who died on the *Independence*, the *Niagara*, the *Comet*, and the *Superior City* are just names on handwritten manifests. There are no widows or children left to object to seeing their pitchers or drinking glasses on a museum shelf.

I walked across the yard to the lighthouse. It's a museum, of course—every Great Lakes lighthouse is a museum, since automation put the keepers out of business. This one, decorated in the calico style of the 1940s, even had a mannequin seated at a desk, dressed in the blue uniform of the U.S. Lighthouse Service, which ran the beacons until the Coast Guard took over. In its flossy white wig and pillbox cap, the dummy looked like the Speedy Delivery man from *Mister Rogers' Neighborhood*.

In the front hallway, I was asking the guide about shipwrecks when a twelve-year-old boy spoke up.

"My dad knows about shipwrecks," he said. "He takes people on wreck dives."

"Does he live around here?"

"Yeah. We own the store in Paradise."

"*And* he does wreck dives?"

"Yeah. And in the winter, we do the snowmobile trails."

There's a single two-lane road from Whitefish Point to Paradise. The Paradise Food Mart is on the right-hand side. Inside are alleys of canned food. Tahquamenon Falls is a few miles further south, and the campers need their Chef Boyardee spaghetti, their deviled ham, and their marshmallows. The storage closet in back is the office for all three of Mike Cook's enterprises. He handed me a Xeroxed brochure for "Captain Cook's Dive-N-Hook Charters": "Dive the crystal clear waters of beautiful Lake Superior, the greatest wreck diving any-where, for the novice diver to the more technical."

The grammar was wobbly, but the boast stood on two legs: divers come from all over the world to poke around the Whitefish Point Underwater Preserve, not just because it is littered with eighteen wrecks, but because cold, fresh Lake Superior has preserved its trophy schooners and ironclads as though they were bottled. The ocean can eat a ship in a few decades, but here, Cook is still leading divers to the corpse of the *John B. Cowle*, a 420-foot ore carrier which sank after a collision on a foggy day in 1909.

7

Boat Nerds

MICHIGAN—SAULT STE. MARIE; ONTARIO—SAULT STE. MARIE

The Great Lakes are the best place in the world to watch ships. On the Lakes, ships have to squeeze through straits, rivers, and canals. Wherever that happens—the St. Clair River, the Welland Canal, the Soo Locks—you'll find a guy standing on shore with a copy of *Know Your Ships*, an almanac of every vessel on fresh water. You can call him a Boat Nerd, because that's what he calls himself.

The Soo Locks turned 150 years old that summer, and the Boat Nerds were thronging Sault Ste. Marie, which sits on the northeast edge of Michigan's Upper Peninsula. June 24 was Engineers' Day, the one day a year the Army Corps of Engineers allows the rabble past the gates. The Nerds were not going to miss a chance to get *that close* to their beloved freighters. The Long Ships Motel, which faces the locks from Water Street, was booked solid. So was the Friday evening Freighter Chasing Cruise, departing from Sault Ste. Marie, Ontario—"Soo, Canada"—the twin city across the Saint Marys River.

I met my first Boat Nerd on Thursday night. I'd just left a bar, after watching the Pistons lose the NBA championship. Across the street was a two-story viewing platform with a message board flashing the ETA of incoming ships. The *Roger Blough* was due in twenty minutes. I ran up the steps. A young man was craning over the railing. If he hadn't been a Boat Nerd, he would have been a nerd for something else: model airplanes, or slot cars. Sweaty, uncombed, soft-jawed, he wore a camera on his paunch, like a medallion, and he was swapping marine trivia with a friend in a T-shirt commemorating the *Stewart J. Cort*, "first 1,000-foot freighter on the Great Lakes."

"What was the old name of the *Saginaw*?" the man in the T-shirt challenged.

"*John J. Boland*," the kid shot back, with quiz-bowl swiftness. He didn't need to look in *Know Your Ships*. He had digested every agate character.

The kid's name was Jason. A twenty-seven-year-old college student from Green Bay, he was using his summer break to stake out the Soo Locks. His boat-widow girlfriend languished in a motel.

"Yesterday, I was here from 6:40 A.M. to 2:40 A.M.," he boasted. "That was my biggest day so far. It was a busy day. I shot twenty-two in one day. I've braved all temperatures. If you're a true Boat Nerd, you'll do whatever it takes to get photos. I've even got a scar. I found a hole in a chain-link fence in Toledo at a steel mill where there was a boat I didn't have a picture of. A security guard chased me. I was coming back out through the fence and I got snagged on barbed wire. Every day, I'm doing something shipping-related. Every year, I fly to Detroit for spring break. We hit Detroit, Sarnia, then we'll go over to Montreal, Toledo, Cleveland, Erie."

Jason posted the pictures on his Web site. To his great agony, he was missing three of the three-hundred-odd freighters plying the Lakes.

"I've got every one but the *Sarnia*, the *Algoport*, and the *Scotia*," he said. "I'm told they travel on the eastern part of the Lakes. That's an eleven-hour trip."

Locking through.

The downbound Saint Marys River makes a right-hand dogleg into the Soo Locks. The *Roger Blough* proclaimed its approach with a dazzling headlamp, magnitude minus fifty. As the boat passed under the ErectorSet arch of the International Bridge, it slowed and slowed, to two knots, one knot, until watching it come on was like watching a snowplow grinding down a long country road. The *Blough* floated into the lock, its rust-streaked hull packing the chamber. The deck-hands were so close you could read the logos on their T-shirts. It was like watching batters warm up from a box seat.

As soon as the watertight doors swung shut, the sailors tossed ropes onto shore. Lockworkers looped them around pegs. The twelve-hundred-foot-long Poe Lock was built in 1968, to accommodate salties from the Saint Lawrence Seaway. North American shipping lines had learned to use every inch of it. The *Blough* was one of thirteen "footers"—one-thousand-foot ships built in the 1970s and '80s. Footers are the most prized photos on the Lakes. Jason and his friend opened fire with their cameras. This is why Boat Nerds love the Soo

Locks: they have captive subjects. The *Blough* could only go in one direction: down. And down it went. A stopcock opened, Lake Superior leaked into Lake Huron, the boat descended. By the end of its seventeen-foot drop, its deck was below the walkway, on display for the picture-snapping Boat Nerds in the stands.

"Are you going on the freighter-chasing cruise?" I asked Jason.

"Oh, *yeah*," Jason exulted.

"I'll see you tomorrow night" I said.

★ ★ ★

Back at my motel, the Laker Inn, I finished reading *Soo Canal!* The jacket smelled of cellar must. The story was hardly fresher: an industrial-age romance about a can-do engineer as dashing as Errol Flynn, it was populated with doubting, harrumphing lawmakers, a brashly adventurous ship captain, and "a wild Irish-Ojibway maid with kiss–and–come-again lips." For 186 pages, I could see the Technicolor Disney version behind my eyes. But the summer stock characters performed before the backdrop of history. The original Canadian lock *was* burned during the War of 1812. Senator Henry Clay of Kentucky *did* disparage the Soo as "the remotest settlement in the United States, if not the moon." Charles T. Harvey *was* in his twenties when he dug his way around the falls in two years, despite a cholera outbreak in the work camp. His reward was 750,000 acres of the UP, still rich in timber and minerals.

★ ★ ★

President Theodore Roosevelt showed up for the fiftieth anniversary of the Soo Locks. His visit was commemorated by a sandstone obelisk on the riverfront. For the sesquicentennial, the member of Parliament for Sault Ste. Marie, Ontario, made an appearance. A one-star general delivered the keynote speech, repeating a statistic all Boat Nerds know by heart: the Soo Locks handle more cargo than the Panama

Canal—it would take three million trucks to haul the goods that float through each year.

The Boat Nerds listened to the speech in a clique. At its center was Roger LeLievre, publisher of *Know Your Ships*. Roger was a Soo native who had inherited the project from its founder, a local engineer named Tom Manse. In high school, he photographed freighters as a gift to his grandfather, who worked on the coal docks. After giving the seconds to Manse, he was invited on a boat-hunting trip to Cleveland. Still, Roger wasn't exactly a Boat Nerd. Nor had he coined the term, which originated on the fan site boatnerd.com. In fact, he seemed alarmed by the freighter cult that knew his book right down to the typos.

"The fewer the boats, the more people that are interested in 'em," Roger said. "*Know Your Ships* sells ten thousand copies a year. I've got people who buy three copies—one for the library, one for the boat, one for the car. Or they'll buy two books, one to keep and one to check off boats they've seen."

★ ★ ★

Sault Ste. Marie, Michigan, is the oldest city on the Great Lakes. Marquette paddled in from Quebec to found a mission here in 1668. The "Soo" is in the UP, but it's not really of the UP. It's in the United States, but it's a suburb of Soo, Canada. This is the one border town where the Canadian neighbor dominates the American. The movie theater is in Ontario. So is the casino. Canadians cross the river for cheap gas. Americans cross for Italian restaurants and government-subsidized milk. For Americans of pre-cable vintage, a Saturday night in front of the TV meant *Hockey Night in Canada* and *Don Messer's Jubilee*. And anyone who went to high school in the 1960s knew a young man who dodged the draft by cab. The football teams play each other, the gangs fight each other, the boys and girls marry each other. Lake Superior State University is in Michigan, but offers in-state tuition to the Canadian Soo. As a result, it has three NCAA hockey titles.

But along came September 11, 2001, and the Department of Homeland Security. The DHS would have been a source of derision, with its speedboats and its TurtleWaxed SUVs, if it hadn't made a run to Canada such a pain in the ass. You could see the problem from the river: the bridge's northbound lanes were a parkway, but the southbound lanes were backed up halfway to the summit. Once the river had united the Twin Soos. Now it was dividing them. Soon Washington would require every American to carry a passport. The plan is hugely unpopular in Michigan, which has two of the three busiest crossings with Canada. When I was at the Chamber of Commerce, collecting maps and brochures, I met Tom Ewing, general manager of WSOO, the local news/talk station.

"In the old days here, it was very informal at the border," Ewing said. "It was like driving into a different state. Since September 11, they've gone and looked up these regulations and started enforcing them. It isn't as bad as it was, but when my wife wants to go to dinner in Canada, I'm not as excited as I am about Bay Mills," an Indian casino in Michigan. "The passport thing, when it would really hurt would be the commuter traffic, people who want to go over to Giovanni's for their chicken dinner on Saturday."

★ ★ ★

That evening, as he boarded the Freighter Chasing Cruise, Roger overheard Jason and his T-shirt–wearing friend, Paul, bragging on their obsession.

"For me, I've gotta catch every boat I see," Jason was saying. "Every time a boat comes to Green Bay, I've *got* to get a picture of it."

"Or you might not have a life," Roger mumbled, acidly.

The rest of the passengers were avoiding Jason and Paul—they were too nerdy even for Boat Nerds—so I sat down at their table. Jason's girlfriend—blond, plainly pretty, mother of his two children—was there, too. She turned away from my notebook as though it were a blinding light. No, she didn't want her name associated with this trip.

"I do a lot of boat watching in Port Huron," boasted Paul, who lived near the St. Clair River. "I get more traffic than here. Any day I go out, I can get at least ten boats. I was into trains before I got into boats. When I moved back to Michigan in 2000, I started with this."

At work, Paul listened to river traffic on a scanner and monitored live webcams from four ports. He sneaked out of his office when one of his favorites was coming. When he watched movies set in the Midwest, he looked for boats in the background: he could identify any laker by its profile, and the logo on its stack. Jason was the same.

"In *American Pie II*, you can see the *Southbound Challenger*," Jason said.

"In *Major League*, the opening credits, they're showing the Cuyahoga River," Paul retorted. "You can see the *H. Lee White*."

Jason would not be topped. He tossed an ace.

"In the *Blues Brothers*, when they jump the bridge, there's an Oglebay Norton boat underneath."

Our boat departed from the Lake Huron side of the river. We had to lock through to Superior to see the big boats coming down from Duluth. The Canadian Locks are much smaller than the Soo Locks, a good fit for pleasure boats. As we approached, the red doors parted with an undertone of thrumming motors. We drifted into the bottom of a concrete chamber. The gate shut behind us. The water was antifreeze green, the walls stained to their brims from thousands of floodings. The air was dank. Soon we began rising like a plastic toy in an overflowing tub. The water spilled from the rubber seam between the western doors. They opened onto Lake Superior and a late, silvery dusk.

Soo, Canada, is nearly five times as large as Soo, Michigan, so it occupies the dirty, cluttered bank of the Saint Marys. Every Third Coast city has its smoky docklands. We passed the paper mill—pyramids of logs on a pounded dirt lot. A steel mill slid by. A Boat Nerd aimed his video camera at a barge laden with steel coil. It wasn't just any barge, the Nerd said. It was the *Chief Wawatam*, which operated as a railroad ferry in the Straits of Mackinac until the 1980s, when it

The *John B. Aird.*

was chopped down to scrap-hauling size and retired to the less glam-
orous Soo. This stretch of the river is called Old Vessel Point. It's a
marine junkyard. Boats too old for open water are harvested for rud-
ders, anchors, gears, and motors.

I pointed at a rusty, stunted freighter. "What was that?" I asked the
Boat Nerd.

"It was a cement carrier," he said.

"It's not very big."

"More than half of it's gone. It's being scrapped. It's being cut up."

But we had paid to see a living boat. And soon enough, the *John
B. Aird* steamed under the bridge. She was 730 feet long, over an
eighth of a mile, with a big humped black hull, like a whale's snout,
and a towering pilot house in her stern. The *Aird* carried all her
weight at the rear, as though reclining on her elbows. (Connoisseurs
prefer a boat with a balanced profile, like a suspension bridge, but piling the pilot house in back leaves more room for cargo.) Painted on
the stern, like a bloodshot eye, was the logo of the Algoma Central
shipping company—a cub prancing inside a red target.

You should have seen the paparazzi crush on deck. The Boat Nerds surged toward the railing, cameras bristling. Our vessel cut a J on the water and harried the *Aird*'s stern. The boat blew a profound salute, right from the depths of its horn. We tootled in response. Sailors waved from the deck.

"Do you have a camera?" a Boat Nerd asked. His lens was as broad as a fire nozzle. I pulled out a flat-front Olympia, with a sliding door.

"Like I said, *do you have a camera?*" He turned away to shoot.

Jason was at the railing. He turned around to holler at me.

"Hey, Ted," he shouted, "*this is what it's all about!*"

When you're a Boat Nerd, your ship is always coming in.

8

Marquette's Only Son

MICHIGAN—MACKINAC ISLAND

Jim Boynton grew up in St. Ignace, on the north shore of the Straits of Mackinac. As a boy, he idolized Jacques Marquette, the Jesuit who founded the first mission on Mackinac Island. When Jim was four years old, his father, the local postmaster, took him to the village's tricentennial pageant. There, he saw an actor stride past in the floor-length cassock of the French Jesuits—the Black Robes, as the Indians called them. He'd found his hero. In grade school, Jim played "voyageurs and Indians." As a teenager, he paddled a canoe to the island, because that was how Marquette had traveled. When he was seventeen, he applied to Marquette University, in Milwaukee. They turned him down. His grades were poor in every subject but history. But it's not the well rounded who make history; it's the obsessives. Jim got into Lake Superior State. One Friday, he was riding his bicycle down Marquette Street, in the Soo, when he was hailed by a man working in a garden.

The gardener was a Jesuit priest who knew some of Jim's relatives. They talked late into the night, and the following Monday, Jim enlisted in the order. During a retreat, he had a vision of Jesus as his brother, so he became a brother himself. But he was a worldly brother, assigned to teach history at University of Detroit Jesuit High School, where he lived in a single room on campus, with his Bible and his volumes of Francis Parkman's *France and England in North America*.

★ ★ ★

Marquette was twenty-nine when he was called to Mackinac. Jim Boynton was twenty-five. In 1992, the Jesuits, aging and dying like the rest of the Catholic clergy, withdrew their priests from the Upper Peninsula. They had been there for 324 years, an unbroken line dating back to Marquette, but the order needed priests in Ohio. Jim was distraught. The young brother resolved to restore the Jesuits himself. He got permission to summer on Mackinac Island. That's not the hardship assignment it was in Marquette's day, when Mackinac was a frozen, isolated wilderness, not a re-creation of William McKinley's America, but he made himself useful around Ste. Anne's Church, building a museum from vestments, stoles, medals, Indian prayer books, and a bell forged in the 1830s. He scanned the parish records to CD-ROM. They went back to 1695, and included his own ancestors.

I had met Jim years before, through my own fascination with Black Robes and voyageurs. France considered the Great Lakes the linchpin of North America, and her priests and fur traders made them the scene of their mythic adventures. Marquette paddling to the Mississippi; La Salle making the long snowy walk from Peoria to Quebec, indifferent to winter's hardships; Nicolet sailing into Green Bay draped in mandarin robes; Isaac Jogues enduring the "caresses" of the Iroquois—these were the Founding Fathers of my native land, and I had always imagined the New World the French would have built had they won the Seven Years' War. A Latin republic, encompassing the Great Lakes and the Mississippi Valley, with a Gallic elite ruling nations of Hurons, Ojibway, Pottawattamie, Algonquins, and Iroquois.

The French didn't covet the Indians' land. They wanted their furs, their souls, and their women—the Métis, a group of mixed-blood descendants, survives today in Canada. Jim Boynton himself is one-eighth Ojibway, an ancestry evident in his vestment-black hair and the faintly olive tint of his face.

When I told him about my round-the-lakes tour, he invited me to spend two nights in the Ste. Anne's rectory. He wasn't the pastor, but he was in charge. He decided who slept where.

In St. Ignace, I boarded a morning ferry for the twenty-minute churn across the straits. From across the water, Mackinac's hazy greenery has the military hue of the spongy sprigs on a model railroad diorama. As the ferry closed in, the colors deepened. The whitewashed cottages revealed themselves. So did the Grand Hotel, an Apollonian temple on a woodland bluff. The summer homes are laid out in Morse code—dozens of dots, and one very long dash.

(The final "c" in Mackinac is silent. Mackinac Island and Mackinaw City, which lies at the tip of the Lower Peninsula, share the same pronunciation. Both names are derived from *Michilimackinac*, an Ojibway word meaning "place of dancing spirits." Why are they spelled differently? Because the French got to Mackinac Island first. But Mackinaw City, the mackinaw boat, and the mackinaw jacket are British creations.)

When the ferry docked, the Grand Hotel's horse-drawn luggage cart was waiting. Cars are banned on Mackinac, so the wharfside scene brings to mind something out of Melville: horses tap out weary canters on the asphalt while broom-and-shovel men sweep up their cloying turds. Main Street, with its buggy traffic and its flat-profiled storefronts, could be the set for a production of *The Music Man*. The tourist count rises with the sun, and by 10:30, we were shouldering past each other to watch confectioners mix planks of fudge. The church is east of downtown. I toted my backpack past the old hilltop fort, and the even more prominent Governor's Summer Residence next door. That gray mansion looks like reason enough to run for office, right there. The most pretentious houses are on the bluffs, but even at water level, you can see turreted Victorians with stained-glass windows. In the front yard of a lavender-trimmed cottage, a woman was gardening. A tourist paused to compliment her.

"You have a nice house," the tourist said.

"Tha-aa-nks," the gardener responded. Her drawn-out vowels spiked her gratitude, making it clear that she knew she had a nice house, and didn't need the approval of some day-tripping vacationer.

Somewhere on this island, the Jesuits were fulfilling their vows of poverty.

The rectory of Ste. Anne's is across the street from the church, and overlooks a hundred-masted harbor. Brother Jim was sitting behind the desk, in the front parlor. It was his room: a black robe drooped from a peg, and beside the piano was his fiddle case, stickered with "Yooper," "Save Tibet," and "Proud to be Chippewa."

"Was I expecting you?" he asked, when I introduced myself. He looked puzzled, but he was quizzing himself, not me. "Yyyess! I was expecting you," he shouted, after a blank moment. And right away, he assigned me my role in his summer pageant.

"You'll be sleeping in the second room in the basement, next to mine"—his crisp Northern accent made him sound even brisker. "Why don't we set up a time to talk?"

He produced a little black book and a pencil.

"How does four o'clock sound?"

My schedule was wide open.

He scribbled in the appointment.

"That'll give you time to visit the fort. There's a real neat museum there. I'll give you my pass so you can get in for free. Just tell them you're me."

Then we were done until four o'clock, and Brother Boynton was on to his next task.

"There's a woman from the local paper coming at noon to do a story about the retreat," he informed one of his priests. "I want to get everyone together for a group photo. It'll be good for vocations."

I wandered off to the fort. It was built by the British during the Revolution, and abandoned by the Americans during the Civil War, when its artillery was needed to shell the Confederates. On the grassy parade ground, young men in Mexican War uniforms drilled with toy guns. Every half hour, they fired a black powder volley. Its popgun echo was a clock chime for the island.

Inside, I read about critical moments in island history:

"In 1900, summer cottager Earl Anthony brought an auto onto the island, frightening horses and wrecking carriages in the state park. Anthony was Mackinac's first and last motorist."

"In the early 1960s, Harry Ryba moved his fudge-making operation to the window of his shop. He also began handing out buttons that read 'Ryba's Mackinac Island Fudgie,' thus coining an enduring term for a Downstate tourist."

I was back at the rectory for afternoon Mass. A dozen Jesuits had appeared from scattered hermitages. They occupied the living room sofas. There was only one woman at this sacred stag party. Auburn-haired, bright-cheeked, she sat alone, in a hard chair. After the service, Jim introduced her.

"I want you to meet one of the only people I know who's really, really, really, really religious"—here, he beamed—"and really, really, really, really fun"—here, she blushed. "This is Katie. She works for the state park."

Our "appointment," which took place on the screened porch, was the only time in two days Jim sat in one place and talked about his work. Thirty-eight is not an age for reflection. There's a career to build. He was organizing English classes for the Mexican gardeners and chambermaids at the Grand Hotel.

"I stayed at the Grand Hotel once when I was in college," I told him. "Are all the waiters there still from Jamaica?"

"Well, they'll hire one or two college kids to make it look integrated, but the waiters are still almost all black. It's only the last four years we've been allowed to teach the workers there. The problem is, they could never come down. The only time they were free is on their lunch hour, so that's when we do it."

This old-fashioned society of masters and servants means that the Jesuits still have work on Mackinac Island. They aren't just here for nostalgia's sake, as actors in a historic reenactment.

"If you look at your missions, Jesuits here worked with the top of society and the bottom of society," he said. "I know a lot of the bluff people"—the vacationers in two-million-dollar homes. "After Mass, the governor says, 'Hi, Jim,' but I do most of my work with the bottom. What I hope to get next summer would be two Jesuit scholastics from Venezuela to teach them English in a formal way."

And then he gave me another role in his pageant.

"The classes are at four o'clock tomorrow. We could use you as a teacher if you'd like to come."

"Absolutely."

"OK. Meet me here at 3:30. We'll walk up."

That settled, he hurried across the street to the church, where he was planning a Spanish Mass.

★ ★ ★

The Grand Hotel doesn't seem so big from the harbor—it's sort of a misty white plantation house, midway between trees and sky—but the closer you get, the more out of scale it looks to its little island, until you think that *no* landscape could absorb a building this vast. A Gilded Age boast of privilege, it's the grandstand at Saratoga, the clubhouse at Augusta National, the railroad magnate's cottage at Newport, blown up beyond robber baron proportions. I once spent two nights at the Hotel, and I remember bracing breezes, long hallways, cramped rooms with hard beds, windows filled to the sashes with views of the water. I remember being scolded for not wearing jacket and tie after six, and being served caviar by West Indian waiters whose role and uniform—white gloves and waist-length blue jacket—were as archaic as a Pullman porter's. This was the setting for the movie *Somewhere in Time*, in which Christopher Reeve travels into the past to romance a woman he's seen on a calendar. He goes to sleep in 1980 and wakes up in 1900. At the Grand Hotel, how can you tell the difference? Your room key unlocks the illusion that the twentieth century never happened.

Outside the gate, Jim recognized Mattie, a rotund chambermaid in a frilled apron. While they greeted each other in Spanish, my eyes zoomed up to the porch. It was beyond human scale—it seemed to be a hundred feet above my head. I felt I'd been digitally shrunk and cast as a hobbit in a resort scene.

It costs ten dollars to walk on the porch—the longest porch in the world, according to *Guinness*—so we entered through the service door, walking past tanks of propane and empty luggage dollies, suffering the starchy humidity of the laundry to reach the servants' mess, a cafeteria called Captain's Cove. Throughout the ascent, Jim had talked on his cell phone while I urged on Father Mike, a hefty, florid priest who paused for breath every few hundred yards.

My student was named Juan Carlos. He was thirty-one years old, from Mexico City, and he was at the Grand Hotel to groom its golf course. Juan Carlos had been on the island for two and a half months, but he lived in complete social isolation from the guests, or anyone else who spoke English. We sat down at a long table. "I don't talk to the guests except what I have to," he said. His baseball cap read "Mackinac Island," but he could not pronounce either word.

"I have been to Iceland one time," he told me.

"Iceland? The country way up north?"

I pointed into the air.

"No." Juan Carlos pointed at the floor. "This iceland."

"Oh. Island."

I explained that in English, unlike Spanish, some letters are silent. I wrote out a phonetic spelling of "island."

"Do you know the name of the island?" I asked.

"Mackinack."

Well, that was no worse than most out-of-staters.

"It's Macki*naw*. What about the name of the state?"

"Mitch-i-gun."

"Uh-uh. Michigan."

"Mish-i-gun."

"Not gun, *gin*."

His head rolled back, and he laughed in frustration.

"Gun, like"—Juan Carlos formed a pistol with his fingers, but on his third try, he almost got the word right.

"What lake are we on?"

"Hoo-ron."

I wrote a phonetic spelling on an index card, then did the same for "carriage" and "cottage." The last word I used in a sentence.

"If I were rich, I would buy a cottage," I said.

"Everyone in America is rich," Juan Carlos responded.

"Not as rich as this. Some of these cottages cost over a million dollars. The governor has a house on Mackinac Island."

"I was there," he said excitedly. "As wider."

"As what?"

"You know, wider. Give drink."

"Oh, *waiter*."

I wrote out that word as well.

Juan Carlos would be working as a waiter that evening, on the porch, in a black jacket and bow tie. But he preferred the golf course. He was studying at a college in Mexico City, and when his education was paid for, he wanted to be a groundskeeper at a school.

This was the free hour between lunch and cocktails. The red-capped bellhops and blue-jacketed waiters filed in for their meals. I got in line behind a Jamaican chef, and started reading a framed article from *Gourmet* magazine, hanging in the hallway. It named the Grand one of the Top 25 Hotels in the World.

"Can you believe that?" the chef scoffed. "It's good to see once. Then"—he shrugged. "They don't even have air conditioning. And it's full of ghosts."

"Whose ghosts?" I was sure he was pulling my leg, but you never know when you're going to hear a good story.

"Everyone who was ever here," he laughed. "I saw one in the kitchen. I hope I wasn't drunk."

★ ★ ★

The square dance began at eight, on the deck beside the church. It wasn't dusk yet, but the time just before, the magic hour, when the light is mellow. Jim unpacked his fiddle. His father, Ollie, had come over on the ferry to do the calling. Katie was there, too. Before the music began, Jim twiddled her ear.

"How are you, my love, my dove?" he asked, rapidly, so it sounded like a light greeting between two friends.

The college students, freed from their shifts in gift shops and diners, sat edgily on benches. Then Jim plugged into an amp and began fiddling a reel.

"Oh, Johnny, oh, now, oh, Johnny oh," sang Ollie Boynton, the retired postmaster of St. Ignace. "Sing oh Johnny oh now, oh Johnny oh."

A couple rose to skip across the planks. Then another. As the benches emptied, I worried that a hand would reach out to recruit my awkward feet. So I slipped across the street to the rectory. It was empty except for Father Rey, the nominal pastor, playing études on the piano. When he took a break in his musical exercise, I asked him how he had come to Mackinac. It was a long story, made longer by his delight in being asked to tell it.

"I consider it all an unplanned accident, even my coming to Michigan," the elderly Jesuit said, still sitting on the piano bench. He had emigrated to America from the Philippines as a teenager, but he had not lost the accent, or the tropical sunniness. "I consider it the plan of God. I decided I could no longer work with the extreme poor. I was working in Brazil, in the Amazon. I wanted to come back to the U.S. But the bishop of El Paso wouldn't take me, the bishop of

Tampa wouldn't take me. The Bishop of Gaylord"—the Lower Peninsula diocese encompassing Mackinac—"was communicating with my supervisor. He took me. I didn't know about the northern part of Michigan. I reported on May 1, and it was the best spring I've ever had in seventy years. Everything was in bloom, and these sprawling fields of cherries and apples. The Leelanau Peninsula—I thought I'd seen all the beautiful places in the United States. And that was the place I needed to find to put into practice what I've learned. They call it the Piece of Heaven."

Father Rey had met Brother Jim many years before, at a conference in Chicago. Jim invited him to the island to work with the Latinos and the Filipinos. It was all part of his plot to install Father Rey as the church's first Jesuit pastor since the 1920s.

"I think he awakened the spirit of the Jesuits here," Father Rey said. "The bishop told me, 'We want Jesuits here, because this is your area.'"

When the story was over, we went back across the street. Thirty people were stomping across the deck, arm-in-arm, in a circle.

"We need one more couple," Ollie Boynton said.

Father Rey stood up to join the square dance. After the song's final note, Ollie dismissed the crowd.

"Until next Tuesday night, good night," he said, "and if you're driving, make sure you have a car."

Jim packed up his fiddle.

"I didn't see someone dancing," he scolded me.

"I was taking notes," I said lamely. "I had to talk to Father Rey."

It was ten o'clock, nighttime even in northern Michigan. A bugler blew taps in the fort. Maybe the cottagers heard it as a signal to rest, but not the Jesuits. Bicycles appeared from the darkness, pedaled by waiters and dishwashers who had just finished work at the Hotel. This was the only time Ste. Anne's could hold its Spanish Mass. I didn't see Juan Carlos in the pews, but two dozen of his countrymen sang along with the soft guitars and prayed before the flickering Virgin candles in their tall glass tubes. Father Rey, now in his white-

and-gold vestment, delivered the homily. The Jesuits had celebrated Mass here in Huron, Ojibway, French, and English. They learned the language of any tribe that found its way to their chip of an island at the meeting of the lakes.

After the service, there were tamales and flan in the basement, and secondhand clothing piled on tables. A few of the workers paged through coats. Nights are cool on Mackinac, even in midsummer.

"How late will the last person be here?" someone asked Jim.

"That'll be me," he said. "In half an hour, this place'll be empty."

He gestured to a maid. They'd been sharing dessert.

"She has to be up at 5:30 and work at 6 in the morning," he said. "And I've got to get up and plan this dinner for two hundred people."

So it was nearly midnight before the church went dark. Where space contracts, time expands. That's why an island is the perfect resort. If you want to experience eternity in a single day, come to Mackinac.

9

The North Country's Other Great Folksinger

MICHIGAN—MARQUETTE

You can date a town's heyday by its architecture. Marquette, Michigan, peaked at the turn of the last century, when iron and copper were crumbling off the mine walls. The old city hall, which rises from the peak of Washington Street, before the steep dip to Lake Superior, is a Romanesque temple, built from red sandstone. The copper-domed courthouse, where Jimmy Stewart hammed it up for justice in *Anatomy of a Murder*, looks like the Old Main of a land grant college, capped with a tarnished planetarium. Henry Ford, in his high collar and lanky boiled-wool suit, would not look like a ghost if he strolled past the main strip's Taft-era storefronts.

The local wildlife sees opportunity in Marquette's decline: on the Saturday I came to town, the local paper, the *Mining Journal*, ran a photo of a bear cub who had wandered into the shrinking city to forage.

I was in Marquette to hear Sycamore Smith, the North Country's Other Great Folk Singer. Sycamore, whose real name I have gratefully forgotten, was once one half of the Muldoons, a duo who delved into the Upper Peninsula's past for carnivalesque ballads about miners, lumberjacks, sheriffs, whores, and saloons. Their CD, with its echoey, garage-level production and numerous kazoo solos, was my UP driving soundtrack. I had rumbled over pebbled roads while listening to "Lake Superior Fireball" and "Shan-tan-titty-town," a song about "a house of ill-repute that's gettin' rave reviews." But the Muldoons had broken up. Sycamore's other half was hermiting in a cabin on a country road. So Sycamore had found a new drummer, and a Saturday night gig at Gallery 231.

★ ★ ★

Marquette is a college town—Northern Michigan University is here—but that alone could not account for the punk-rock scene inside Gallery 231, a performance space behind an art gallery. Five bucks at the door, Magic Marker on your hand. The floor and the stage are plywood, the pressed tin ceiling peeling to its wooden beams, the burgundy back wall chalked with graffiti. And just in case any of the acts play the national anthem, there is an American flag, defaced with a duct tape cross.

Every hipster north of the Mackinac Bridge was working this room. I saw bug-eyed sunglasses, a "U.S. Space Camp" T-shirt. Sycamore's drummer, Sammy Name, was wandering around in a black-and-white sailor sweater when he was suddenly, unexpectedly, hit on.

"I like that sweater," a girl said.

Sammy thanked her, then described the garment's provenance: "I got it in Japan. It's from Denmark."

Sycamore Smith was the midnight act. Tall and gaunt, like the tree whose name he took, Sycamore had a long forelock of brown hair, scything out from under his Gay Nineties bowler. Once he took that long-legged step onto the stage, he loomed over the room like a seven-foot preacher. Sycamore fitted himself into a wire-metal kazoo holder with the sign "This Machine Kills Itself," and curled over his guitar,

Johnny Cash–style. The big ones have to. The drums snapped three times, the guitar strings jangled, and Sycamore began hurling lyrics about Rosie and Flanagan, two of the dancers at "The Razor Ball":

"There's a big crap game in the hall
Everybody fightin' and yellin'
Rosie hit the floor when Flanagan rolled
Because he fired the dice at her melon
Rosie got up and said goddamn it all
Grabbed old Flanagan and threw him through a wall
And he landed on a beehive as I recall
Down at the Razor Ball."

Then came the break, a stomping kazoo turn that buzzed the room like a swarm of hornets. Sycamore sang about Old Doc Rouch, the lewd sawbones of "Bottomless Town," who goes to the gallows for playing doctor with the sheriff's daughter. He sang "Little House on the Black River Falls," in which he set out his disappointing bride on a boat, "tied her to the anchor, ran along the bank, and shot it till I sank her." It was the best kind of folk-rock, a Northern version of The Band's re-creations of Civil War Dixie. The music sounded modern, even though it was played with traditional instruments, and the lyrics evoked old-timey characters, while reminding us that their passions were no different than ours.

Sycamore ended his show with "The Nantucket Waltz," a litany of bawdy limericks. This was the kicker:

"If your husband's a dumb fuckin' frickin' bore
If he comforts you some, but you bicker more
If you're quite undersexed,
And it's making you vexed
Then you best go lie under a Sycamore!"

★ ★ ★

The Portside Bar is across an alley from Gallery 231. After the show, I drank beer on the deck with Sycamore and Sammy.

Writing songs in the UP is a tough racket. Most barflies demand Tom Petty covers. Marquette's biggest brush with rock-and-roll fame occurred on the day the Rolling Stones jetted in to attend the funeral of their Yooper road manager, Royden "Chuch" Magee. The Muldoons began trying to break out in the late 1990s, when Sycamore returned home after two years of hanging out in Brooklyn. They played their first gig in the basement of a porn shop. By the time they broke up, they were a North Country phenomenon, with a following from Fargo to the Soo. Chicago wouldn't book them, but they connected with music fans in far-flung small towns. As a solo act, Sycamore had recently slipped away from his job as a janitor in the VA hospital to play a tour that took him to podunks like Logan, Utah, and Fort Collins, Colorado. Every little town had a stage like Gallery 231, said Sammy, the drummer.

"For a town this size, that's so far removed from a major city— we've got eight hours to go to Detroit or Chicago—we're stuck in our little island of inaccessibility, so we had to create our own scene."

"When I lived in Brooklyn," Sycamore said, "I worked full time at a bar full of every kind of person, from twenty-one-year-olds to eighty-two-year-olds, all walks of life, all obsessed with talking about movies, books, and music."

"It's just you and me here," Sammy said.

Sycamore and Sammy were both sons of Detroit-area migrants and had inherited their parents' metropolitan values. They weren't interested in deer hunting and snowmobiles, like their Yooper peers.

"Before Sam and I played here, we used to sit around and talk about records," Sycamore said.

"If it weren't for the Internet, I would have moved to the big city five years ago," said Sammy, who was twenty-three. "But I can get any music I want here. I figure I can live in a big city when I'm older. I like living here when I'm young, because I can go out and go hiking. I can sit in front of a desk when I'm older."

Sammy wanted me to see his favorite hiking spot—Wetmore's Landing, a roadless cove on Lake Superior. It was two o'clock in the morning, but we all agreed to meet at ten, at Dead River Coffee.

★ ★ ★

The Dead River is the daytime headquarters for Marquette's scene-sters. You can buy a *Morning Journal* or a *New York Times* across the street at Book World, then spend the morning drinking coffee and waiting for a pickup Scrabble game. The cafe is owned by a gray-haired hippie named Theo, who long ago belonged to an Ann Arbor food co-op. Going north was the right move. There's a misconception that Ann Arbor is Michigan's gateway back to the 1960s. The back-to-the-land types slipped away to northern Michigan, and they're still here, judging by the stacks of environmental pamphlets in the Dead River.

Sycamore walked through the front door in full hipster regalia: oversized shades, a shirt patterned with oak leaves, stovepipe jeans, and motorcycle boots. He ordered a Styrofoam vat of coffee.

"Are you going to have any?" he asked, sipping the first jolt.

"It's too early in the morning for coffee," I said. "I'm drinking papaya juice."

Sammy was still asleep in his parents' basement, so we drove over to pick him up in Sycamore's Ford Explorer. All the way, a CD of songs that influenced Bob Dylan played on the speaker.

Wetmore's Landing is five miles north of Marquette. The trailhead is at the summit of a half-bowl of sloping woodland and sandstone cliff. We stair-stepped downhill like crabs, pausing for footholds on stones and hemlock roots.

"This is a path that's good for a city boy," Sammy said, leading me down a gentle grade.

"We don't have hills in Chicago," I said. "But if we were in Chicago, we'd probably all be going out to brunch instead of hiking."

"When I visited my friend Eric in Chicago, we went to this cafe called Lula's where he had some artwork," Sammy said. "The waiters had the most indifferent attitude."

Sycamore brought up an episode of *This American Life*, in which the correspondent asked friendly waiters to act blase. They got bigger tips.

"Maybe the customers were afraid of them," I said.

The beach was walled off from the rest of Michigan by the five-story bluff. A family roamed the sands, but they had arrived by boat. There were days, when the wind blew the topwater inland, that Lake Superior was warm enough for swimmers. We didn't test it that morning. As we hiked back up through the red pines, Sycamore recited a lyric he'd been noodling with:

"Flanagan was drunk / But not drunk as a skunk / No—more like drunk as a trunk full of skunks / I didn't know what to think / I only knew what I thunk / He was pitching like the *Fitz* pitched / Just before she sunk."

"People might not get that line about the *Fitz*," Sammy said. *He knew it was the Edmund Fitzgerald, but the Trolls . . .*

"Everyone in the UP calls it the *Fitz*," Sycamore protested. "My mom used to bake a cake every year on the day that it sank."

Sycamore drove back into town with the Velvet Underground on the CD player. We'd just passed the "MARQUETTE 19,661" sign when I spotted a brown animal crossing at the light ahead of us. It was the size of an Irish setter, but it was moving like a sloth—lazily, fluidly. It was too slow to be a dog.

"That's the bear!" I shouted. "That's the bear I saw in the paper!"

The bear was leaving a storage facility, in search of more garbage. The authorities had urged the public not to hassle the cub, so traffic halted while he crossed the street. Everyone wanted to gawk, anyway. Sycamore didn't know whether to be fascinated or embarrassed.

"Uh-oh," he said to me. "Now you're going to think Marquette is the wilderness. That's the first time I've ever seen a bear in Marquette. I've seen a lot in the Keweenaw, but never in Marquette."

10

A Long Way from a Long Way from Anywhere

MICHIGAN—ISLE ROYALE, IRONWOOD

Isle Royale is a long way from a long way from anywhere. To catch the once-a-day ferry to the dolphin-shaped island in the northwestern corner of Lake Superior, you have to drive to Copper Harbor, the northernmost village in the UP. It lies at the tip of Keweenaw County, a barely inhabited land of fir-covered mountains and volcanic rock.

I went to Isle Royale with one goal in mind: to see a moose. Once I crossed the channel between Houghton and Hancock, it was a long, steep haul up U.S. 41, past Coppertown, U.S.A., an abandoned mine pit south of Calumet, and past the Jampot, where monks make jelly out of thimbleberry, a boreal shrub that thrives in cool Northern forest. At Eagle River, where this pop. 2,000 county is run from a courthouse the size of a one-room school, I turned onto the lakeshore highway.

For dramatic coastlines—the intertidal battlegrounds where insistent waves burst against ancient rocks—you cannot beat Big Sur on the West Coast, Maine on the East, or Keweenaw on the Third. The road threads the ledge between billion-year-old hills and a frenzied beach where the tide slaps over copper-tinged boulders, forcing surges of froth through the gaps.

In the summer, Copper Harbor is the embarkation point for Isle Royale. This is the end of the road for U.S. 41. The highway was a snowbird migration route in the 1930s and '40s, and there's still a mileage sign for those seeking warmer islands: "MIAMI FL 1,990."

In the morning, the *Isle Royale Queen IV*, a two-story, one-hundred-foot boat, nudged its bow against a gravel parking lot, still greasy with the night's rain. The *Queen IV*, a retired New York city ferry called out of a Florida retirement, had just replaced a smaller, slower vessel known to travelers as "the Barf Barge." Bigger and faster, the *Queen IV* saved an hour, and innumerable breakfasts.

Isle Royale is the least visited national park in the Lower 48. About fifteen thousand people set foot there each year—fewer than an afternoon crowd at Yellowstone. The eighty hikers shrugging their packs onto the luggage cart were different from the brat-grilling RV campers I'd tented with in state parks. These were lean adventurers, urban outdoorsmen stepping directly from the cubicle maze to the wilderness. One man browsed *Wired* magazine. Another wore wool, from bush hat to trousers—the getup of a mid–twentieth-century Alpinist.

The boat set sail under black powder clouds. The wake peeled away from the stern; the evergreen hills softened behind the spray. Never in my life had I lost sight of land, but it wasn't long before Copper Harbor revolved over the horizon, and then we were churning through a compass of water, encircled by mist. It was like sailing on a watery planet. You couldn't judge the distance to the horizon. The boat might have been floating in a water tank, a hundred feet across. It might have been drifting across the North Atlantic.

The landing at Rock Harbor is the only developed corner of Isle Royale. There's a camper's commissary, a gift shop, and a lodge with soft beds and a china-plate restaurant. But by law, only one percent of the island is set aside for civilized comforts. The rest is wilderness. This must be the most remote spot in the continental United States: where else, even in the mountain west, could you find yourself so far from the nearest automobile? The island was not always so isolated from human commerce: the Ojibway canoed in to chip copper, Norwegian fishermen from Minnesota wintered out in cabins, and hay fever victims cottaged here before antihistamines made ragweed less of a misery. When the Park Service took over in 1940, it granted lifetime leases to landowners; the shrewdest wrote down the names of their youngest grandchildren, so there remain a half-dozen cabins, and one family still fishes. Nobody winters anymore. The island closes November 1, and from then until spring, the only visitors are scientists who fly in to count the moose and the wolves. The moose swam over from Ontario. A herd of five hundred supports thirty wolves, descended from a pack that walked across the ice in the winter of 1948. Moose sightings are common—moose have no sweat glands, so when the temperature rises past fifty degrees, they are neck-deep in coves, harbors, or inland lakes. But only one hiker in a thousand ever sees a wolf.

I had two nights on the island. I couldn't go far enough inland to find a wolf. But I wanted to see a moose; now that I'd seen the bear in Marquette, it would complete my Lake Superior menagerie. I began walking west, in the direction of Windigo, the ferry dock on the island's western edge. That's a five-day hike; I hoped only to get as far as Daisy Farm, the second campsite on the trail. It was seven miles away, and I still had a long Northern evening.

Isle Royale is the essence of the North—wolf, moose, fir, rock, water—reduced to 133,000 acres. My backpack was stuffed with beans, noodles, canned soup, and peanut butter, but I worried out my *Trees and Flowers of the Great Lakes* and searched for wildflowers that have been choked out of less insular country. I saw thimbleberry, its tiny pods not yet budded to fruit; wild rose; wood lily; ox-eye daisy; and, every time I lifted my eyes from the trail, the spindly profile of a spruce.

I got lost twice on the way to Daisy Farm. John Updike once wrote that "New England wears its bones on the outside." So does Isle Royale. My boots danced around puddles, sidestepped rocks. By the time I found my way, the light was smoky in the overcast evening. I decided to stop at Three Mile, the first campsite on the trail. This late, the mosquitos were hunting in earnest. I slapped them into rouge smears on my cheeks and hands. Then I unknotted the rain jacket around my waist, pulled the hood over my head, and yanked the cuffs past my fingers.

At Three Mile, I found a screened-in porch: plank floor, sloping roof, concrete-block pillars. The walls recorded the sentiments of past campers. "Troop 104 Slept Here." "Dave Varro, Warren, MI, 7/30/74." "I Need Nookie"—a timeless wilderness complaint. I ladled a pot of water from the lake, boiled it on my camp stove, and drained it into a plastic bottle. The lake was infested with parasites, so this was the only safe way to drink. Then I heated a can of soup and pitched my tent on the wooden platform, just as the rains began dribbling down. Even under a roof, I needed the extra layer of shelter: the temperature fell to the mid-forties, closer to freezing than to bare-arm weather. I slipped directly from my jacket to my sleeping bag. Clicking on my hiker's headlamp, I read my loose-paged *Anatomy of a Murder*, the book that gave the Upper Peninsula its one and only turn in the Hollywood spotlight. One of the great courtroom procedurals, *Anatomy* helped nudge the legal thriller from the crusading of *Perry Mason* to the moral ambiguities of *Presumed Innocent*. Its narrator, Paul Biegler, is no Atticus Finch: he's an ex-prosecutor representing an Air Force captain who killed a man to defend the honor of his sluttish wife. In some ways, the book is too dated for modern readers—it is sordid in a way that was only possible in the 1940s and '50s, when there was an enormous gap between public virtue and private vice—but the movie is still popular in the UP. Outside Ishpeming, I'd passed a bar that declared "SEEN IN *ANATOMY OF A MURDER*."

The next morning, I made it to Daisy Farm Camp, slipping over mud, roots, and rocks every step of the four-mile walk. I sat down to

Moskey Basin, Isle Royale National Park.

lunch on a can of sardines. Loons paddled in Moskey Basin. The water was a grained mirror. At the mouth of the cove, I could see the Rock Harbor Lighthouse, and the ruined shacks of an old fishery. It was only eleven o'clock in the morning. I couldn't keep hiking west, to Lake Richie or Chickenbone Lake. I'd never make it back to Rock Harbor for the next day's ferry. I decided to head north, and hike the Greenstone Ridge. It was the spine of Isle Royale, far above the bug-swarmed shoreline.

Getting there was like climbing a staircase, a mile and a half long. The trail finally flattened out at Mount Ojibway. A three-story look-out stood on the summit. It was as spindly as an electrical tower. Standing beside it was the wool-clad hiker I'd seen on the ferry. He was with his wife, a woman so palely beautiful I figured she must be one of the local Finns. I was wrong. He was the Finn. Galen Ojala was an Air Force captain from Iron Mountain. He'd purchased his hiking outfit—combat boots, herringbone pants, button-up vest—at a military surplus store. He insisted it wasn't hot. On Isle Royale, you

The view from Mount Franklin, Isle Royale National Park.

couldn't be warm enough. We both started up the steps. I thought maybe I could see a moose cooling itself in Lake Ojibway. Halfway up, I felt the tower shuddering in the unbroken northwest wind. I retreated. Galen kept climbing.

"It's too windy," I told Galen's wife. We watched him scout from the highest platform.

"That's what I thought," she said. "I tried to go up there before, and I only made it up the first set of stairs."

Galen came down from the tower, shouldered his pack, and headed west, to Lake Ojibway. His wife followed. I turned east, hiking alone to Mount Franklin. It's named for Benjamin Franklin, who swindled Isle Royale from King George III at the Treaty of Paris talks, in 1783. One historian says that eighteenth-century maps misplaced the island in the middle of the lake; another that Franklin heard stories of fabulous copper deposits.

Atop the mountain, I stepped into a rock ledge, and looked around. To the south, I saw meadows of summer-faded grass, flecked with yarrow and thistle. To the north, past a jungle of evergreens and miles of gloomy water, was the Sleeping Giant, a range of hills shaped like a reclining man. It was fifteen miles away, on the tip of Ontario's Sibley Peninsula, but sharply drawn beneath clouds that overarched like a drawn-up curtain.

A milepost pointed the way to Three Mile Camp, but I nearly lost the trail as I zigzagged down a rock shelf. At some point, the cairns marking the path crumbled to shapeless rubble. I found myself stranded on a volcanic slab, with no map, and very little water. Tobin Harbor was straight ahead, but thick undergrowth blocked my path. Dropping my pack, I tried to blaze a trail. Within ten yards, I was up to my chest in leaves. The branches resisted like a police line. Half an hour is not so long to be lost in the wilderness, but it's enough to bring you to the suburbs of panic. I paced the rock face, feeling edgier with each lap. Finally, I found a hole in the tree line. Stepping through it, I set my boot on a path.

I still had hours of walking. I sipped from the bottle every mile, but I was so dehydrated I slipped on a damp rock and tumbled forward, skinning my wrist and pitching my pack into the dirt. The last three miles, the path lengthened with each step. I suffered the same delirious cravings I'd felt during marathon training runs—for milkshakes, Whoppers, pretzels, corn chips, and malted milk balls. When I saw the seaplane drag race off the water, I knew I was close to Rock Harbor.

By the time I gained the commissary, I had hiked thirteen miles, under a full pack. I tore a thirty-two-ounce bottle of Gatorade from the shelf, drank it in a single chug, and chased it by crumbling a package of Oreos into my mouth. Outside the store, I met three girls and their mother. Their hair was lank, their faces were sweaty and greasy, and they smelled like tramps.

"We were out there four days," the mother said. They had gotten as far as Chickenbone, the wishbone-shaped lake. That exhausted night, they ate a cold supper: beans from the can.

"Did you see a moose?" I asked eagerly.

"We did see a moose," she said. "It was acting bizarre. It just kept charging through the water, like it was running at something. Maybe it was trying to get the flies off itself."

That evening, I asked a ranger the same question.

"Where are all the moose?" I demanded.

"I don't know where all the moose went," she said. "There was one right here in front of the auditorium on Tuesday. It was standing right on the asphalt path."

I didn't see a moose on Isle Royale. But I wasn't prepared for wilderness hiking. Any big-city wuss can set up a nylon tent in an RV park, with a car parked on the campsite, and an ATM in the party store up the road. Isle Royale is Camping 401. Stuffing cans into my backpack sustained me for forty-eight hours, but that's not enough time to explore this exotic kingdom. A man from Petoskey passed by my tent. He'd been on the island a week. It was his third trip: he'd dehydrated twelve pounds of beef down to two pounds of jerky, packed sun-dried tomatoes—and seen a moose, bathing in McCargoe Cove, on the north shore.

The next afternoon, as I waited for the ferry, four young bucks paddled up in a canoe. Their beards were somewhere between Humphrey Bogart in *The African Queen* and Erik the Red. They toted a quiver of fishing rods.

When I got back to Copper Harbor, Don Kilpela, captain of the *Isle Royale Queen*, was in his office.

"One thing about Isle Royale," he said. "They say it's the least visited National Park, but the most re-visited. I have people on that boat who've gone every year I've owned the boat. If I knew what it was, I'd sell it."

Maybe they're still trying to see a moose.

★ ★ ★

On U.S. 41, my gas gauge quivered near "E." In Keweenaw County, this is a serious issue. Pressing lightly on the pedal, I rolled through

Delaware, and Central, hoping to find a gas station, but those settlements had made more of an impression on mapmakers than on the landscape. Finally, in Phoenix, I passed a general store with a single pump in the parking lot. The nozzle was holstered in the side—you can only get premium on the Keweenaw—and the price was recorded by spinning tumblers. Inside, the warped, varnished planks said this place had once sold coffee, newspapers, and beans to copper miners. Nope, they didn't take credit cards. The $2.50 in my pocket bought less than a gallon—enough, I hoped, to get me to Calumet.

I badly wanted to visit Gay, where locals drink in, yep, the Gay Bar, but it was down a county road in the southeast corner of the peninsula and I was too tired for that drive. I did see the "Keweenaw Snow Thermometer," a vertical billboard commemorating the winter of 1978–79, when 390.4 inches fell. The thirty-two-foot sign dares the Witch of Superior to bury it, but that's not likely to happen these days: the year before, 202 inches had fallen, still a blizzard short of the twenty-foot average.

When I checked into a motel in Houghton, my cheeks were shaded with whiskers, my hair was mashed under a baseball cap, and I was breathing the thin air of exhaustion. I asked for a room with a tub.

"You just come off the island?" the clerk asked.

It gives you that look.

★ ★ ★

Ironwood, the westernmost city in Michigan, is 350 miles from Fargo, and 600 from Detroit. That's a lot of space in both directions. Ironwood has used it to build two entries in the Great Northern World's Largest Derby. Copper Peak, the better-known monument to Bunyanism, is the world's longest ski jump. It was built in 1969, during the Jean-Claude Killy era of Alpine chic, to lure European athletes to the UP. For awhile, it did. Finns, Norwegians, Austrians, and Japanese all hurled themselves off the lip of the 469-foot chute. But

The world's largest fiberglass Indian.

the wooden hill has not launched a jumper since 1994. Its track needs new planks. Today, Copper Peak is marketed as a scenic overlook.

I had visited Ironwood the previous autumn, and paid ten dollars to ride a chairlift to the foot of Copper Peak. The chair swung from a cable, squealing like a gull as it rolled upward. Dangling twenty feet above a snowbank may not feel like a cable-snap from death, but it's different when you can see the rocks and the scrub that will break your fall, and your legs. On its range of wooded hills, Copper Peak doesn't look like a Brobdignagian folly. It looks like an old mineshaft. There's an eighteen-story elevator to the top.

As I'd made toward the jump, the chairlift operator called to me. I recognized his face from a newspaper photo in the visitor center: he was the only Yooper ever to qualify for Copper Peak. The leap had nearly maimed him.

"You know you can walk up," he said.

"Are there stairs?"

"No. You can walk up the hill. Just hold on to the railing. I do it all the time."

So I'd walked, never looking back at the ever-lengthening tumble I'd take if I lost my balance. Once I summitted, I was looking over the quilt of autumn, with patches and threads of yellow, pumpkin, and crimson. Supposedly, you can see past the blue curve of Lake Superior, all the way to Minnesota's North Shore.

Ironwood's other "world's largest" is the World's Largest Fiberglass Indian, an inflated lawn ornament looming over downtown like a water tower. It is allegedly a likeness of Hiawatha, the mythical Ojibway hero who lived in the Superior Country, but it's dressed in a Sioux war bonnet and a turquoise breechcloth, so maybe it's meant to honor all Natives, the way a figure in a Viking helmet and a toga would honor all Europeans.

On the very last block of the UP, before U.S. 2 crosses the Montreal River and becomes honky-tonk Silver Street in Hurley, Wisconsin, you'll find Joe's Pasty Shop. No oven produces crisper, flakier, meatier pasties than Joe's. The pasty (pronounced PAST-ee, as opposed to the tassels that swing from burlesque girls' breasts), is the UP's signature delicacy. It was brought to the North Country by the "Cousin Jacks," the Cornish miners who crossed the sea from coal to copper in the nineteenth century. Their wives, the Cousin Jennys, wanted them to carry a full meal into the mines, so they invented the pasty, a stew folded into a turnover shell. The original pasties were as complete as frozen dinners—some had jam baked into a corner compartment, as dessert. The miners threw away the corners or "crimps" not only to avoid arsenic poisoning from their coal-dusted fingers but also to feed the "knockers," the ghosts that lived underground. A classic pasty is filled with beef, potatoes, and onions, but in America, they've become as much a dumping ground of ethnic foods as pizzas. Joe's serves the Reuben pasty, the bacon cheeseburger pasty, the taco pasty, the pizza pasty, and the Cajun chicken pasty. I like the Cornish pasty, which is the original filling, plus rutabagas. You can't leave the UP without eating one.

11

Highway 61 Visited

MINNESOTA—DULUTH, GRAND MARAIS

The *Ziemia Łódzka* spent the Fourth of July anchored in Lake Superior. The Polish freighter was visiting Duluth to load grain, but the longshoremen weren't working on the holiday, so it made no sense to pay a thousand-dollar docking fee. The bulky ship, with its owner's name, Polsteam, painted large on the hull, made a picturesque nautical float for sightseers on the port cruise. And the sailors got to watch fireworks from Duluth *and* Superior, its sister city in Wisconsin. Superior's were better, they all agreed. More garish, more bombastic, more American.

Nobody at the Norshore Theatre, the restored movie palace on Superior Street, was interested in watching fireworks. Too bombastic, too militaristic. Inside the Norshore, they were throwing a counter–Fourth of July, a "Peace Is Patriotic" rally, featuring a long bill of poets and folksingers from Duluth and the Iron Range.

★ ★ ★

Minnesotans are notorious for their progressive politics. Hubert Humphrey, Eugene McCarthy, and Paul Wellstone all went to Washington to noodge their fellow senators on civil rights, the Vietnam War, and poverty. Bob Dylan sang "Masters of War" at the Grammys during the Gulf War, although most viewers couldn't understand the lyrics. Garrison Keillor, who started *A Prairie Home Companion* in front of fourteen people in Saint Paul, is public radio's only superstar. A "Peace Is Patriotic" night seemed like the perfect place to observe the Minnesota Liberal. I hail from a Big Ten college town, so I know that the Upper Midwestern left isn't angry. It is earnest, wholesome, nonconfrontational, and a little hurt that the U.S.A. settles its conflicts with violence. It goes to church and volunteers at the nature center. Its car is rusty. It needs a new pair of Rockport walking shoes. It pays ten dollars to hear folk music at the Unitarian fellowship.

Those were the folks at the Norshore. The organizer was a tall country doctor who had been drawn to the antiwar movement after treating veterans at his family practice in Pequot Lakes. He handed me a card reading "Every Church a Peace Church." It was from his peace group at Our Savior's Lutheran. I asked him whether there was something peculiarly Minnesotan about this event.

"There's such a thing as Minnesota nice, and there's a lot of socialist types in the Range," the doctor said. "There's a lot of people interested in the environment. And the Scandinavians, the Finns, they were socialist. There's also been a lot of mining and logging. The unions."

The doctor had to run—the show started in ten minutes—so I turned to a girl wearing a "Wellstone" button. The senator had died in a plane crash while running for re-election, but his followers were still campaigning.

"He was a teacher, not really a politician," the girl said. "He tried to make things better for other people, not himself. And he had the green bus. It was part of his campaign. There are many people up here who still question whether the plane crash was an accident."

The lights were flashing, so I hurried along the literature table, picking up *The Third Way of Jesus*, *Out Now!*, *Youth for Socialist Action*, *Questions Recruiters Don't Want You to Ask*, and *The War Prayer*, by Mark Twain.

The doctor was a diffident, homely emcee, in a Gandhi T-shirt, knee-length shorts, white socks, and sneakers. His audience was middle-aged, gray—veterans of the struggle against the Vietnam War. One man wore an American flag with corporate logos in place of stars. The sad thing wasn't that they were still protesting war. The sad thing was that there were still wars for them to protest.

"I love my country so much that I'm wiling to have a lover's quarrel with it," the doctor said. "There's a lot more of us out there than we think."

He introduced the first folksingers—Cindy, blond, rosy and maternal, and Dan, a balding man in round glasses who sat motionless except for his long, plucking fingers. He looked like Picasso's painting of a guitarist.

"This song is called 'How Do We Teach the Children?'" Cindy said. "It was written during the first Gulf War, when I was a graduate student at the University of Wisconsin in Madison, and unfortunately, war doesn't seem to go out of fashion. There's always a need for antiwar songs."

The music was as gentle and graceful as the lyrics were blunt and awkward: "Our might has leveled cities," Cindy quavered. "Untold damage has been done / And we sit back in our arrogance / Tell me what is it we have won? / How do we teach the children / There's got to be a better way / The only hope for the future / Is shining in their eyes today." It is fine work, making poetry out of agitprop. Duluth is only big enough for one Dylan.

The duo was followed onstage by a man who read a poem about why he wouldn't fly a flag in his yard. Here my notes read "incense wafting from exits." The doctor returned to the stage.

"We're going to take an intermission for the obligatory fireworks," he said. "Unless nobody wants to see the fireworks. Seen one, seen 'em all, right? It's pretty toxic stuff that comes raining down, so don't stand downwind."

I wanted to see the fireworks. I sneaked out through the incense-scented exit.

If the quiet, uncompetitive folks at the Peace Is Patriotic rally were ever given power (they're not the types to seize it themselves), they probably wouldn't use it to build the tallest skyscraper, or explore Mars. It is an irony of politics that progressives resist progress, and conservatives don't want to conserve anything. But we'd all be able to see a doctor. And we'd never go to war.

★ ★ ★

The *Ziemia Łódzka* began loading in the morning. Duluth is where the Great Plains meet the Great Lakes, so the harbor is ringed by grain elevators as big as housing projects. The ship parked itself under a funnel, which sprayed wheat into its holds. It would take on eighteen thousand tons here, then top off for the ocean voyage at Trois-Rivières, Quebec. The sailors hadn't been ashore since Milwaukee, where the *Ziemia Łódzka* had dropped off steel. They hadn't been to Mass since leaving Poland, two-and-a-half months before. That afternoon, a priest arrived from the Seafarers' Center. Father Robert Sipe had once led a Polish-American congregation in Minneapolis, so he could sing their hymns and recite their Lord's Prayer. He was ushered into the captain's office, where Piotr Mikolczyk, the boyish, round-faced captain, greeted him gratefully. The *Ziemia Łódzka* was a society of twenty men. Any visitor was welcome.

Father Bob and Piotr sat down at a round table in the captain's office. A depth chart of Duluth-Superior Harbor hung on the wall. Piotr poured coffee and laid out cookies.

"I am so glad you are coming, even to say hello," Piotr said. "So many people forget about the seafarers."

"I retired a year ago, and I didn't even think about the seafarers," Father Bob said. "It really is a world apart."

Piotr Mikolczyk, captain of the *Ziemia Łódzka*

"I have been sailing twenty-two years, so it's almost half my life. When I am off the vessel, I only see the sea on the TV. It's OK. I am sick of it."

"Your wife hasn't divorced you?"

"No," Piotr laughed. "I hope not. You get used to it. This is vacation time in Poland, and I proposed to my family, 'Come to Cleveland,' but there was no time. They had to go to Warsaw and see the consul. Now we are planning to get them to Portugal," where the ship would drop its load of wheat.

Father Bob was on a sales call. A good salesman knows how to make a connection with his work. He asked Piotr what he knew about Maximilian Kolbe, the Polish priest who died in a German death camp.

"I hope that soon they will have the pope make him a saint," Piotr said, his eyes flashing. "He was a saint, man. All Poles love him."

Father Bob asked if he could come back the next day to celebrate Mass. The captain said of course.

★ ★ ★

The Seafarers Center, which sent Father Bob to the *Ziemia Łódzka,* is in an old Catholic parish house on Duluth's seedy West End, not far from the port. Sailors wash ashore in this neighborhood, so you can also find several flophouses, including the Seaway Hotel. Charles "Lucky" Lane, the Texas missionary who ran the center, described the Seaway as "the bordello of the west side."

"They had women in there who would set seafarers up, someone would lie in wait for 'em, roll 'em. There's probably a half-dozen of 'em here in Duluth. One of them is notorious for meth, one is notorious for coke. They all have their reputations." Some pimps made it even easier for the sailors. The police had broken up a ring that delivered women right to the ships. The Russians loved Scandinavian girls.

The center has computers, so foreign sailors can check their e-mails. It has piles of coats for the Filipinos who arrive during the cold "shoulder seasons" of spring and fall, and a dozen beds for sailors. That night, only two were occupied: one by Father Bob, the other by Bernie Aus, a middle-aged mariner who'd tried to quit the Lakes, but couldn't make it on land. He was living at the mission while he studied for the seaman's test. Lucky had given him chores, but mostly he seemed to watch baseball in the TV room and smoke on the stoop. A lanky man with long, thinning hair, a goatee, a faded Harley shirt, and a wistful grin, he'd obviously been born for the rootless life.

"My father sailed, too, so I guess it's in my blood," he said, when I caught him with a Marlboro. He exhaled his words as softly as cigarette smoke. "I don't have a wife or any kids. I grew up in Superior, so I used to winter over on ships in the harbor. I'd live there with another crewmember. 'Bout six years ago, I decided to quit and get a job onshore, but I couldn't find steady work. I'm too old to go to school, so I guess I'll go back to sailing."

That evening, Lucky drove the van down to the docks, to take the crew to a shopping mall. Poles are easier to work with than Russians, he said. Most Russians don't have visas, and since the terrorist scare had begun, an armed guard stood at the bottom of the stairway, to prevent them from placing one foot on U.S. asphalt. On the way to the mall, Lucky handed out phone cards, while Jan, the chief engineer, talked about finding a jean jacket for his wife, and extra memory for his digital camera. He really preferred Cleveland to Duluth, he said.

"Cleveland is close to downtown. Last time, I went with captain to music center."

The sailors returned to the van lugging bags full of candy bars, work boots, solar lamps, detergent, and trousers.

"You going to be back tomorrow?" Jan asked Lucky.

"Father Bob will be back at one tomorrow to say Mass," Lucky said. "I hear they're having some problems mixing the protein they're putting in the grain, so if you're here tomorrow night, I'll be back at six."

★ ★ ★

During the night, the *Ziemia Łódzka* had shifted forward, so the elevator could fill its last hold. The stairway at the bow could no longer reach the dock. Father Bob had to climb a rope ladder. He stood beside the ship, in his priestly collar and his Minnesota Golden Gophers cap, his wine and his surplice locked in a briefcase.

"Morning," the captain called down. "Will you manage to climb up?"

"If I climb up, you'll go to confession," Father Bob shouted.

The captain lowered a rope. Father Bob tied it to his briefcase handle.

"One second, we will bring the safety," the captain said.

A crewman descended with a harness. He fitted it over Father Bob's shoulders and locked it around his waist.

"I'm only seventy-two," the priest said, as he was hauled up, plank by plank. "In a few more years I won't be able to do this."

When he reached the top, Father Bob clapped Piotr on the back.

"That's ten years in purgatory," he promised. "Think anybody will show up for this?"

"They say that Poland is a ninety-five percent Catholic country," Piotr said.

"So people still go to church in Poland, even after all those years of having a communist government?"

"When I am at home, I go to Mass every Sunday. It is the main part of the day. The noon Mass. I try to be a good Catholic."

Mass was in the movie room, which was equipped with a flat-screen TV and a long shelf of videos: *Ziemia Obiecana*, *Mr. Bean*, *Zamsla Ganstera*, *Forrest Gump*. Over the table, Father Bob spread a white cloth embroidered with the logo of the Apostleship of the Sea, an order of maritime chaplains. He had joined after retiring as a parish priest. So far, it had been a pleasant transition from work to heaven: he had sailed as a shipboard priest on cruises to Hawaii and the West Indies.

We waited for the crew to ease the ship back into place. In the meantime, Father Bob talked. He was gregarious, and since he was a priest, he was used to people listening to him.

"There are two things you'll never find in politics," he pronounced. "A compassionate Republican and a pro-life Democrat."

I had to admire his bipartisan cynicism.

After half an hour, Piotr rushed into the room, with a freshly baked loaf of bread, and apologies.

"Sorry we waste your time," he said. "We don't know what's going to happen any minute that is our life."

Ten sailors followed him through the door. They were hard-looking men, their faces turned to stone by the stoicism of lonely months at sea. But in the presence of a priest, they became as downcast and fidgety as altar boys.

While the captain translated, Father Bob talked of Czestochowa and Medjugorje, Eastern Europe's shrines to the Virgin Mary. He knew how to play to a congregation.

"Mary told us some beautiful things," he said. "Don't just pray, pray from the heart. Go to Communion often. Take the Eucharist

Father Bob says Mass.

often. Fast. And read the Bible. These are the five stones. Just as David took five stones and slew Goliath, these will slay the devil."

And then, in a colorless pulpit baritone, he crooned a hymn in Polish. Every Polish Catholic knows *Serdeczna Matko (Beloved Mother, Guardian of Our Nation)*. All the sailors sang along, in mumbled, self-conscious tones.

The Catholic liturgy makes fathers of the priests, and children of the congregants. As Father Bob carried his wafers from sailor to sailor, each opened his mouth like an infant expecting a spoon.

After Communion, the captain made a speech, praising Father Bob and the entire U.S.A.

"America is a country where you can see all kinds of people living together," Piotr gushed. "Black people, white people, people with different religions. If every country were like the United States, there would be no wars!"

Father Bob chuckled.

"Well," he said. "I wouldn't go that far."

★ ★ ★

Oh God said to Abraham, 'Kill me a son'
. . . Abe said, 'Where'd you want this killin' done?'
God said, 'Out on Highway 61'

—Bob Dylan, "Highway 61 Revisited"

If you live on Minnesota's North Shore, U.S. Highway 61 is "the road to Canada." If you love old roads, it's the Avenue of the Saints, because it follows the Mississippi River through Saint Paul, St. Louis and New Orleans. Highway 61 also links Duluth to Clarksdale, Mississippi, birthplace of bluesman Robert Johnson. It's the north-south axis of his "Crossroads." Did Dylan have this in mind when he named an album after the road? He's not telling us. He never tells us anything. But *Highway 61 Revisited* is Highway 61's claim to fame.

The road narrows to two lanes at Two Harbors, just past the taconite port, and then slices through shoreline cliffs that crumble into pebbly beaches. We're due west of the Keweenaw, so the rock is just as old, and as full of treasure. This is the Iron Range, where the *Edmund Fitzgerald*'s "load of iron ore" was mined.

I was headed to Grand Marais, to spend a morning on Harley Toftey's fishing boat. At one time, there were four hundred Norwegian fishermen in Minnesota. The North Shore reminded them of their native fjords, and its cold waters teemed with fish. Then the Saint Lawrence Seaway opened in 1957, and lampreys swam in, killing the trout. A decade later, waste from the Silver Bay taconite plant drove the herring far from shore. When the plant began pumping its silt to a pond, the herring came home, but now only two dozen men pursue them. Harley sold his catch at the Dockside Fish Market, a restaurant/deli run by his wife. I got the number from a fishing museum down the coast, in Tofte. "I'll be glad to have ya up to the rest'runt," Harley said when I called. "I'll even take ya out on the boat. I usually leave at seven in the morning, so be on the dock by then." He didn't say much more. I got into Grand Marais on a Wednesday night, rented a cabin on the hill above town, and set the alarm for six.

Harley's skiff was tied up behind the restaurant. He was in the fish-cleaning room, dressed in orange waders and overalls, loading his boxes with ice. The television was tuned to Fox News. A charred London bus appeared on the screen.

"Some o' these countries got more serious about terrorism, wouldn't be no more o' this," Harley grunted, hefting a box out to the boat. His dog, Cubby, followed, and jumped into the bow.

"He's got to go out every day, or else he gets mad," Harley said. He pointed at my shoes.

"You might want some rubber boots. It gets kind of wet out there."

I found a pair of wellies in a jumble box, and then we buzzed out on to the lake. Gulls gathered behind the stern, their papier-mâché bodies sharp against the bright sky. As they pumped their wings to keep pace, Harley picked up a box of fish guts, and heaved the gory remains of yesterday's catch onto the water. The birds splashed heels-first into the lake, to peck at heads and lungs with scimitar beaks.

"You feed 'em, they leave you alone when you're pickin' the guts," he explained.

A few determined gulls kept up the chase. Harley pushed the throttle into fourth, and soon the birds looked like moths against Grand Marais' green hills. Once he cut the engine, the lake smoothed to blue vinyl.

Harley gripped his nets with gloved hands, and hauled them across the deck. Maybe one hole in two hundred held a herring, twisting and flashing in the sun. Harley popped them free and punctured their air-bloated bodies with a metal spike that fit over his hand like brass knuckles. He tossed his victims onto the ice boxes, where their panting gills feathered out final breaths. The Evinrude engine was set to growl. It nudged the boat sideways, so the net streamed across the deck. While Harley plucked herring, I lifted the depth lines over the bow.

Every once in awhile, a stray gull harried the boat. Harley sicced his dog on it. "There he goes, Cubby, get 'im. Get that bird. Get 'im, Cubs. Get that bird!"

Cubby planted his paws on the gunwale, whining as the gulls flew away.

"They poke my nets full of holes and ruin 'em," Harley said in a tone of jovial disgust. "Once in awhile, they'll pull a fish out. I got a shotgun there, I'll shoot it in the air once in awhile to scare 'em off. It's the young seagulls, don't know anything. Eventually, they'll watch their buddies get in trouble."

Harley Toftey had his opinions, but he wasn't a conversationalist. I suppose that came from being Norwegian, and from spending his mornings on a boat, with no one for company but Cubby, the seagulls, and the fish. Since writers work with words, we perpetrate the fallacy that only articulate, "quotable" people make good subjects. But if we paid as much attention to what people do as to what they say, we would realize that men who work with their hands are as worthy of our words as actors or television anchors.

Harley was back on land by a quarter to ten, with two hundred pounds of fish.

"It ain't great," he said, "But for this time of year, it's average or a little bit below average. It's been raining, and it puts a little silt in the water. Fish don't like that."

There was a sign over the cleaning room: "LOCALLY CAUGHT—From Our Boat To Your Table—Herring, Whitefish, Brown or Spec. Trout—Cured Smoked Fish." Harley dumped his catch into the scaler, a metal cylinder with a fish-skinning screen. He pumped in water as it whirled. Silver flakes drifted into the drain.

Two old fishermen wandered in. Dick and Leonard came by every day, when the boat docked. Leonard grabbed a knife, began slicing the flanks off filets. He ribbed Harley about his politics.

"I call him George W.," Leonard said.

Harley sliced the cartilage off a herring, tossed it to Cubby.

"You know, a lot of kids around here are Republicans now," he said.

"Yeah, but when they go to school they'll learn to be Democrats."

Harley carried two tubs of fish upstairs to his wife, Shele. They'd met in Alaska, during one of his summer fishing trips. When he brought her to Lake Superior, she thought she was still fishing the ocean, it was so rough and mean. It took her two weeks to realize she wasn't on salt water anymore. Shele had known dangerous waters in Alaska—she'd lost a boyfriend in a boat wreck. But in Grand Marais, "there's waves that come bookin' in, and there's water on the downtown streets and rocks in, especially when we get a good easterly."

The summer she was pregnant with the twins, Harley was up in Alaska, so Dick helped her pull up nets. "We're settling down," she told her husband. They opened the fish market, and now they'd expanded it to a restaurant, serving fish and chip baskets. It was open twelve hours a day, seven days a week between April and November. In the winter, Shele waitressed in a ski lodge while Harley fixed the machines that groomed snowmobile trails. Freedom isn't free. It's harder work than servitude.

Shele had a seafood tip for me. You can tell your fish is straight from the lake by the way it curls in the fryer.

"So make me fish and chips with the fish we caught today," I said. "That's got to be the freshest fish in the world."

"You want today's catch? OK. Go wait in the restaurant."

I sat by the window, looking out at the docks. Ten minutes later, Shele came out with a basket of herring. Whorls and corkscrews of herring, flopping on a bed of French fries. I picked one up. It fell apart. I stuffed it into my mouth. The flesh was so soft, it disintegrated. That's why you get up early to fish.

★ ★ ★

Pigeon River, at the sharp point of the Minnesota arrowhead, isn't one of the busier border crossings, but it's the only road into Canada between International Falls and the Soo. When I told the customs officer I planned to spend five-and-a-half weeks in her country, I had to pull over for questioning.

I shoved my book contract and my passport through a bulletproof window, to a young woman, just out of college. (It would always be so on the border. The Canadians were kids who asked a few polite questions: "Citizenship, whereyougoing, howlongyoustaying?" The Americans were crew-cut SWAT commandoes in wraparound sunglasses, bulked up with flak jackets, leading German shepherds on leather leashes. They wanted to know your hometown, your occupation, your destination. They asked their questions with humorless stares that said they'd drag you onto the pavement for a boot party if you were lying.)

The wait in that empty lobby was the most suspenseful fifteen minutes of my trip. If I couldn't get into Canada, I'd have only half a book. Finally, the customs official reappeared.

"How much money are you carrying?" she asked.

"Five thousand dollars in traveler's checks. Plus I've got a credit card."

She studied my contract.

"How much do you expect to make on this book?"

"Enough to pay for the trip, I hope."

"Hmpf." She slid my papers through the slot. "You can go ahead."

12

Above Lake Superior

ONTARIO—THUNDER BAY, PAYS PLAT FIRST NATIONS RESERVE, SCHREIBER

Sixty kilometers past the border, I turned off the Trans-Canada Highway, headed for downtown Thunder Bay, Ontario. I never got there, because there is no such place. Thunder Bay is a mash-up of two old colonial outposts, Fort William and Port Arthur. They merged to form the biggest city on Lake Superior, but it's a city without a center, or a street life. In search of the lakefront, I drove for miles down the Harbour Expressway, the rusting seam that welds the two halves of Thunder Bay together. It's a boulevard of motels, chop suey takeouts advertising "Chinese and Canadian Food," and donut shops serving Persians, a frosted bun indigenous to this town. Every building looked weathered and weary from the snow-driving winters and bleaching-bright summers—even the Inter-City Shopping Centre, a mammoth white mall anchored in a lagoon of asphalt.

Finally, I found Cumberland Street, which follows the curve of the lake to the remains of downtown Port Arthur. The brown bulk of the Prince Arthur Hotel cast a cool shadow on second-story barristers' and insurers' offices. I parked the car and began walking my rounds, looking for cheap lodgings. Past a laundromat, past a grocery store where a Native family was loading sacks into the trunk of a domestic beater, I found a forty-dollar motel. Its smeared plasticine windows looked steamed over. The carpet was trodden to its fibers, like the putting green on a miniature golf course.

"We're full up," the clerk said, looking up from her miniature TV. "It's Blues Festival weekend."

So I checked into the Prince Arthur. It was one hundred dollars a night, but it was Canadian money, then worth four cents on the Jefferson nickel, and I figured I deserved luxury after three weeks of tents and discount motels.

"Do you take traveler's checks?" I asked the concierge, who wore a necktie.

"If you're going to pay that way, you should cash it at the Charity Casino across the street," he said. "They'll give you an extra one percent."

When I returned, after collecting $121 and a free soft drink, I met another concierge. This one wore beads. She whipped a booklet out of her back pocket.

"Extra set of tickets to the Blues Festival," she said. "Do you want them?"

I took the tickets.

"Come back to the hotel tomorrow night." She waggled her necklace. "We're having New Orleans Night."

Blues Festival? New Orleans Night? Thunder Bay is due north of the Mississippi Delta, but the bluesmen got off the train in Chicago, halfway between the two. Yet their music carried this far. At the edge of Lake Superior, Thunder Bay is in a perfect spot to pick up fifty-thousand-watt WLS from Chicago. While the CBC force-fed Anne Murray and Gordon Lightfoot to the rest of the nation, the Lakehead was listening to Muddy Waters. King music nerd Paul Shaffer, a Fort William native who later played with the Blues Brothers and headed David Letterman's TV band, became a living iPod by absorbing Chicago radio. In the 1960s, Thunder Bay was a hideout for American hippies fleeing the draft: blues jams broke out in the back room of the Co-op Book Store, with the immigrants teaching Skip James, Son House, and Bukka White to their new country, until the music caught on enough to support blues nights at the Finn Hall.

Fort William was Neil Young's first stop after busting out of Winnipeg in search of rock stardom. He was only nineteen, but he wrote "Sugar Mountain," recorded his first demo, with local deejay/scenester Ray Dee, and met Stephen Stills, his sidekick in Buffalo Springfield. After eight months, he took off for Toronto in his broken-down hearse, Mort, the car memorialized in "Long May You Run."

So Thunder Bay has two lines in the history of rock and roll. And that weekend, it had Dr. John. Years before, in New Orleans, I'd asked a street mime, "Where can I find Dr. John?" The mime didn't know. I'd finally located him here, at the opposite end of Highway 61.

Dr. John's New Orleans sidemen seemed startled by the harsh Northern climate. I hadn't seen so many black men in one place since I'd left Chicago.

"We just flew in from Winnipeg," the drummer marveled to the ten thousand crowded into a meadow by the lake. "We were playing a festival over there, and I swear I had a bug sandwich, and a bug shake. I'm still picking the bugs out of my teeth."

The band worked up a fanfare, and then Dr. John eased himself onstage, portly in a white planter's suit and feathered dandy's hat. As far as he was concerned, this was Tipitina's. At sixty-five years old, he squashed his pedals, he abused his keys, he played two keyboards at once, and on "Right Place, Wrong Time"—as essential to a Dr. John performance as a duck walk to a Chuck Berry show—he threw his head back with such sly pleasure you would have thought he had a girl hidden under the piano. Dr. John played the sun out of the sky, and was still making the night vibrate when I walked back to the Prince Arthur, for New Orleans Night. On the way, I passed a busker singing "Goin' Up the Country." I tossed a dollar coin—a loonie—into his guitar case. Later, I ran into the busker in the lobby. He was waiting for a crosstown bus.

"I live over on the other side," he said.

"The other side?"

"Yah," he said. "Over in Fort William."

★ ★ ★

I'm going to call them Natives, although others prefer the term Indians, aboriginals, or (the politically correct Canadianism) First Nations. They were everywhere in Thunder Bay—begging in front of flophouses on Simpson Street, wearing tribal gathering T-shirts in the laundromat, feeding loonies into slot machines at the Charity Casino. I helped a Native teenager make a long-distance call from the hotel lobby. As an American, I was startled to see Natives so integrated into urban life. It would be an unusual sight in most Canadian cities, too, but Thunder Bay rests on the border between white North America and the galaxy of Native villages speckling Northern Ontario's impassable network of rivers and lakes. If you're a young Cree or Ojibway looking for city life, Thunder Bay is the place.

That Saturday afternoon, I drove to a strip mall in Thunder Bay North and parked in front of Ahnisnabae Art Gallery, where I'd made an appointment to see Louise Thomas, the widow of Roy Thomas, one of the painters who popularized Native art in the 1970s.

A Cree from Alberta, Louise was a small, quiet woman, but she was eager to show off her late husband's work—brightly colored, phantasmic turtles and bears, outlined with bold black strokes, like traditional rock paintings. Louise had opened the gallery after Roy's death, that past November. The paintings were "all I have left of him," she said, and she needed a job. She had never lived on a reserve, and didn't intend to.

"You have to be doing something," she explained. "If you are doing nothing, they'll say, 'That lazy Indian.' Too many people want a handout. I had never had a job before, but I couldn't imagine work-ing for someone else for the money they would pay me. This was Roy's studio. I knew a lot of Native artists through Roy. People will pay more if it's an aboriginal artist."

Louise lent me a book of Roy's artwork. I took it back to the Prince Arthur and read it cover to cover. Imagine Oliver Twist grow-ing up to become an art world phenom, and you have the life of Roy Thomas. He was born in 1949, to a family of hunters and trappers in Pagwachuan Lake, a "fly-in" community accessible only by airplane, dogsled, or canoe. They lived in a log cabin, wore rabbit-skin clothes, and ate smoked moose meat and dried blueberries. His grandmother rubbed bear grease on his head, to ensure it would never gray, and nicknamed him *Ahmek*, or "Crow." At age nine, he was sent to a Catholic boarding school in Fort William. Four years later, his parents were killed in an automobile accident. His grandmother froze herself to death in grief. Roy moved to a reserve, and drank. One night, after a binge with some ex-cons, he crawled into a boxcar, waking up in Winnipeg. While looking for work, he passed a Native art gallery. The paintings reminded him of boyhood visions of spirit animals. A Salvation Army captain gave Roy art supplies, and the gallery bought his painting of a buffalo dance, paying him enough to rent a room and buy a bus ticket to Toronto, to visit his sister. There, he sold another painting, to the Royal Ontario Museum.

Woodland art was in vogue. As a genuine Native artist, Roy Thomas found himself with more money than his subsistence upbringing had prepared him to deal with. After netting five thousand dollars from a show in Toronto, he rented a suite at the Royal York Hotel, ordered a dozen shirts and a dozen pairs of pants from a men's boutique, then called a limousine to take him to the airport for a flight to Vancouver, where he continued to party.

Roy met Louise at a square dance in Edmonton, and they moved to Thunder Bay to start a family. Here, he'd been able to sup-port their sons with his painting: his biggest commission was the mural in the Charity Casino—a turquoise fantasia of turtles and fish.

"There are a lot of tourists in Thunder Bay interested in aboriginal culture," Louise told me when I returned the book. "There's wonderful artists in this area. But a lot of them live in fly-in communities. They're not visible, eh. It's just like the black people in the United States. There's just a handful of aboriginals."

Louise pointed at a collection of eagle paintings in the corner. They were the work of Moses Beaver, an Ojibway from the Far North. He represented the Woodland school as well as any living artist.

"I had a doctor come in last week and buy one of Moses's paintings," she said.

Louise got on the phone to Moses's girlfriend, to see if he could come down to the gallery. But Moses was out of town. He was living in a tent, at Pukaskwa National Park, on the northeast corner of Lake Superior, where he was that summer's artist-in-residence. Louise pointed it out on a map.

"I'll be going by there," I said. "I'll stop and look him up."

★ ★ ★

My cell phone didn't work in Thunder Bay, and I wasn't going to let the Prince Arthur dun me for a long-distance call, so I bought a phone card at a convenience store on Cumberland Street, and tried to call Domenic Filane. Dom Filane was famous all over Lake Superior. Even the customs agent in Pigeon River knew his name. A ten-time light-flyweight boxing champion of Canada, an Olympian, he'd been named a "Champion of the Coast" by the Ontario government. He was about the only Champion who still lived on Lake Superior. Paul Shaffer had buggered off to New York. Roberta Bondar, the Soo astronaut, was in Peterborough. But Dom Filane had returned to tiny Schreiber, Ontario, to open a gym.

The pay phone was broken, so I borrowed the store's cordless and dialed the number Dom had e-mailed me. It was the Falling Rock

Motel, one of the family businesses. I got Dom's father, Cosimo, on the line. "Cos" was, reportedly, an even bigger character than his son, known for crooning Jerry Vale–style *bel canto* numbers on the Thunder Bay Cystic Fibrosis Telethon.

"Well, you can stop by the motel," he said. "I can't guarantee I'll have time for you. You know how it is when you run a business. Where are you from, anyway?"

"Chicago."

"Chicago!" he said excitedly. "WLS! I recorded a song in Chicago. Dick Biondi played it on the air."

"He's still there. He does oldies now."

"Is he? He did me a big favor. Today, you have to have money or know someone."

"It's still that way. Pay to play."

"Well, listen," Cos said, completely won over, "stop by Monday and we'll have a cup of coffee and talk. You know us Italians. We're shy and quiet and reserved. It's called the Falling Rock Motel. A guy from Chicago named it. I was opening this motel and I was going to call it Big Eagle, and he said 'Falling Rock,' and I said, 'Why do you want me to call it that?' He said, 'You see all those signs on the road? Falling Rock? It'll be free advertising!'"

★ ★ ★

The Trans-Canada Highway curves like a bow over the roof of Lake Superior. A two-lane road, made to feel narrower by whooshing RVs and long-bedded lumber trucks, it scribbles a route between reddish boulders and lakeshore pines. The landscape is more Western than Midwestern: to the north, the thinly forested hills are broken off in jagged faces where the road crews dynamited. Sometimes, the hills dip and saddle to reveal polished blue lakes, speckled with evergreen islands. To the south are waters so pale and shallow that one can wade chest-high to the offshore islands. In the chilly evenings, the inlets become bowls of mist. According to the Thunder Bay paper, the American midlands were suffocating: in Chicago, it was ninety degrees. From the summit of Lake Superior, where it was always cooler than seventy-five, the heat wave seemed as faraway as a South Seas tsunami.

I was minding my own drive to Schreiber when I passed a sign welcoming me to "Pays Plat First Nations Reserve." The reserve consists of a gas station, a restaurant, and a few dirt roads spaced with dull wooden houses wearing eyeless TV dishes. A hand-lettered board for "Dave's Smoked Fish" pointed down a dead-end street. On any other afternoon, I would have driven right through that stingy Native settlement. But this was Powwow Sunday, the one day a year Pays Plat turns colors and comes to life.

The powwow was in full swing. Inside a paddock, men in eagle-feather bustles hopped and jingled to a drum circle—eight heavy-armed guys doom-doom-dooming and wailing under a gazebo supported by stripped logs. The dancers wore woodland buckskins, with one anachronistic touch: their feathers fanned out from compact discs reflecting slick rainbows. Under canvas tents, women peddled dream catchers and fox pelts. The food wagon served hot dogs and bannock, a bland but hearty fry bread. I bought a cherry slushy, leaned against the fence, and listened to the music. The singers followed no melody, but would suddenly skip an octave, as though trying to voice many notes at once. To English ears it was wordless, tuneless, but you could hear the plaint nonetheless. A rabbi once said that the essence of Jewish music was the expression of ecstasy and sorrow in a single note. The Ojibway had lost their land (the reserve was one square kilometer), their religion (everyone here was Catholic), and their language (the powwow caller spoke English), so they required the same harmonic grammar.

A cadre of veterans raised the Maple Leaf and the Stars and Stripes, on long branches. The Ojibway were once the most powerful nation on the Upper Lakes, so they had fought for, and against, both flags. In the late fifteenth century, the tribe migrated from Hudson Bay to the Soo, eventually conquering most of Lake Superior and Lake Huron. In the west, they defeated the Sioux; in the east, the

Iroquois. They so dominated the fur trade that French trappers learned their language, and married their women, creating a mixed-breed people known as the Métis. Their legends inspired Longfellow to write *Hiawatha*. The Ojibways' remote Northern lands were not coveted by settlers, so their presence, and their culture, still persist on Lake Superior. In the Soo, they're considered a third nation, alongside the United States and Canada.

An old Canadian Army veteran made a speech: "Many people think powwow is a religion," he said, in the singsong drone you hear from Natives on both sides of the border. "I'm a Roman Catholic. I've been doing this for twenty years. When I started doing this, my father didn't understand. He said, 'I didn't raise you that way.' But my grandmother came from this country. We have to remember the long history we have on this land . . . "

As I was scribbling this in my notebook, a young man approached me. He wasn't wearing a dancer's costume.

"Are you a writer?" he asked.

"Yeah, I guess so," I said. I'd been writing furtively. I didn't know whether notetaking was allowed at a powwow. "I'm writing a book."

"If you're writing a book, you have to meet the chief."

He led me to a heavily authoritative man, settled in a lawn chair. Raymond Goodchild looked as comfortable as a hammock-sitter, but he stood to shake my hand.

"This is a pretty small powwow, but what can you do?" he said, as though he would have organized a bigger powwow if he'd known I was coming. "We're one of the smaller reserves."

Then he asked if I had any tobacco.

"We have to throw some tobacco in the fire, and then I will tell you all about the reservation and the spirits."

I had brought along a pouch of pipe tobacco, because I thought smoking would repel mosquitos. I fetched it from the car, handed it to Raymond, and followed him across the paddock.

"The secret is offering to the spirits in the trees, in the ground, in the lake, in the river, in the plants, and our ancestors," he said.

Raymond halted beside the campfire—a few flickering orange shoots, just hot enough to crack twigs. He dug out a pinch of tobacco and sprinkled it on the flames.

"Hello," he recited. "I pray to my bear spirit, I pray to the eagle spirit, I pray to all the animal spirits, plant spirits, water spirits. I pray in the direction of the east, the west, the south, the north, and all the traditional lands of the Pays Plat Nation."

We walked back to his lawn chair. His wife was sitting there too, holding their nine-year-old daughter, a Cree orphan they planned to enroll in the tribe.

The Pays Plat Nation numbers three hundred people. Only one hundred live on the reserve. Raymond had spent many years in Thunder Bay, working as a police officer and a social worker. It is the only place a Native can get a job, an education, or even a bed. In Pays Plat, there aren't enough houses to go around.

The reserve's only resources are wind, trees, and water. The band is building turbines, and plans to log the woods for furniture. They're also trying to snare truckers with tax-exempt gas pumps and a new diner, Wiisniwin Gamiing. That sounds like a casino (the government won't let them build one of those), but it means "Eating by the Water."

I asked Raymond Goodchild whether he'd heard of a proposal to pipe water from the Great Lakes to dry regions of North America. His features darkened, tightened.

"To my beliefs, and my values, it's all my land," he said. "When a corporation or a business tried to do something, they would hear from my people. There's medicines in the water that belong to the people. I will die like my ancestors died for the lake."

"In the United States," I said, "there are states trying to get the Great Lakes water. We're saying no."

"If that happens, you will die. I will die, all the Chinese people will die, because the lake will work against us."

The caller, who was sitting in a little wooden booth, like a high-school football broadcaster, announced a "snagging dance"—the

powwow version of a Sadie Hawkins. A short, round old woman gal-
loped out of the paddock and seized my hand. I'd been snagged. Soon
I was a link in a line of dangers jogging around the gazebo to the
four-step drumbeat. I wasn't the only *Shaganash* in the chorus: a few
hands down was a pale, toothless man who wore a full Ojibway costume and a beard too abundant for a Native face. He was a pensioned
doctor who had worked on northern Ontario reserves for decades,
earning him a welcome at any powwow. The line split in two, square-
dance style—men curled north, women south. When we circled back
together, my old woman and I were hand in hand again. I felt like a
sparrow adopted by a flock of parrots: the dancers wore white buckskins with flying fringes. Their beaded vests were strapped over bold
red frocks gaudy with eight-sided stars and zigzag stripes.

"You're going to have to get married," the chief teased me when
the drumming stopped. "Diane's husband is in line. He's going to be
jealous."

(Diane's daughter was in line, too. She wore a T-shirt with a picture of Geronimo and the slogan, "Homeland Security: Fighting
Terrorists Since 1492.")

Children in turquoise vests walked up and down the line, presenting the dancers with gifts and handshakes. A girl handed me a pin.
"*Mi-gwetch*," I thanked her, employing my one word of Ojibway.

"There's drums from all different nations, eh," the chief said when
the music started again. We were both finished dancing—the chief
because he was middle-aged, I because I felt like an interloper.
"There's a powwow here this weekend, and next weekend, there's
going to be a powwow at Lake Helen. It's a spiritual ceremony. Some
of these people are praying right now to the Creator. They'd say this
is our Red Path. One of the things you don't do is go out and drink.
You don't go out and do drugs. Right now, there's powwows going
on all across North America, celebrating being on the Red Path and
obtaining your ceremony."

I went into the diner, and ordered a wheel of bannock. Jason, the
young man who'd first noticed my notebook, fried up the bread. I was

his only customer. After I finished eating, we went outside to watch the last dance of the afternoon.

"Do you have forest fires in the United States?" Jason asked. We were both leaning against my car. It was just a question to get a conversation going.

"Sure," I said. "Out west. That's where Smokey the Bear came from."

"I fight fires in the summer. This winter, I'm trying to get a concession to deliver logs to the elders for their stoves. You have to do a lot of different jobs here. I'm lucky because I inherited a house from my grandparents."

Chief Raymond Goodchild offered to let me pitch my tent on the powwow campsite, at the edge of the woods. Turning him down is the biggest regret of my trip. Refusing hospitality is always an insult. Pays Plat didn't have much land, but the chief had offered me a patch for one night.

"I've got to meet someone at ten o'clock tomorrow," I said lamely. "I need to stay at a campsite with a shower."

"You could wash up in the bathroom," he suggested.

"Mmmm."

"OK," he said, but when I headed for my car, his goodbye wave was limp.

That night, in Neys Provincial Park, which isn't much bigger than a highway turnoff, I had trouble sleeping, for the tide of eighteen-wheelers in my ears.

★ ★ ★

Cos Filane spent his mornings in the coffee shop/general store/gas station next door to the Falling Rock Motel. The Falling Rock was one of two motels he owned in Schreiber. He also owned a restaurant, Cosimo's Room, where he sometimes roamed from table to table, serenading the diners with "One Hello" or "I'm Beginning to Think That I Love You," songs he'd recorded in the 1960s, when he was trying to become the Frank Sinatra, or at least the Al Martino, of northern Ontario. In the coffee shop, he dealt with truckers and tourists off the Trans-Canada. They wanted gasoline or motor oil or granola bars, but in case they were music lovers, Cos displayed the old LPs on a shelf above the counter: *Small Town Boy*, recorded when his hair was dark and thick, and *This Is It*: Cos posing in front of the motel, a portrait with the artificial tints of a vintage postcard.

In Schreiber, the Italians had thrived. The fathers had come across to pound spikes for the Canadian Pacific Railroad. The sons and grandsons owned Speciale Hardware, Villa Bianca Station Inn, Costa Apartments, Rocco's Bar. The Filanes had made it bigger than anyone: Domenic's portrait was on the "Welcome to Schreiber" sign, with boxing gloves ready to strike. Cos was named in the town brochure as a "Canadian recording artist." Yet he didn't quite belong to Schreiber. A generation removed from the Old Country, he had the same explosive mannerisms, the same hungers, as a guy from Bensonhurst, Brooklyn. His personality was too big for this town, but his voice hadn't been strong enough to reach the world beyond.

"I think I had some ego I wanted to be an entertainer," Cos said, pouring me a cup of coffee. "I left Schreiber to go to Toronto to be an actor. I was in a few movies: *A Heart and a Diamond*. I was a carnival barker in *The Witch Doctor*. I was always, you know, the one they say, 'You ride with me, kid.' From there, I went into singing. I thought singing would open the door to being an actor. I had a song called 'My Girl.' It hit the CHUM charts."

But to really make it as a singer, you had to cross the border. You had to sing for Americans. Not even Canadians wanted to hear an album recorded in Canada. One summer, a couple from Chicago vacationed at nearby Rainbow Falls, buying their weekly groceries at Cos's store. They had a friend who owned a studio, so Cos paid to record "One Hello" there. Then he called Dick Biondi. And called. And called.

"I kept phonin' him and buggin' him, and finally, he played it a few times, and finally, I was driving in Chicago, and he played it. In those days, to get a record played, you had to know somebody. I was just a pain in the ass."

"One Hello" didn't get him out of Canada. Neither did *Small Town Boy*. Even after touring England with the Country Hoe-Down Show, Cos ended up back at the motel. His tenor was just too thin. It was lost among the nightclub strings and hurricane horns of the backing bands. Still, he found ways to call himself a singer. The motel's profits paid for more studio time. He recorded three more albums in Los Angeles, one with Burt Bacharach's singers, another with a guy who'd played guitar on *The Dukes of Hazzard*. That summer, he was performing at the Festa Italiana in Thunder Bay, and of course, everyone watched him on the Cystic Fibrosis Telethon.

Cos got up from his stool and fed a cassette into the VCR above the counter. There, up on the TV, Cos and his son Sal were standing in front of a gilded curtain, singing "Fuhgeddaboutit," a new Cosimo Filane composition, a tarantella. Sal has gone just a little farther in show business: he sings commercials in Toronto, and played Hercules on a Disney cruise. He got out of Schreiber.

Before I left the gas station, I bought a copy of Cos's novel, *You Can't Win Them All*. The story: Tony Caruso, ex–hockey player turned lounge singer, meets youth coach Dean Filane on a tour of northern Ontario. They team up to build a new arena for Dean's team, Filane's Flyers. It was Dream Cos meets Real Cos. (On the jacket was a picture of Cos herding the real-life Filane's Flyers onto the ice.) Entrepreneur to the end, he'd published it himself, and extracted a blurb from *Hockey Night in Canada* blowhard Don Cherry.

"A fellow dared me. He said, 'If you can get Don Cherry to say something about it, I'll buy a dozen copies.' So I phoned him up. It was originally meant to be a movie. I asked Alan Thicke how much he wanted to write the script. He said $100,000. I said, 'You crazy? That's a lot of money for a script.' I think it would make a great movie. I don't have a million or two million to spend on it. This stuff never dies. Music dies on you, but books never die."

While we were talking, a traveler asked to use the bathroom. She looked distressed.

"We don't have any water today," he told her.

"No water?" She clamped her legs together. "I drank too much water today."

"You're going to have to go another four miles."

After she left, I pointed at my coffee cup.

"You had water to make coffee," I said.

"I know. I just tell 'em that. Otherwise, everyone would be in here."

★ ★ ★

The storefronts of downtown Schreiber are like headstones, memorials to an era when the Canadian Pacific sustained the town. Now all the business was up by the highway, and the windows of the flat-roofed buildings on Scotia Street were papered over with crisping newspapers. As I inspected a plaque honoring Sir Collingwood Schreiber, the engineer who had blasted through the rocky hills, I heard a grinding sound, like the buzzing of a seaplane engine. Looking up, I saw a jointed snake of railcars edging up the tracks. It passed the old brick station, with SCHREIBER etched into a concrete doorway dingy with age, then burrowed into a stand of trees, and climbed the ridge to my east.

Across the street, behind a glass door labeled with stick-on letters, I found Hollywood Filane's Sportswear. And behind the showroom jammed with pristine tennis shoes and puffy warmup jackets, I found Domenic Filane. In his red track suit, he still looked like a compact scrapper, even though he was a dozen pounds heavier than his fighting weight of 106. His handshake was tight and brisk. It drew you in his direction.

If Cos Filane saw Schreiber as a base for his sallies into showbiz, his son saw it as a retreat. He'd conquered his world, and he was glad to be home. Dom had fought on every continent—in Toronto,

Auckland, Mumbai, Barcelona, Atlanta, Biloxi, Rome. From 1990 to 1999, he won the Canadian light-flyweight championship every year, fighting in the Olympics and playing in celebrity golf tournaments with bigshot hockey players Tie Domi and Mats Sundin. The hallway between the store and the gym was Dom's Hall of Fame. Dom with Jesse Jackson, Dom with Carlos Santana, Dom with his idol, Muhammad Ali ("He doesn't talk much. He talks with his eyes. He has an aura about him."), Dom with the Queen. He'd met her at the Commonwealth Games, in New Zealand, thrusting a Canadian boxing pin over the shoulders of her security phalanx.

Dom led me into his empty gym. I asked him for a photograph, so he pulled on sparring gloves and posed uncomfortably beside a hanging bag. ("That enough?" he asked, after two snapshots.) Then he found me a bottle of water and sat down at his coach's table. Unlike his father, Dom is a sober North American; he cringes at the old man's operatic antics ("Sometimes we'll be at a restaurant and he'll start *singing* to people"). But he built his career through agonizing discipline, not exuberance. To make weight, he subsisted on one thousand calories a day, and ran morning, noon, and evening.

"But once I made the Canadian team," he said, "it was like living a movie star life. Just being there, you're sitting next to Magic Johnson. Walking into the Opening Ceremonies of the Olympics, it sucks all the life out of you. You're standing in the middle of the track. You can hardly believe it."

Dom never won a medal, and he didn't make much money. Fight fans don't pay to see the little guys. After missing the 2000 Olympic team, he quit his Toronto gym and retired to Schreiber. He's tried not to have regrets, but no athlete enjoys surrendering his sport to younger men.

"I always thought it would be an easy transition," Dom said. "It's not. In boxing, you wake up in the morning, you've got something you got to do. You've got to go running. You've got these calls: 'We're going to Italy. Can you be ready?' It's a lot slower. You always say you're not going to get depressed. My wife made that map"—on a

Dom Filane.

bulletin board in the gym, his wife had tacked up a world map, punc-
turing each of his stops with a pin, until the planet looked infested
with black flies—"and I was thinking, 'I should go there. The team's
going there.' It might have been easier if I'd been on the Olympic
team in 2000."

He was glad to have traded Toronto for Schreiber, though. Yeah,
he was a big fish here, with invitations to sports banquets and boxing
exhibitions in Thunder Bay. And of course, his name was on the town
sign. But that wasn't why he'd come home. All the Filanes were here,
and his kids could walk the streets safely. They could live an outdoor
life.

"I wanted to raise my family in a small-town atmosphere," he
said. "If you're a hunter or a fisherman or a hiker, there's no better
place. A friend of mine came down. He said, 'This is amazing.' He was
actually looking for a house where he could go ski-dooing."

Being a Champion of the Coast was a nice honor, but Dom confessed he had no idea what his duties were. I think that speech ful-
filled them perfectly.

13

The Ojibway Way

ONTARIO—PUKASKWA NATIONAL PARK

Moses Beaver was not hard to find. Everyone at Pukaskwa National Park knew where he was, and what he was doing. An Ojibway ranger gave me directions.

"He's at his campsite, painting," the ranger said. "Campsite 13."

As I walked up the double-rutted path to the clearing, I saw an eight-foot canvas, wild with half-painted loons, lakes, and spectral women. And then I saw Moses, sitting on a folding chair, sipping coffee, as though he'd been waiting for me all morning.

"Louise Thomas told me to look you up," I said.

Moses pulled up a cooler for me to sit on, and explained what he was doing here in the woods.

"I'm the artist-in-residence," he said. "I'm supposed to build a kayak from roots and trees. It's a survival skill, eh, in case you ever get caught in the wilderness. I built one last week. I used dogwood and spruce for the poles, and then I wrapped a tarp around it. It's in the water now. You can see it. I'm building another one this Friday. Then

I'm going back to Thunder Bay. I got here Friday last week, so I'll be here three Fridays."

His campsite looked lived in. Laundry hung like prayer flags from a line tied to the rain flap of his tent. Through the gaping zipper, I saw a suitcase and a wadded-up sleeping bag. The picnic table was covered with tins of paint—what hadn't been brushed onto the canvas, or spattered all over the artist. Moses's lavender T-shirt and gray cords were smudged with every color on his palette.

"So what's the painting for?" I asked.

"The painting? This one I'm just donating to the park. They didn't never told me what to paint."

An art critic might have called the canvas "busy." A wolf howled in one corner, a loon swam in another. A stream flowed, the transparent face of a woman peered over a file of evergreens.

"It's more like a spiritual painting, when you see faces in the landscape. That's just the way we paint, eh. We believe there are spirits in everything. My mother used to tell me the trees talked to each other. Most people when they're alone in the bush, they think they're alone, but they're not."

Louise had pointed out Moses's native village on my Great Lakes atlas. Summer Beaver was at the margin of the map, five hundred kilometers above Lake Superior. You can get in and out by turboprop only. In Summer Beaver, they still speak the old language. There, Moses is called Amik—Ojibway for "beaver." That's how he'd signed his earliest paintings, he told me. He'd started out drawing stick figures with charcoal from the fire, sketching onto the cardboard that insulated the walls. As his eye became surer, he drew sacred animals: turtles and wolves and eagles and his namesake beaver. He dropped out of school after grade seven, making his living as a carpenter, and as the owner of a video store (Summer Beaver gets two TV channels). He never stopped drawing, though. The white nurses and teachers from southern Ontario paid him forty-five dollars for an animal. And then the government paid him five grand for a mural in the nursing station. That wasn't huge money for Summer Beaver, where gas was a dollar fifty a liter, but it made him think he could survive as an artist. He moved to Thunder Bay—"there's more art supplies there"— where the Ontario Arts Council paid him to teach painting in the public schools. Moses was a widower—the "Sally Lucy Beaver" tattoo on his fleshy forearm was a memorial to his wife, and he signed SLB on all his paintings. But now he lived with a white woman who answered his e-mails and kept up his Web site.

"Did you ever see the Northern Lights?" I asked, when he'd finished talking about Summer Beaver. I suppose that was as naive as Jason asking me if there were forest fires in the United States, but I'd only seen the Northern Lights once, in Michigan, and there they were a faintly greenish white, like milk spilling down the sky.

"Oh, yeah," he said. "They used to warn us when we were kids not to look at them too long, or they'd take us away."

We'd been talking for an hour by then, but Moses had barely made eye contact, and I could hardly see his face behind its stage-left curtain of black hair. He never seemed bored with my questions, or irritated by my intrusion, but when he wasn't answering me, he stared at his painting, or sipped his cooling coffee. I figured he wasn't curious about me at all. I'd interviewed hundreds of people who never looked past my notebook, and I almost expected it from artists. But then Moses stood up and walked over to his canvas.

"You want to paint one of the birds?" he offered.

"Aren't you afraid I'll mess it up?" I asked. "It's your painting."

"It's OK. If you do, I'll just paint over it."

Moses handed me a brush. I stabbed black paint across the empty profile of a loon, careful not to violate his outline. While I was working, four middle school girls, Ojibway children from the Long Lac Reserve, bustled into the camp, heralded by laughter. In front was willowy Candace, who already knew she was pretty enough to boss the others around. Then came round-faced Hope, whose rabbity teeth made her conscious of smiling, then Dakota, and finally Ariel, who rolled behind the others in a wheelchair, her foot swaddled in a cast.

Moses and his mural.

"You want to put your hand print on there?" Moses asked them. "You can be part of the painting. I need your handprint, because you're the future."

There was one girl for each of the Ojibway colors. Black, white, yellow, and red represent the cardinal directions, and the races of man. Dipping their hands in Moses's pans, the girls stamped prints on the canvas.

"If this becomes famous, you can say you were part of my painting," Moses said. He must be the least neurotic artist ever, I thought.

"How come you sleep in a tent?" Candace asked. She was staying in an RV.

"I grew up in a tent," Moses responded. "I used to go spend two months in de boosh with my uncles, hunting and trapping. My whole family was hunters and trappers. We used to eat bear meat and moose meat and fish. In the winter, it got down to forty-five below, so we stayed in a cabin. The only time we came out was to get firewood and check the nets under the ice."

★ ★ ★

I'd planned to spend Tuesday night in Pukaskwa, then head down the coast, to the wilderness adventure outpost of Wawa. But I decided, what the hell, I'll hang out until Friday and watch Moses build his kayak. Pukaskwa (pronounced PUCK-a-saw) bleeds the urgency from a traveler. It's the only spot on Lake Superior where the Trans-Canada swings away from the coast, to avoid intruding on the back country. Most of the park is accessible only by hiking boot, or canoe. I pitched my tent in the semi-civilized campground, at the end of the road from Marathon. Even there we had a nearly transparent inlet, Hattie Cove, surrounded by cliffs of ancient, bulbous rock. Fossilized bubbles, they are older than the first tree, and they will still be here in Pukaskwa after all the green has faded from the Earth, and the waters dried up. So why was I in such a hurry?

★ ★ ★

In the afternoon, I went down to the "Ojibway village"—a bark wig-wam, a fire tepee, and a picnic table—to hear a talk on Native spiri-tuality. The teacher was Collette Goodchild, an elder from the nearby Pic River Reserve. Collette wore a khaki uniform with a "Parks Canada/Canada Parcs" patch. When Moses ambled into the clearing, they greeted each other in Ojibway. Moses greeted me by comment-ing on my Michigan State T-shirt.

"You know what 'Michigan' means in Ojibway?" he asked, deadpan.

"What?"

"Pubic hair," he giggled.

"Come on," I said. "It means 'big water.'"

"It means pubic hair, too." His downturned eyes were full of laughter. I decided to ask Collette, later.

There were four *Shaganash* at the picnic table: myself and three Israeli tourists. Before the lesson started, Collette burned a potpourri of cedar, sweet grass, sage, and tobacco, passing the smoking dish around the table, so we could inhale its scent. Then she taught us to make tobacco twists. Except for the nineteen-and-over smoking paraphernalia involved, it was an after-school crafts project. We were given squares of cloth, in the four colors, and told to sprinkle a pinch of tobacco onto each. We twisted them into pouches, and tied them together with a length of yarn. The result looked like Halloween ghosts hanging from a clothesline.

"You have to say a prayer now," Collette said. "Keep it for four days, and then drop it in the river or hide it in a tree, where no one can see it."

I prayed for a safe journey and decided to hide the twists in my glove compartment, until their medicine ripened.

★ ★ ★

Last Friday's kayak was beached on the dock at Hattie Cove, behind the interpretive center. Moses had insisted I paddle it, but when we reached the dock, the girls were there, clamoring for a trip. Dakota stepped in first, and crossed over to the cliff while Hope and Candace waded behind her in the waist-deep water.

"The kayak was an Inuit invention," Moses explained. "We were more canoes. It was mostly the Europeans who did the ships."

Once Dakota finished her lap, I lowered myself into the kayak. It was a floating anachronism: a pre-Columbian relic, a skeleton of sinewy roots and heavy-boned branches, wrapped in a gray tarp that glistened like sharkskin. I could feel the wooden cradle bow under my buttocks, but it didn't sink. It was watertight. Moses handed me the paddle—a pair of roughly carved birch blades lashed to a spruce bough—and my craft waddled off toward the cliff. It was a hundred yards of awkward paddling—birch doesn't sweep away water as smoothly as molded fiberglass. By the time I returned to the dock, my arms were aching.

In his two-and-a-half weeks at Pukaskwa, Moses had organized a little society, with his campsite as the capital, and he invited me to take on the role of sidekick/errand boy. The next day, after hiking around the cove, I stopped by Moses's tent just as he was finishing four hours of painting. He'd dappled white spots on the loon's back, and added an eagle.

I told him I was going to the reserve, for a newspaper. That was the only way to get baseball scores in Pukaskwa. Cell phones didn't work here, and Northern Ontario radio towers were too weak. Pukaskwa was an analog backwater on a digital continent.

"Can you get me some condensed milk?" He ducked into his tent, and came out with a toonie and two quarters. "This is all the cash I got."

Twance's Store, across the street from the reserve's weedy baseball field, held on its shelves a threadbare supply of bread, sardines, canned beans, peanut butter, and soda pop. I picked up a Thunder Bay paper, a can of Heinz spaghetti and a Cadbury bar. There were no vending machines in the park, either, so I was craving sweets. Then I found Moses's milk: $2.19 a can. But he knew I would have paid any deficit and not complained about it, either. Art patrons were the same. As a government-approved Native artist, Moses could charge two dollars a square inch for his paintings. Later that summer, he was getting three thousand dollars, plus expenses, to teach a class in Ottawa. It had to be satisfying to turn colonialism on its head like that.

In the evening, Moses and I shared a bachelor supper. He was too tired to start a fire, so I fetched my propane camp stove, which was powerful enough to heat his Chef Boyardee ravioli and my spaghetti.

"Hey," he said, as I was packing away my camp stove. "You got a car, right?"

"Yeah. I got a car."

"You can help me get the roots and branches I need for my kayak. I have to get them out on the reserve."

"Sure," I said. "I can do that."

I'd been planning to propose that trip myself.

★ ★ ★

"I don't have a driver's license," Moses said the next morning, as I drove him out of the park. "My girlfriend's got a car, but it's falling apart."

At the guard shack, the Canadian flag was back at full staff. It had been a week since a terrorist attack on London. I pointed this out to Moses.

"They had them at half-staff for the people who died in the subway bombing," I said.

"Where was that?" Moses asked.

"London."

"London, Ontario?"

"No. London, England."

We crossed the Pic River, flowing flush with its banks, and followed the empty road between sloping stands of hardwood forest. The clouds were so faint it looked as though someone had pounded chalky erasers against the sky. Moses motioned me to pull over. Brandishing his hatchet, he leapt over a water-filled ditch and stumped across a spongy bog, until he found a moose trail. We followed it deep into the woods, to a clearing. There, Moses got down on his hands and knees and peeled away the peat with his work-gloved hands. Underneath were roots, tough as the wires in an engine block. Moses chopped at them. He was wearing a sleeveless T-shirt, so I could see "Beaver" tattooed on his bicep in faded ink.

"Do you always bring a hatchet into the bush?" I asked.

"Or a big knife or a handsaw. You always have to have that, eh. I learned to make a kayak out of necessity. I was fighting fires and I wanted to visit a friend across the lake."

Moses cuts branches for the kayak.

In need of thicker bindings, he stripped the bark off a spruce, leaving a branch as naked and damp as a plucked chicken.

"The tree will try to heal itself, but it'll probably die," Moses predicted. "If you paint over the wood, it would live, eh."

After all that work, his blade was coming loose, so he bound it to the handle with duct tape. He kept a roll in the pocket of his jeans.

"Always bring duct tape," he advised.

"Do you ever watch *Red Green*?" I asked.

"All the time," Moses grinned. (*Red Green*, a CBC sketch comedy show about a handyman who fixes everything with duct tape, is big all over the Great Lakes. I'd seen it in Thunder Bay on a Detroit station that showed up on cable.)

Now Moses needed diamond willows. They're flexible trees, so flexible he'd bent them into bows and rabbit snares when he was a boy. We found a roadside park where the reserve road met the Trans-Canada. Moses chopped down a poplar, and flexed it over his knee. It snapped.

"Too weak," he mumbled.

Finally, he found his willows. He shoved the branches through the open window of my car, until my back seat was covered with a pile of kindling and wormy, dirt-shedding roots that looked like unstrung tendons. We picked up a slender spruce on the rez, and Moses had everything he needed for a kayak frame. Back at Pukaskwa, I helped him carry it all to the cove. He dumped the roots and the bark into the water. By morning, they'd be as supple as leather.

★ ★ ★

At that afternoon's Ojibway class, Collette had a map of the park, which she unfolded on the table. She wanted us to know the Ojibway names of Pukaskwa's landmarks.

"Black River," she recited. "*Mkade Ziibi.*"

"Beaver Lake. *Amik Zoogigan.*"

"Big Eagle log. *Gitchi Magizi Gwatikgoun.*"

Of course, I was more interested in an anatomical term. After everyone else had gone, I whispered Moses's translation to Collette. She didn't look flustered. She puzzled over the question for a few moments, then said, "*Michiganic?* Maybe."

That day, Moses finished his painting. As a final touch, he wrote "www.mosesbeaver.com" in the lower-right-hand corner.

"I've got to put my Web site at the bottom," he said. "I'm going to donate this painting to the visitor center. It'll be free advertising. A lot of people visit the park."

★ ★ ★

"Hey, you should have come by this morning!" Moses shouted when I met him at the visitor center for the kayak-building class. "These women from the reserve brought me breakfast: scrambled eggs, hash browns, cinnamon rolls, toast, coffee, pancakes. I needed to eat. I been here two weeks, and I gotta hold up my pants with suspenders."

Moses's hair was bunched in a topknot. A bear-tooth necklace grinned across the collar of his acrylic sweater. Today was showtime, and Moses wanted to look as Ojibway as possible.

"You're going to help me, right?" he asked. "It's Dan, isn't it?"

"Ted," I said. "Yeah, I'm going to help you."

Moses laid three willow trunks lengthwise on the deck, lashing them together with water-softened roots. If a root was too thick, he gnawed a notch in one end and gradually peeled it in half. My job was to plant my foot on the middle trunk and haul up the gunwale trunks while Moses bent the spruce branches beneath them.

"We gotta make sure the kayak is the right depth," Moses said. "If it's too deep, it'll tip over."

Half a dozen campers watched from a bench on the cove overlook. The women were enraptured with this long-haired man of nature who could walk into the woods empty-handed and walk out with a boat.

"Have you been doing that for hundreds of years?" cooed a schoolteacher from Stratford.

"No," Moses said. "I just started."

(Yeah, I remember that line from *The Milagro Beanfield War*, too.)

"Moses," said a matronly schoolteacher from Marathon, "do you remember when I was teaching in Summer Beaver?"

"I'm not sure . . ." he said.

"I brought my daughter fishing with you," the teacher prodded. "You skinned the fish so fast that the skin was still quivering and you could feel the pulse in the meat. My daughter has been to New Zealand, but she still says that's one of her top ten experiences."

Moses remembered the daughter. "Oh, yeahhh," he said, brightening. Then he looked at me.

"I'm thirsty. Hint, hint."

I didn't take the hint. I was busy tying knots.

"There's pop inside," I said.

The schoolteacher took the hint. She jumped off her bench and lunged toward the visitor center, asking "What do you want, Moses?"

When the roots and bark strips were snug, Moses dragged a bunched-up tarp from under the bench. Quickly, he found a flaw: a pinprick hole that could sink the entire craft.

"The best way to plug it is with moss," he said. "You can also use a stone."

He found a pebble on the beach, stuffed it in the hole, and wrapped a root around the protrusion.

"It's just so *obvious*," the teacher from Stratford gushed.

But the kayak still wasn't lake-worthy. Hope stepped into the cockpit. A few paddle-strokes from the dock, she felt her feet dampening.

"There's water coming in," she moaned to Moses.

Well, getting wet was nothing to whine about. Once Hope beached the kayak, Moses took over. He lowered himself onto the craft, laying across it lengthwise until it sank.

"Did you get a picture of that?" Moses asked me, as he hauled himself onto the dock, dripping like the Swamp Thing.

I hadn't.

"Sometimes"—he shook his sleeves, spattering water on the planks—"you gotta entertain people."

★ ★ ★

Moses was due in Marathon at six o'clock for the bus to Thunder Bay. Some admirer or other would give him a ride. While I sat in his campsite, eating breakfast leftovers from a foil husk, a ranger came to measure the painting for the visitor center. It was, he discovered, too large to fit through the door. Moses hadn't thought that far ahead. The painting had been a lark.

"I just did it for fun," he said. "I was just supposed to build boats, but I said, 'Bring me some wood.'"

"We'll get someone to take it to the administration building," the ranger promised. "Maybe we can have someone from general services remove the sliding door so we can get the painting inside."

I don't know if they ever went to that much trouble. The last I saw of the painting, it was riding away from Moses's camp, in the bed of a Parks Canada pickup truck.

14

The World's Largest Freshwater Island

ONTARIO—MANITOULIN ISLAND

Only one bridge joins Lake Huron's Manitoulin Island to the mainland. It is one lane wide, and its pavement has been worn through to the wooden planks, so that a stripe of asphalt runs down the center of the road. Every hour, traffic stops as the bridge swings ninety degrees to open a nautical passage between the North Channel and Georgian Bay.

I was looking for a fishing charter on Manitoulin. I'd given up on my pole after snagging a branch overhanging the Tahquamenon River. I needed professional help. The government landing is in Providence Bay, on the south shore of the island. Driving there, I passed the Native village of M'Chigeeng and slowed through downtown Mindemoya, with its tavern, hardware store, and Loonie Toonie dollar emporium. Flat gray roads, ditches dusted with samplers of Queen Anne's lace, spools of hay in open meadows, the water never more than a few curves away. *I've been on this island*, I thought, and then I realized when: Manitoulin was the Lake Huron twin of

Washington Island. I opened my atlas. Yes. Both floated at the same latitude. Michigan and Huron are mirror-image lakes, and those islands were mirror images, as well.

When I found the dockmaster, he was inking figures into a ledger that vied for desk space with unspooled maps. He was a paunchy man, with a flop of sandy hair and a ruddy, veiny Celtic complexion. His summer-people costume—untucked oxford over Bermuda shorts and topsiders—suggested he hadn't spent his life in a dank trade like policing boats. In fact, the dockmaster was an out-of-work principal whose school had been turned into a restaurant. On an island where dairy farmers were being crowded out by cottagers, that seemed like a natural evolution. He himself had been born on Manitoulin, which made him a "Haweater," a descendent of the desperate settlers who'd eaten hawthorne berries to survive the nineteenth-century winters. There were twenty thousand year-rounders left, but many were Natives, living on reserves.

"I suppose I could tell you something about the island," he said, settling back in his chair with an air of desk-bound authority. "The number of farmers have decreased tremendously in the last ten or fifteen years. You only have a few big farmers, eh. You could count the number of dairy farms on one finger."

Every brochure in the Welcome Centre declared Manitoulin the largest freshwater island in the world. That was quite a distinction, but the dockmaster seemed skeptical.

"There'll be a place in the former Russia that'll argue that point," he allowed. (Ostrov Ol'khon, in Lake Baikal, if my map reading is correct.) "We *do* have the largest lake within a freshwater island in the world, and that can't be argued."

We had been talking for five minutes or so when the dockmaster's ears suddenly registered one of my broad Upper Midwestern vowels. It set off his Ameridar.

"I detect an accent," he said. "Are you American?"

That damned elongated "O." Cahhhmmon. Pahhhp.

"I am," I admitted. "I detect an accent, too. Are you Canadian?"

In fact, his speech sounded Scottish. Did Haweaters speak an insular dialect, closer to the Old Country than to the rest of Ontario?

"I am," the dockmaster said, ducking his head and grinning.

I described the purpose of my journey, telling him it was probably a good thing the Great Lakes were divided between two nations. The United States would never drain them, for fear of offending Canada.

"I don't know how much the U.S. is going to listen to Canada," the dockmaster snorted. "I don't think you pay much attention to us at all. We pay a lot more attention to you. I don't know if you're a Republican or a Democrat or don't care to say, but I think a lot of Canadians know more about your presidential campaigns than a lot of Americans."

This wasn't the first time I'd been baited into a political discussion. It had happened on the Boat Nerd cruise ("So, you must have a lot of divisions in your country these days"). Canadians love to talk about American politics for the same reason they prefer watching NBC to CBC: the show across the border is far more entertaining. That very month, the Canadian Senate had approved a bill legalizing gay marriage. Imagine the United States Senate following suit: tens of thousands would march on Washington, prayer vigils would gridlock the Capitol, dueling TV pundits would spit "homophobe" and "decadent" into each other's red faces. Here in Canada, a religious group from the Prairie Provinces was appealing to the Queen to withhold royal assent on the bill. It was a last-ditch gesture, with no hope of success. This was, after all, a country with an official multiculturalism program.

"I've only been in Canada for two weeks," I said, "but I think I understand the difference between Canadian and American politics. In Canada, politics is about finding ways for diverse groups to live together, while respecting everybody's differences. In the United States, it's about trying to force your way of life on the rest of the country."

The dockmaster grinned, nodding his head. "I think you've figured it out," he said, with a scholastic's pride.

"You don't have the religious right here in Canada," I continued. "Personally, I blame the South. That's the most conservative part of the country, and they've got more power than ever. Every time there's a new census, all the Great Lakes states lose congressmen, and the South and West gain them."

Even Canadians buy into the caricature that America is fifty states of Texas, with every section of the bleachers howling for blood as our legions rampage through Mesopotamia with Bibles in their left hands and guns in their right. I wanted the dockmaster to understand that the Great Lakes states could no more be blamed for America's bloody wars and executions than they could have been blamed for slavery or Jim Crow.

★ ★ ★

I hate to interrupt a fish story with a lecture on politics, but I didn't get started on this topic. The dockmaster did. To bolster my argument, here's a quote from the Pew Global Attitudes Project that demonstrates that while North America's international border is along the Great Lakes, its cultural border is the Ohio River.

> Canadian social and religious values are much closer to those held by Europeans than by Americans. On many public issues, however, geography may have as much to do with public attitudes as nationality. On a range of issues, the views of Americans who live in the northern border states are much closer to values held by Canadians than are the values of Americans living in the U.S. South. For example, a strong majority of Canadians (68 percent) believe that people do not have to believe in God to be moral. Most Americans living along the Canadian border agree (62 percent). Only 38 percent of people living in the American South share that view. Similarly, Americans living in the northern tier of the United States have views on homosexuality that are closer to the Canadians' than those of their fellow citizens of the South.

★ ★ ★

The dockmaster led me down to the water, in search of a charter.

"We've got a few here," he said. "There's one down there now, he charges $250. There's another who charges half that much. I don't think he's here."

At the end of the pier was a little skiff flying a Newfoundland flag, half-eaten by the wind. The dockmaster introduced me to the captain, then retreated to his office, so we could dicker alone. Three-hour cruise was $250, the captain said, but when I balked, and said I'd heard about a $125 cruise, he reconsidered.

"Is it just you? I'll take you out for $150. You don't want to go now, though. It's too choppy. The waves are four foot. The wind should go down this afternoon, though. How does five o'clock sound? We could go out from five to eight."

"Do I need to bring my pole?"

"I got everything. Just bring a bottle of water."

On the way back to the car, I stopped by the dockmaster's office.

"He told me he'd take me out for $150," I reported.

"That's good. He probably wouldn't have lowered his price if I hadn't mentioned the other guy."

★ ★ ★

At five o'clock waves were still bobbing and sliding around, so Captain Tom Power asked me to follow him across the island to the Ojibway dock at M'Chigeeng, on the sheltered North Channel. I helped Tom lower the *Sandra-Kelly* into West Bay, and we set off at twenty-five miles per hour, an arrowhead wake behind us.

A pair of mounted rods dragged lines baited with twinkling spoons. Beside the wheel was an electronic fish finder: schools of black dashes ticked across the screen. It made angling look like a Pong-era video game.

"Sandra-Kelly, that's my daughter," Tom explained. "That's a Newfoundland tradition. You name your boat after your daughter. Or your wife."

Tom was fifty-seven years old, which meant that, technically, he had been born not in Canada, but in the Dominion of Newfoundland. The island was so poor it had to look beyond its coastlines for support—it first became a British dependency, and then, in 1949, joined the nine Canadian provinces. In Tom's hometown of Grand Falls, the only industry was a doddering paper mill. He could have worked there, as a seasonal laborer. Instead, he migrated, along with three-fifths of his high school classmates, to central Canada, where he found a job in the nickel mines of Sudbury. An Inco service ring bulged from his hand like a zinc knuckle. The joke in Canada is that Newfies leave their island so they can earn enough money to move back. Since retiring from the mine, Tom had spent his summers as a charter captain, but business was declining: Manitoulin is infested with cormorants, shaggy-feathered birds of prey that dive for alewives, the salmon's favorite meal.

"They're eating the bait fish," Tom complained. "If the feed is not here, the salmon won't come here. Over the last five, six years, the salmon are getting smaller. I once caught a thirty-pounder, but that was eight years ago."

The cormorants had caused a huge local controversy. The Ministry of Natural Resources oiled the birds' eggs, but most fishermen favored a more drastic solution. Earlier that summer, sportsmen had posted flyers on the island, announcing a "cormorant hunt." The Ontario Provincial Police stepped in, setting up roadblocks near the bridge, checking all visitors for weapons.

Here I pocketed my notepad—writing on a swaying boat was making me queasy. We waited silently for the first tug on the lines. Then Tom said, "Things must have changed a lot in your country since 9/11."

"I haven't seen any changes in everyday life," I replied. "Although after the London bombing, I am a little leery about riding the 'L' in Chicago."

"The what?" Mining blasts had dulled Tom's hearing, and "L" was an unfamiliar term.

"The train," I said.

"I had a group on here from Idaho the other day. They were all for the war."

"That's not surprising. Idaho's about the most conservative state there is."

"Is that right?" Tom said. "I just hope the war isn't just about money. It'd be terrible if all those kids were dying just for that."

As an American, I am so used to the stereotype of the hard-hat patriot that I was startled to hear a middle-aged miner make an anti-war speech. But Tom's home riding, Nickel Belt, is a stronghold of the New Democrats, Canada's most socialistic party, and he held opinions that would have made him a Marxist crank in the United States. Of course he believed in universal health care. Every Canadian believes in that. When the CBC held a survey to name the greatest Canadian, the winner was Tommy Douglas, father of the nation's health care system. But Tom also believed no one should earn more than $200,000 a year.

"I mean honestly," he wondered. "What are you gonna *do* with all that money?"

Suddenly, the tip of the rod bent toward the water.

"There it is," Tom cried. "You've got one!"

I dropped my pen and worked the handle out of its holder, bracing my belly against the side of the boat as I cranked the reel. Tom rushed to the bow to coach me.

"OK, that's it," he urged. "Let it drop when you reel it, and then pull up on it."

A flapping salmon leaped from a swell, then splashed back into the channel.

As I tightened the reel, I could feel the fish's will ebbing—it was transmitted through the slackening line like a telegraph of surrender. When I finally lifted him on board, Tom swept him up in a net, yanking the hook out of his eyelid with a pair of pliers.

"There you go." He handed me the fish. Six pounds of slick muscle bent between my hands. Tom snapped a trophy photo with my camera.

"Ya caught a good one," he said. I didn't feel like I'd done anything. Tom had piloted the boat, found the school, and landed the fish. I'd just paid $150.

"What do you want to do with it?" Tom asked.

"I guess we should throw it back," I said. "I don't have anything to cook it on back at my campsite."

Tom pitched the salmon into the water, but it didn't swim away. It floated on the surface like a dead goldfish. A gull found it, and began tugging on the skin.

"I think we should have kept that one," he fretted. "I think that one's gonna die. I think we drowned him. If you hold their mouth open too much, they drown. Maybe that's a Newfoundland saying."

We caught one more fish. Tom tossed it into a hope chest. His wife was in their camper, waiting for supper, so I told him he could keep it.

"We'll just fry this one up on our grill," he said eagerly.

Back on that dock in Providence Bay, I'd thought I'd made a sharp deal. But as Tom drove away, with the *Sandra-Kelly* hitched to his pickup truck, and my salmon in his cooler, I wondered just what I'd gotten out of that fishing trip, other than a receipt for $150.

★ ★ ★

There was still light when I got back to my campsite, so I hiked into the woods and hid my tobacco twists in a bush, just as Collette Goodchild had instructed. After sunset, I read by lantern at a picnic table. Then I crawled into the tent, turned on my headphone radio, and listened to WLS. It was everywhere on the Upper Lakes. For some reason, this breeze-fed island relaxed me more than any stop since Door County. It took me all evening to figure out why: I wasn't slapping bugs.

★ ★ ★

The ringleader of the thwarted cormorant hunt owned a hardware emporium in Mindemoya, catty-corner from the Loonie Toonie. I'd read about him in one of the island weeklies, so on my last morning on Manitoulin, I walked into the store. Behind the wooden counter was a tight-faced clerk with a chest-length beard.

"I'm looking for Blaine Nelder," I said.

After a moment's hesitation, he owned up to the name.

"I heard you're part of the anti-cormorant effort," I said, talking as quickly as I could, trying to keep the look of glum wariness on his face from turning completely to stone. "I'm writing a book on the Great Lakes, and I want to put something in there about this."

I was armed with a pen, which probably allied me with the enviro-wacko-journos from Toronto, but Blaine Nelder was one of those men whose resentments are so strong, and so pressing, that he'll vent them to anyone. He edged out from behind his counter.

"You know what the problem is," he said, his voice deep, his shoulders clenched, his arms folded. "The problem is these big-city types from Toronto coming up here and trying to impose their PC environmental agenda on Manitoulin. They've completely paved over the best farmland in the entire country, and now they're trying to tell us how to manage our wildlife. We also got bleeding-heart media on our case. CNN was all set to cover the cormorant shoot before it was called off. Come on upstairs, and I'll give you a flyer on all this."

I followed Blaine up an unfinished staircase, to the fishing-tackle room. On the wall was a red poster labeled "The Libranos," a *Sopranos* parody with former prime minister Jean Chrétien as the don. Beside it was a bumper sticker, "Gun Control Means Getting Your Aim Right," and a T-shirt of a raggedy cormorant labeled "Public Enemy #1." The man had been born on the wrong side of Lake Huron. He would have fit right in with the Michigan Militia, a group of hunters who banded together in the 1990s to defend the state from the United Nations. In the United States, the rural-urban rivalry goes all the way back to Jefferson vs. Hamilton, and is even now a source of conflict on guns, gay rights, abortion, and a dozen other issues that divide ignorant fundamentalist hicks from godless big-city sodomites. In Canada, it's a more lopsided contest. Despite its international reputation as a wilderness, Canada is one of the most urbanized nations in the world: over 80 percent of its people live in cities of ten thousand or more. There's no elected Senate or Electoral College to over-represent the countryside, so Toronto, Montreal, and Vancouver lord it over the nation. Manitoulin's sportsmen were suffering the anger of the powerless. Blaine handed me a flyer titled *Save Our Trees & Fish.* I'll reprint the boldfaced sentences: "*Manitoulin Island is plagued by an overpopulation of cormorants* . . . In the past twenty years, Ontario's cormorant population has exploded to over half a million—that's 250 times historic population records. *Recently, the animal rights extremists mobilized their members and threw a costly wrench into this year's cormorant cull at Presqu'ile Provincial Park.* Clearly the government needs to listen to all of us who really care about the environment—*not the International Fund for Animal Welfare, Animal Alliance, Peaceful Parks Coalition, and other animal rights groups.*"

"The cormorants are ruining the charter fishing business, the tourism business," Blaine snarled. "I know people who've sold their places because they can't catch any fish."

He stared at me, searching for a sign of sympathy. *Down in Toronto,* that look said, *they care more about some ugly birds than they do about us.*

After word spread about the hunt, "the government brought in lots of armed goons. They hired a camera crew to film everybody. Then, even though it was called off the night before, they had all kinds of OPP and all kinds of MNR K-9 units pulling people over who entered Manitoulin. They were asking if they had guns. People don't like that."

It could have been a rallying cry for revolution, but Canada is not the sort of place where disputes are settled with guns. Only a few angry sportsmen would wish it so.

★ ★ ★

I had entered Manitoulin on a bridge. I left it on a ferry. The *Chi-Cheemaun*, which sails from South Baymouth, is much better maintained than Highway 6, the road to the island. It communicates with Southern Ontario, whose burghers expect luxury. In the onboard cafeteria, I ate my first butter tart. Butter tarts may be the one uniquely Canadian pastry: they're on sale in every corner shop, bakery, restaurant, chip wagon, and duty-free shop, but they never cross the border. You can't find one in Detroit, Buffalo, or even Soo, Michigan. Perhaps the recipe is a national secret. Or perhaps it's because we Americans have our own version: the pecan pie, a giant butter tart, with nuts.

When the ferry docked at Tobermory, where the long arm of the Bruce Peninsula reaches up to catch boats, the North Country was behind me. I wouldn't see it again until Michigan's Lake Huron coast.

15

Emancipation Day

ONTARIO — OWEN SOUND

After the edge-of-civilization rusticity that surrounds Lake Superior, Owen Sound felt like a settled, foursquare Canadian village. This was the Ontario I remembered from a boyhood visit to Stratford, where the bed-and-breakfast owner's daughter went riding in a red jacket and breeches. Owen Sound is a North American city, struggling out of its British shell. In front of City Hall, wind-bellied banners commemorate local heroes, including Tom Thomson, father of Canadian painting, and three of the Victoria Cross winners. The Sydenham River, reflective in both the smoothness of its surface and its unhurried journey to Georgian Bay, is as indecisive as the Isis, in Oxford: one can barely detect a muscle of current beneath its torpid glass. On the east bank was a chip wagon, selling *poutine* and hamburgers. On the west, a grain elevator, white as a Greek temple, feeding a ship's hold.

Hungry, I rounded a corner and found a Scottish pastry shop, Oor Wee Bit. A "Thank God I'm Scottish" sticker clung to the glass door. Pipe band CDs and tartan directories were on display beside the register. The owner, Mrs. Wallace—an auburn-haired, freckled woman with tight, fussy lips—was the daughter of a lowland doctor who had emigrated to Canada. Oor Wee Bit sold comfort food to Ontarians a generation removed from Britain: sweet dollops of cherry nested in a crust as neat as a folded napkin; doughy, hearty meat pies, first cousin to the miner's pasty.

As I ate a meat pie, Mrs. Wallace told me how the New Canada was pushing out the Old Canada, right here in Owen Sound. That summer, the Orange Order had asked to display its colors outside City Hall. The Orangemen, a Protestant order founded in Northern Ireland, were once the most respectable outfit in Ontario. Toronto's July 12 parade, which celebrated King William's victory at the Battle of the Boyne, was the province's grandest fling. But Owen Sound turned the Orangemen down. Their emblems offended Catholics. On the other hand, Mrs. Wallace said disapprovingly, a gay pride group was allowed to fly its flag.

"It seemed like there wasn't much controversy when Parliament legalized gay marriage," I commented.

"I don't know if it was without controversy," she said. "They kind of put it through without anybody getting a say on it. I don't think they should be able to get married in a church, because it says in the Bible that's wrong. So they shouldn't be able to stand up in front of a minister and get married. If they want to get married in front of a judge, or a justice of the peace, that's something else."

★ ★ ★

Outside City Hall was a plaque with a black-and-white portrait of an old black man. Dressed in a bowler hat, shabby overcoat and cane, he looked like a character from a Stephen Foster song. Jim Crow relics were rare enough in the American North. How had this one found his way to Owen Sound? I bent to read the inscription. John "Daddy" Hall had been the town crier, announcing each morning's news in a

Kentucky baritone. Allegedly, he'd lived to the age of 117, fathering twenty-one children by five women.

At the town museum, a short float upstream from the grain elevator, I asked a docent about Daddy Hall. An escaped slave, he'd settled here because Owen Sound was the last stop on the Underground Railroad. Sitting at the apex of a triangle with Niagara Falls and Windsor, Owen Sound was civilization's northernmost station. For a black man, escaping to Ohio or Pennsylvania was not enough, especially after 1850, when Congress passed the Fugitive Slave Act, enjoining Northern lawmen to hunt down Southern "property." With the aid of American abolitionists, tens of thousands crossed the Great Lakes frontier—Erie, Pennsylvania, where George and Eliza stowed away on a steamer in *Uncle Tom's Cabin*, was just over one hundred miles from the Virginia panhandle. Today, Owen Sound is full of their descendants. The docent gave me the phone number of an artist who'd designed a monument to escaped slaves in Harrison Park, along the river. I called Bonita Johnson–de Matteis from the museum. She seemed puzzled that anyone would want to write about Owen Sound, but she told me to meet her in the park on Saturday.

★ ★ ★

If I'd been a schoolmate of Bonita Johnson–de Matteis, I never would have guessed that her family tree grew out of Africa. Rose petals shone through her beige skin, qualifying her for that classic standard of whiteness, blood in the face. The leavening of an English mother had relaxed her hair. It rolled toward her shoulders in stiff waves. To use a Jim Crow term, she could have passed.

On the other hand, I never would have pegged her for Canadian, either. As she approached the picnic table where I'd spread out my notebook, her whooping voice was a riff on prim CBC English. "You must be the *writer*," she called, in a shout that carried over the grass and seized me by the shoulder.

Bonita had grown up in Niagara Falls, Ontario, worshiping every Sunday in her grandmother's British Methodist Episcopal Church, listening to hymns and sermons the slaves had brought up from the South. The biggest event of her summer was the Emancipation Day picnic, which drew all of black Ontario to Owen Sound.

"I grew up believing it was a family reunion," Bonita said. "It was like 'I'm in the biggest family in the world.' The kids dressed in white, and we'd have biscuits, black-eyed peas, chicken, okra, sweet potatoes. There would be singing, a lot of gospel songs. There would be children's races and prizes. There was always music playing. There was a shelter, and the bands were there all day."

Niagara Falls had a tiny black community, but since it was on the border, Pullman porters laid over in Buffalo came over looking for dates. Bonita's Aunt Beatrice married a man from Alabama.

As a girl, Bonita was shushed from talking about her blackness. If the neighbors couldn't tell, they didn't need to know. Her aunt had been denied a spot in nursing school because of her skin. The local MP found her another school, but she was so stung, she finished her education in the West Indies. Proud of her ancestry, Bonita stole Little Black Sambo books from the school library and brought them home to her grandmother, insisting they were "derogatory" to blacks. When anyone asked about her background, she'd tell them she was "colored" because anyone could be colored. The whites said, "Oh, you're not really black?" Blacks said the same thing. In today's Canada, most blacks come from the Caribbean. They don't consider the descendants of American slaves—lightened to mulatto, quadroon, or octoroon after so many generations—"real" blacks.

"There is a love-hate relationship between us and blacks from the islands," Bonita said. "But I decided a long time ago, if I can be put up on an auction block, let's go."

When she took a trip to New Orleans, they understood. They knew right away she was creole: "I've never felt so comfortable anyplace. Everyone's mixed up. But they could tell. They'd be like, 'You one of those long-lost brothers or sisters.'"

Once she married (to a white man) and moved to Owen Sound, Bonita became more forthright about her background. The city is proud of its black community: Owen Sound was multicultural before the rest of Canada heard the term.

Bonita led me to the monument, chuckling.

"If my grandparents knew there was all this hoopty-hoop about the cairn, they'd be, 'Why'd they bring this up?'"

It was called a cairn, but the quilt-patch stones were set in the ground, like the steps of a children's cakewalk. One rock had been ballast in a slave ship; another built a Cuban slave market. They were inscribed with mournful incantations from moaning spirituals: "Swing low, sweet chariot, comin' for to carry me home." "When Moses was in Egypt land, let my people go." "We are free at last." A metal frame shaped like a church steeple cast a spindly shadow. As the great-great-great-grandson of a Georgia dirt farmer who went to war to keep blacks enslaved, I was stingingly aware that these square yards of grass belonged to my country's history, too. The United States projects itself everywhere: we have graveyards in France, and flags on the moon. If I came back in a week, Bonita promised, I could see more than pictures of long-dead slaves. I could see this park animated with *their* great-great-great-grandchildren.

★ ★ ★

The picnic is always held the first weekend in August—the date, in 1833, that the British Empire freed its slaves. By then, the practice had long been outlawed in Ontario. Its climate was wrong for plantations, so even in the 1790s, it was safe for Lieutenant Governor John Graves Simcoe to take an abolitionist's stand against any law "that discriminates by dishonest policy between the Natives of Africa, America or Europe."

Bonita stood beside a picnic table, organizing a Tupperware buffet of fried chicken, green beans, and diced potatoes. It was a burnished afternoon, the summit of a southern Ontario heat wave. I stag-

The Johnson family reunion.

gered up to the table behind truck-stop sunglasses. Looking startled, then delighted, Bonita clapped a hand on my back.

"You made it!"

I grinned, warmed even further by her greeting.

"This is why they knew you were one of them down in New Orleans," I said. "It's not the way you look. It's your manner."

An old woman in Sunday clothes spoke up.

"Is this your husband?" she asked, offended by my familiarity. "Is he allowed to talk to you like that?"

Bonita introduced us.

"This is my aunt."

As we shook hands, limply, another Johnson appeared at the table, sighing away the exhaustion of a hot car ride from Toronto.

"This is my brother Nick," Bonita said. "He looks like Tom Hanks and Steve Martin rolled into one."

Actually, Nick looked an Atlanta politician. His fluffy white hair was combed straight back, a mustache sobered his smile, and he could have aced the brown-paper-bag test at a cotillion club. More siblings arrived. After jumping the border, the Johnsons had hopscotched the color line, too. Linda was pale enough for a Lutheran church supper, but Susan had skin dipped in walnut juice and hair let down in poodle waves. Valerie looked Jewish, with a sharp nose and a short, kinky crop.

The picnic was a humming gathering of hundreds. Cousins of all colors greeted each other with broad laughter and slapping hugs. The gestures weren't just black, weren't even American. They were *Southern*, the same as you'd see at a family reunion in Mississippi.

I was introduced to George Green, an elder of Owen Sound's black community. We walked together down the Freedom Trail, a pathway milestoned with photographs of black sergeants and black preachers. Bonita took George's picture beside a spruce tree planted in his parents' memory.

When George was growing up, in the 1940s and '50s, cooking on a freighter was the best job a black man could get. Every autumn, the BME church held a "sailor supper" to welcome them home.

"I'll tell you, you never had a dinner," George enthused. "They had turkey. My father cut it."

Canada wasn't as prejudiced as the United States, George said, "but don't think there weren't problems. We had problems here in Owen Sound. When my wife and I got married, people didn't want to rent to us. My sister had a hard time at RBW [a print shop]. I worked at RBW when I was a teenager, and I thought I'd get a job after high school. I didn't. You know why?"

"Because you were black."

"Yeah, that's it. I went to work as a deliveryman for a creamery. I had problems one day. One day, I went to my boss, and he said, 'I got a note on my desk. This guy doesn't want you to deliver. I told him, "We don't want that kind of customers.""""

I imagined Canadian blacks would have had a rooting interest in Martin Luther King Jr. I asked George what he'd thought when he saw fire hoses and police dogs on TV.

"Gee," he said, "good thing it's not happening here, eh."

There was music under the yellow-and-white-striped tent. Every generation brought its songs to the picnic. An old man crooned Louis Armstrong's "What a Wonderful World," then yielded the stage to a burly, pious pounder in a straw hat, who sang "Every Day I've Got the Blues," tapping out a hobbyhorse Chicago blues beat on the keyboard. Mama and the Three Soul Sisters did "This Little Light of Mine, I'm Gonna Let It Shine." A history of African American music, in a single hour. It ended with an aspiring rapper from London, Ontario.

"I'm gonna do a little freestyle," Titus rolled out. "I need a topic."

"Freedom!" someone shouted.

"Underwear!"

Titus chose freedom.

"Talk about the things we had back in the days," Titus chanted, "Like the freedom that came from the slaves."

In the United States, your street cred is your "ghetto pass." Canada has no ghettos that can compete with the sagging hopelessness of Chicago's West Side, or Detroit's Black Bottom, so I wondered whether young black Canadians envied the poverty and discrimination that had given their American cousins "authenticity." A different generation might have been proud of its favored position. They'd been clever enough to escape. A young man wore a T-shirt that said "Over 400 Years of Oppression Has Made Me Who I Am." But he lived in a society that was neurotic about minority rights. Rap had its origins in Jamaican "toasting." It would have been a natural import to Toronto. Instead, it had found more fertile ground in the jagged sidewalks and arsoned tenements of the South Bronx. There had not been a great African Canadian rapper. What was there to rap against? But

Titus was trying. He had his own Web site, titushiphop.com. He asked the crowd for an object. Someone held up a purse.

"I got a lunch bag, what's that, Louis Vuitton? Where you workin', mom? You got it goin' on."

Titus freestyled on a cigarette case, a Corona beer, and a watermelon.

"Emancipation Day, makin' it hot for your mom one time. Emancipation Day, are you having a good time? I want to hear everybody sing. I know y'all know the words to this song. It's not even my song. I need one thing from you. I need you to sing along. If you've got a bad voice, sing even louder."

A keyboard player plinked the toy piano chords of "One Love," a late–twentieth-century spiritual written by Bob Marley, the son of an English army officer and a woman descended from Jamaican cane cutters. To Marley, the entire New World was "Babylon," a strange country where Africans were held in captivity. Even if life was better in Canada, Titus wanted his listeners to feel a solidarity with blacks in Brazil, Jamaica, and the United States. The ones who never escaped.

16

Southern Ontario Gothic

ONTARIO—POINT PELEE NATIONAL PARK, LEAMINGTON, PORT DOVER

Robertson Davies, the Canadian novelist, grew up in the South-western Ontario village of Thamesville. From that backwater of the British Empire, he rose to study at Oxford, take a deanship at the University of Toronto, and write the Deptford Trilogy, on which he hung his unrewarded Nobel Prize bid. Margaret Atwood, Canada's other world-renowned writer, dubbed this literary territory "Souwesto" and its school of storytelling "Southern Ontario Gothic." Davies' trilogy begins with a snowball striking the head of a small-town minister's wife, and expands to take in the Great War, the Prince of Wales, saints, magicians, traveling carnivals, Jungian analysis in Vienna, vaudeville, and the unsolved death of a sugar baron. Of course such a tapestry could only be woven from cloth milled in a humble settlement.

In Davies's description, Deptford "lay on the Thames River. . . . We had an official population of about five hundred . . . we had five churches . . . a canning factory . . . also a sawmill and a few shops." It was a sketch that fit Thamesville perfectly.

Southwestern Ontario is infamous for its blandness—it is unrelentingly middle-class, Protestant, Anglo-Saxon, and suburban; its signature dishes are doughnuts and chips with gravy; its native pastime is curling; driving its main highway, the congested 401, you see the same flat farmland repeated at every milepost; and the greatest expression of shock its mild-mannered inhabitants can muster is a considered "OK," accompanied by a leery retreat of the head and shoulders. That's why it's just as full of surprises today as it was in Davies's early-twentieth-century youth. Anyone who investigates a small Souwesto town can expect to discover the alien, the tragic, the eccentric, the close-mouthed native, and of course, the local secret.

★ ★ ★

Lake Erie's upper shore is known as "Canada's Deep South." It's covered by the same broadleaf forest that makes the eastern United States so verdant. Canadians find it exotic, and flock here for bird-watching. Once I passed Harrow, heading east, I began to see roadside stands offering trays of deeply colored tomatoes, cherries, cucumbers, plums, strawberries, and carrots—fruits and vegetables that swelled to ripeness in the humid gardens. By then, I was almost south of Chicago. I could dip below the 42nd parallel at Point Pelee National Park, a stalactite of land hanging off the underbelly of Ontario.

Point Pelee's chief naturalist was a young woman who had come all the way from stony Newfoundland to oversee this lush strip of her native country. In Tammy Dobbie's office was a terrarium containing a prickly pear cactus and a five-lined skink, two almost-all-American species that find themselves at home on the Point, but nowhere else in Canada.

"We're very unique down here," Tammy said, leading me into a room with a wall map of "Carolinian Canada"—Ontario's Green Zone, it lies south of a line running from Toronto to Grand Bend.

This is one-quarter of one percent of Canada, but it holds 25 percent of the people, and grows 25 percent of the crops.

"The sandwiching of this area between the Great Lakes makes it so temperate," she said. "Point Pelee being out into Lake Erie, the moderating effect makes the trees in the park bud out two weeks earlier. It stays warmer in the fall, and there's more lake-effect snow. I think we are the warmest place in all Canada. They call this the Banana Belt, the Sun Parlor, the Sun Belt. We're on the 42nd parallel, the same as Rome and Barcelona."

Carolinian Canada belongs to the same temperate zone as Lower Michigan and upstate New York: travelers use it as a bridge between Detroit and Buffalo. Politically, the Great Lakes are divided between the United States and Canada. Geographically, they're divided between an Evergreen Nation and a Broadleaf Nation. Lying north of the 45th parallel, the Evergreen Nation is a sparsely populated, wintry land of snowmobiles, Natives, hunting lodges, taverns, and silty, rocky soil that yields little food. Read any Jim Harrison book, and you'll be in Evergreen Nation. South of the 45th parallel, Broadleaf Nation is the industrial engine of the continent, its mills and cities consuming Evergreen Nation's wood and ore. Flat, fertile, urban, and modern, Broadleaf Nation follows the southern curve of the Lakes from Milwaukee to Toronto, appearing as a continuous blotch of light on satellite maps of North America at night.

Every fifteen minutes, a trolley left for the tip of Point Pelee. When it pulled up to the park office, I sat down next to a bearded ornithologist who'd been brought in from Banff to lead birding expeditions. There were warblers here, he said, Carolina wrens and red-bellied woodpeckers, birds that flew as far north as Pelee, and no further.

The trolley dropped us on a plank path shaded by elms. The forest air tingled with dampness. To our left was a modernist sculpture: the number 42 striped in maple-leaf red, marking the 42nd parallel. Ahead was a beach. We walked down Point Pelee until it dwindled to a narrow point splashed by the waves of Lake Erie. It wasn't quite the end of Canada—that was Pelee Island, an hour's ferry ride from here—but it was as far as you could go on foot. On the walk back north, the ornithologist pointed at something that looked like a calcified shell, sticking out of the sand.

"A gull's skull," he said. A flock of birds flushed out of the trees, slashing over our heads. "Those are barn swallows and starlings. I'm really looking forward to this place. There are all kinds of birds I've never seen before."

★ ★ ★

Geography is destiny. In Leamington, I saw things I never expected in Ontario. Like Mexicans. Leamington bills itself as "the Tomato Capital of Canada." But Canadians won't pick that crop, so every summer, a work gang crosses two borders to reach the vines. They bicycle up and down Erie Street. They have their own church, Templo Cristiano de Leamington. For lunch, I went to Tacos Tony. A Mexican dollar was taped above the Jarritos cooler. The menu was printed in Spanish, English, and German. While I tried to figure that last one out, a woman in a black head covering walked through the door. Leamington has Mennonites, too.

"Hola," the Mennonite wife greeted the counterman, with a Spanish 101 accent. "Coma esta?"

The chicken tacos were as good as any from the barrios of Chicago, and in my own Spanish, I learned from the cook's father that four thousand Mexicans come here every summer. A thousand stay year-round.

"¿Adonde trabajan?" I asked.

"Los campos," he said. The farms.

★ ★ ★

The farms belong to an earlier group of immigrants—the Italians. The next morning, driving the lakeshore highway in search of a grower to explain Leamington's lushness, I stopped at a produce stand

Fruit stand outside Leamington.

belonging to Mastronardi Farms. It was tended by an old woman who
spoke Chico Marx English after forty-five years in the New World.
She was selling zucchini from her garden. Most days, nobody at the
stand, she said. She left the price on the bucket, the customers left
money.

"My husband started in 1957," Marie Mastronardi explained. "He
worked on a farm in Italy, and he heard about Leamington. Some
friend, he call him, and he tell him to come over. He came back after
he buy the little place, and then he married, and we kept going on
the farm."

It was not a little place anymore. Beyond the stand was a crystal
palace of greenhouses. If I wanted to know about those, I'd have to
talk to her son Jerry. He was working in the fields. I walked down the
dusty access road, past fluttering vegetables. Jerry was sitting on a trac-
tor, holding court with his farm managers. He was having a hell of a
day, he said, looking at his watch. Why didn't I try his cousin Carl?
Carl had a little farm off toward Windsor.

Tourist information booth, Leamington.

Carl Mastronardi was born on this side of the Atlantic, but "you can't tell by listening to me that I'm Canadian," he boasted. His speech was as colorful as the trays of cantaloupes, tomatoes, beans, peaches, raspberries, and honeyrock melon he sold to travelers. Canadian? American? The Mastronardis would have been no different if they'd landed forty miles west. They were here for the land, not the Queen. To a British Canadian, a word is as precious as a toonie. If it weren't for immigrants, Ontario would be as silent as an Anglican prayer service.

"The climate here, obviously, being by Lake Erie, the climate's good for growing," he said. "It's a heavier sand. It does give you a slight microclimate, and it does give you water to the greenhouses and fields."

Every year, Carl grew sixteen million pounds of tomatoes, and shipped 99 percent to the United States, filling supermarkets in Detroit, Chicago, and the Carolinas. For most of his life, America had exerted a stronger pull than Canada. He'd married a Michigan girl, he watched American TV, he was a Tigers fan, and he thought of Detroit as "his" city. He still went there all the time to see his mother-in-law.

"We used to be the sixth biggest city, and now we're what, eleventh? It's terrible! They can't tear down houses fast enough."

It took 9/11 to remind him that he was marooned across a border from the country that provided his living. In the weeks after the bombing, the trucks were backed up twenty miles, waiting to cross into the States. Police set up port-o-johns for the drivers.

"Well, some Americans thought Canada's immigration laws were too lax," I pointed out.

Suddenly, Carl was a red-and-white Canadian with maple syrup in his veins. He struck an indignant pose and raised his voice. I was delighted. I hadn't heard a cross word in weeks.

"Why are they blaming us?" he raved. "There are millions of people coming across the border with Mexico. Have any terrorists come through Canada?"

I didn't have an answer for that. After a moment, his spasm of national pride settled, and he was boosting Leamington again.

"We have almost every country in the world here," he bragged. "There's Vietnamese, Nicaraguan, Indians, Somalians. We have Iraqis, we have Lebanese, Portuguese. The majority of the greenhouse growers are Italians and Germans. And now we have a huge Mennonite and Mexican population. I used to have students pick for me, but I haven't had a student come here in six years. I wish I had time to show you my greenhouses, and the dorms I have for my workers."

"I'll be around tomorrow."

"Tomorrow, tomorrow. Ah, I can't do it tomorrow. I'm goin' over to Cedar Point on my partner's boat."

★ ★ ★

Back in town, I saw a hockey fan in a Red Wings T-shirt reading the *Detroit Free Press* in the doughnut shop. The big news: the Wings had cut Leamington's own Darren McCarty. In the barber shop—

Mastronardi's—I waited while a less distinguished local jock had his head shaved.

"Give it to me straight to the bone," he ordered the elderly barber, sweeping a hand over his stubbly skull. His inflated arms were inked with cave paintings. "That Miracle Gro isn't working in front."

The barber asked a question that's as much a part of his trade as the striped pole.

"So what are you doing these days?"

"Ah, I'm still in the AHL. I got traded from Quebec to Houston. I'm likin' it down there in Texas. That warm weather. I'm also getting ready to do this thing called *Ultimate Fighting on Ice*."

"How does that work?"

"They drop a puck on the ice, and two guys fight over it. There's a $250,000 prize if you win. I'm doing it for the publicity. It won't be too bad to bring home the money, either. It's gonna be on pay-per-view, because they don't want the kids to see it."

There ought to be a course in barbering at every journalism school.

When it was my turn, the barber shared his disgust with the goon.

"That's why I don't like hockey," he mumbled, even though the tip was in the till. "The fighting. I don't want to see all the fighting. I want to see them play the game."

★ ★ ★

Port Dover looks like the set of the movie *Popeye*: in a harbor at the bottom of a hill, fishing shanties cluster around the docks. Tires, chained to the cracked concrete piers, buffer the homecomings of the tugs. The cinderblock ruins of a processing plant sit across a weedy alley from a shack scraped to bare boards by the elements. Its graying sign reads "Bait & Boats Rentals."

At the harbor's mouth is a statue of three fishermen hauling a net. "This monument is dedicated to those commercial fishermen who have lost their lives on the lake," it reads. "It will serve as a lasting memorial celebrating the heritage of our fishing ports and the unique and hazardous way of life of our fishermen."

Carved in the plinth are twenty-eight names. The oldest, William Smith, died in 1844. The youngest—Gary Speight, Dean Felker, and John Walsh—in 1991. They were preceded, seven years earlier, by another crew—Jim Saunders, Daryl Clement, and John Mummery. This was no historic pillar. It was a community memorial—and there was space for more names.

Port Dover, according to an old guidebook, is "the home of the largest freshwater fishing fleet in the world." That was why it had sacrificed so many to the lake. It seemed like a horrific cull for such a small town.

The Harbour Museum is in the old fish-packing district. It gave me my first clues about those fishermen's deaths. Port Dover is at the northeast corner of the Erie Quadrangle, a shipwreck field extending from Nanticoke to Port Burwell on the north shore, and from Barcelona, New York, to Conneaut, Ohio, on the south. Four hundred twenty-five vessels have gone down in this shipping trap, making it four times as deadly as the Bermuda Triangle. Eastern Lake Erie is shallow, so storms boil up quickly. During rough weather, ships try to reach safety by shooting through a canal dug across Long Point, the sand spit that shelters Port Dover. Not all of them make it.

In a corner of the museum, I found a shrine to the victims of 1984 and 1991: photographs of the boats—the *Stanley Clipper* and the *Captain K*—pencil sketches of the crews, and a Great Lakes ballad about the wrecks, typed and framed. It begins:

We all remember April 30, nineteen-eighty four
When the waters rose to a fury, and lashed against our shore.
The wind came over the waters, in a mighty gale.
Dark clouds hung so heavy, and the sky was pale.

Morning had brought the sunshine, but by noon it was gone.
Then came the waters rising, lapping at our backdoor.
The Stanley Clipper *was on the lake with about a dozen more.*
At their last call the waves were high, the water took them down.

After writing this down, I found a docent.

"What happens in Port Dover when a boat goes down?" I asked.

"We grieve," she said. "Because everybody knows somebody who was on that boat. The memorial service for the *Captain K* was so huge, they had to hold it at the community center."

It's a scene that's been repeated at maritime towns all over the Lakes, from Rogers City, Michigan, to Grand Marais, Minnesota, wherever men earn their livelihood on the volatile waters.

I walked up the hill to the Port Dover Board of Trade, the local chamber of commerce. The Board was as bare as a campaign office: one receptionist, two telephones, tourist brochures piled on a folding table. But it had a president who knew her small town as intimately as an old-time telephone operator. Milly Coulthart had the frosted hair, the glitzy blouse, and the upright, all-business manner of a successful Realtor. We made small talk about Port Dover's economic fortunes. Well, she said, the town has the Fish Fest in July, and every Friday the 13th, it's over-run with bikers. Her biggest project was restarting the ferry to Erie, Pennsylvania, which last ran in the 1940s. (Port Dover has a kinship with Erie. During Prohibition, its smugglers supplied Pennsylvania with booze. Now, pleasure boaters cross over to shop in stores advertised on Erie TV.)

When I asked about the *Captain K*, Milly's sober PR delivery wavered.

"We all stand on the dock and pray," she said, choking up. "That's how we respond."

Milly composed herself, breathing deeply, patting dry the bridge of her nose with a tissue. I decided to drop the question, but she continued.

"There are five or six thousand people in Port Dover," she explained. "Everybody knows everybody. It's almost as though we have this brotherhood—there's us and the tourists. We need them, but they're not us. The sailors, it's pretty much like they're your relatives."

Asking the locals about the *Stanley Clipper* and the *Captain K* felt like grave robbery. There was a more considerate way to get the story. In the office of the *Port Dover Maple Leaf*, a modest weekly paper whose newsroom could be seen from the ad desk, I asked an editor to copy the front pages from those grim weeks. According to the *Maple Leaf*, the *Stanley Clipper* went down in a storm, after the captain sent an emergency message reporting that "several large waves had washed over the ship and they had taken much water on board. At the time of the distress call, winds were of gale force and had churned the water into mountainous waves." The *Captain K* was plowed under in heavy fog by a Coast Guard cutter servicing buoys for freighters headed to the Welland Canal. It sank in 130 feet of water, trapping the captain in his wheelhouse and the crewmen in their beds. Late March was too stormy for salvage, so their bodies lay entombed for two weeks, until the crumpled fish tug was raised.

"This week's mishap is a frightening repeat of the sinking of the tug *Stanley Clipper* in March 1984," read an editorial titled "Three Lost." "When the life of a commercial fisherman is claimed by Lake Erie the ongoing love/hate relationship with that body of water which is so much a part of our community is renewed."

Port Dover knows that shipwrecks didn't end with the *Edmund Fitzgerald*.

★ ★ ★

I pitched my tent in a provincial park along the road to Buffalo, and went swimming. It was the hottest week of the summer, in the hottest part of Canada. Lake Erie was as gentle as a pond. There were no waves. The water tucked itself into a neat fold when it arrived at the beach. The temperature was just cold enough to make me hesitate before a headlong dive, but not cold enough to raise gooseflesh when I finally subsided into the water. A few miles down the shore, I saw the bristling chimneys of a steel mill, looking like an abstract tree line. Maybe that's why my skin felt oily. That's Lake Erie. It's the most industrialized lake, and the shallowest, so it can't clean itself. It was still a lovely evening for a swim. Floating on my back, like an otter, I could see the mown lawn of the park, and the cotton-trimmed sky. If, at that moment, the world consisted of anything but water, grass, and clouds, I wasn't aware of it.

17

Greetings from Niagara Falls!

ONTARIO — NIAGARA FALLS, HAMILTON

The Great Lakes don't play a big role in North American folklore. The Copper Rush didn't produce the money-mad prospectors of the California Gold Rush. The War of 1812 was a tie. Hiawatha in his canoe didn't cut the same desperate figure as Geronimo, or Sitting Bull, riding into battle for one last stand against the white man. The Cape Cod whalers went to Tahiti. Great Lakes sailors go to Cleveland.

There is one magnificent exception to this lack of legends: Niagara Falls.

It is the quintessential postcard: a garishly colored photo of the rapids, under the megaphoning message, GREETINGS FROM NIAGARA FALLS. It was the original tourist trap—Disneyland before Walt Disney was ever born, Las Vegas when Nevada was only a desert outpost peopled by senile silver miners. As early as the 1850s, the Falls were a come-on for sleazy midways of "tattoo artists, five-legged calves, fortune tellers, and fat ladies." Its name was synonymous with "honeymoon," and daredevils from all over the world tried to

Niagara Falls.

prove their bravery by conquering its booming waters. The French tightrope walker Blondin crossed the Falls dozens of times, sometimes with a terrified passenger clinging to his back. Captain Matthew Webb swam the English Channel, but drowned in the rapids below the Falls. The first barrel-rider was a woman, Anna Edson Taylor, who in 1901 locked herself inside a steel-bound vessel, weighted with an anvil. Her successors have included a jet-skier, who died when his parachute failed to open, and a semi-suicidal drifter from Michigan who survived the plunge in street clothes. He was banned from Canada for life, but got a contract with a traveling circus.

Niagara Falls' aura of love and danger has obscured its original appeal: it is the greatest natural wonder east of the Mississippi River, and the greatest near a big city—Buffalo is only twenty miles upstream. The Falls do their own advertising. First, a visitor sees the skyscraper of mist, an industrial-colored plume that hangs over the water like smoke from a steel mill. Then comes the audio. From a distance, it sounds as though someone left the tub running upstairs. When you finally descend to the viewing terrace, there are the waters of Superior, Michigan, Huron, and Erie in a violent, boiling race to the precipice, a lemming leap 165 feet down to the rocks. The concave Horseshoe Falls, a heelprint stamped into the river, is a braided curtain of water, thousands of showerheads set on "pulse." The Falls glow with a green fluorescence, and boom with the energy of a never-ending explosion. Niagara Falls is proof that water is the most powerful force on Earth. That's why it conquered two-thirds of the globe. The Falls make the Great Lakes seem bottomless. Every minute, 150,000 gallons of water spill over Niagara, and it keeps coming and coming and coming, still flowing as swiftly as it did under Blondin's feet.

Down in the gorge, the *Maid of the Mist*, a boat full of slicker-clad gawkers, circles the cloudy pillar, looking like a bathtub toy. In some patches, the river froths with eddies. In others, it is so placid that algae grows on the creamy scum. All up and down the railings, tourists in plastic ponchos record this once-in-a-lifetime scene with enough digital equipment to fill a Manhattan camera boutique.

Niagara Falls belongs on the life list of the most casual North American traveler, so the town is still full of bush-league Barnums, out to wow the rubes. "In Blondin's day," wrote Lloyd Graham in his book *Niagara County*, "both sides of the river . . . were filled with all sorts of gaudy, catch-penny, private enterprises that the New York state and Canadian governments eventually took a hand, believing their low-comedy character to be entirely unfit to be associated with the majesty of this great natural phenomenon."

In the end, the mountebanks won. Downtown Niagara Falls, Ontario, looks like a carnival that has put down roots and incorporated itself. There may not be a sucker born every minute, but there is one checking into a local motel. Hiking up the steep midway of Lundy's Lane, I marveled at the larger-than-life marquees of Dracula's Haunted Castle, Movieland: Wax Museum of the Stars, Guinness World Records Museum, Marvel Super Heroes Adventure City. I had only enough money for one admission, so I chose Ripley's. Growing up, I'd devoured that breathless feature in the classified section of my local newspaper. Before the Adventure Channel, Middle America depended on Ripley's for its exotica: the cartoon always featured a body-piercing fakir, or a duck with molars. Ripley built his flagship museum in Niagara Falls, on the theory that one wonder deserves a thousand more.

Right inside the door I saw a stuffed buffalo with eight legs. Was it a freak of nature, or a taxidermist's trick? It was too late for that question. I forged on through the winding exhibit rooms, witnessing a model of Kensington Palace, built with dryer lint, a photo of a cigarette-smoking chicken, a medieval chastity belt, a Chippendale chair designed for an eight-foot, eight-inch man, a spiked collar, and the collected whiskers of Jacob Acoste Jr., who "grew a bushy walrus-style moustache every September and shaved it off every April." It was the story of a man's life, in black and gray.

Did you know, reader, that a "Light Bulb Fell 12 Stories and Did Not Break!" It happened at the Perrine Building, in Oklahoma City. Did you know that "Elza Fire of Bedford, Iowa, visited every state in the United States and collected a soil sample from each!" The dirt was on display, glued to a map. Did you know that a rock cod caught off Bellingham, Washington, was wearing glasses? Did you know I paid twelve dollars to see all this? It was worth it. Seeing the Falls is one thing, but no visit to Niagara is complete until you've been swindled.

★ ★ ★

The Niagara Peninsula is actually an isthmus, between Lake Erie and Lake Ontario. Since it is bordered on the third side by New York, it looks like a peninsula on a map of Canada, and nationalists who'd like to make the United States disappear have dubbed it so. As the barrier between two Great Lakes, it is rich grape-growing country. On every road between Niagara-on-the-Lake and St. Catharines is a sign that looks like an inverted pyramid of cannonballs, with a curling fuse. This stylized bunch of grapes stands for winery. Niagara must be North America's wine cellar: nowhere else do so many vines crawl over such a small patch of dirt. At Hillebrand Estates, tours started on the hour. A three-man combo delicately offered smooth jazz to semi-drunken diners at umbrella tables. I went into the tasting room to kill time.

"Would you like to try a glass of ice wine?" a bartender offered. I had never heard of it.

"It's very popular in Japan and Saudi Arabia. It's made from grapes plucked when the temperature reaches minus-ten degrees Celsius. Then it's pressed in a frozen state, when the sugar is most concentrated."

Ice wine is fermented from pure juice and so requires eight to ten times more grapes than a normal bottle. The bartender handed me a flute. It was the thickest, sweetest, most honeyed beverage I'd ever tasted.

"It's sixty dollars a bottle," he said. "You'd better buy the ice wine now, because soon there's gonna be no more ice wine. Global warming."

The tour gathered in front of a row of vines, tethered to a wire fence. Gord, our guide, began with a geography lesson. He pointed at a hazy bluff to the south.

"That's the Niagara Escarpment," he said. "That's one of the reasons this is a great wine-growing region. The other is Lake Ontario. Because we're on the lakeshore, there's a warming effect that prevents spring frost. It brings the temperature up five degrees and extends the growing season in the fall. Cab Sauv and Cab Franc all need longer seasons. What happens is the air is warmed over the lake, carried over the Escarpment, drops down, cycles back to the lake, and gets reheated. It's an endless cycle that makes this a perfect microclimate."

(Southwest Michigan and the Finger Lakes of New York, the Third Coast's other great wine countries, are also low-lying areas next to lakes.)

Niagara is the most expensive grape-growing land in the world. The Napa Valley, the vineyards of Burgundy—they are rural, but Niagara is part of the Golden Horseshoe, the megalopolis that covers the western bell-end of Lake Ontario, from Toronto to Buffalo. That's why this tour costs five bucks.

An assistant handed out glasses of chardonnay, and Gord taught us to taste it the way a jazzhead listens to Sonny Rollins. The nomenclature of wine tasting is just as obscure as the review columns of *Downbeat*.

"There's a little cork taint in here," he said. "and some citrus melon, tropical fruit. About thirty or forty percent of this was fermented in oak barrels, so there's some burnt toast, nutty, vanilla flavor."

Gord swirled his glass, like a contemplative villain in a melodrama. This was "opening up the wine."

"You need to run air over the surface"—he lifted the rim to his nose, and took a draft. We all did the same. "You can taste by smelling. Let it get to the back of the nasal cavity."

Olfactory appreciation was not enough to prepare us for a taste. We had to peer through the liquid's yellowed transparency to see the evening sun, mellowed by the medium of wine. Tilt your glass back, Gord said. See how the wine pales at the edges. That's the meniscus. It's the sign of a quality vintage. By then, my tongue was gooseflesh, in anticipation of the chardonnay's chilly tang. I lifted the glass, letting its cargo spill over the dam of lip and teeth.

"Move it all over your mouth," Gord encouraged. "Pick up the sweet, sour, bitter taste in different parts of your mouth. Treat it just like mouthwash."

I didn't truly taste the chardonnay until it sparkled over the back of my tongue. Then I was browsing a tropical orchard of pears, apricots, mangos, and peaches.

Our second wine was a gamay noir rose—a red to wash away the white. This got some earthy reviews from my fellow bibblers.

"I got quite a lot of strawberry!"

"Easy drinking."

"Great with a hot dog."

"Great with pizza."

It tasted a little Faygo Red Pop to me, but I prefer the Northern astringency of a good white.

★ ★ ★

No TV program portrays Third Coast culture better than *The Red Green Show*. An Up North cross between *Hee Haw* and *This Old House*, it follows the exploits of fishing lodge handyman Red Green, who solves every home repair problem with a roll of duct tape, and leads his guests in the Man's Prayer: "I'm a man, but I can change, if I have to, I guess." *Red Green* had followed me all around the Great Lakes. It was on every motel TV from Escanaba to Windsor. Its appeal is strong in the Upper Midwest, where PBS stations give it the Pledge Drive slot, but it was filmed in Hamilton, Ontario, the steelmaking hometown of its star, comedian Steve Smith. *Red Green* ended its run in 2006. I was there for the filming of the final "Handyman's Corner," a segment about Red's crackpot inventions.

Steve Smith's trailer was parked beside a hill at the Christie Conservation Area, outside Hamilton. Inside, the star was in full costume: beard, flannel shirt, red and green suspenders, and a shapeless Canadian Army field cap stained with the sweat of fifteen seasons under studio lights. After so many weeks of living outdoors, I wasn't used to low ceilings, and as I tried to take a seat, I bumped my crown on an overhang.

"That's the kind of thing that happens on your show," I said weakly.

"Except we do it on purpose," he said. A comedian can't resist a wisecrack, especially after a setup like that. But then he was completely gracious. He was going over a storyboard with his director, but we could talk between shots.

"I just had three shots of you duct-taping stuff together," the director said.

"Hey, did you know they fixed the Space Shuttle using duct tape?" Smith said. It was in the day's news. Canadian engineers had made the repairs.

"What kind did they use?" the director asked. "It's got to be stronger than our stuff."

"They've been watching too much *Red Green*."

Meeting over, Smith and his crew tromped uphill to the set. The prop master had laid out a baffling agglomeration: corn stalks, a trash barrel, a propeller, a lawnmower. Smith took his mark, behind a work-bench piled with encyclopedias.

"This is our last Red Green Handyman Corner," whispered the producer, Sandi Richardson. "Steve is turning sixty, and he's ready to hang up his hat."

There was a sound problem, so Smith returned to the trailer. I followed. This time, I didn't hit my head. He took off his cap, and I asked him whether his show was based on a real-life Northern lodge.

"There used to be this show called *Scuttlebutt Lodge* on CTV, with a guy named Red Fisher." He was in another character now: Steve Smith, Interviewee. His pitch brightened, he shifted to the edge of his bench, he cupped an invisible beach ball with his hands. "It was a fishing show, and there were episodes where he wouldn't catch any fish. They would sit there and talk about fishing trips, and he had poems, and he would read his poems on the air, and it was 'Why God Loves Moose.' I was just making fun of him. My wife and I had a sketch comedy show called *Smith and Smith*, and I was doing this character."

After *Smith and Smith* went off the air, Steve debuted *Red Green* on a station in Hamilton. It was canceled almost immediately. After the sacking, the station got letters reading "Forget the Whales, Save Red Green!"

"In Canada, a lot of TV is government-subsidized art stations," he said. "The Canadians know that, and they resent it. To get Canadians complaining about a Canadian show going off the air is amazing. Usually, they're street-dancing when a Canadian show goes off the air."

Red Green got another break when it was picked up by the PBS station in Detroit. WTVS was hoping to attract viewers in Southwestern Ontario. But Michiganders love hunting, fishing, and auto repair, too. The show became a regional hit, airing in Marquette, Toledo, Milwaukee, and Elkhart.

"I think Canada generally is very much like the Midwest," Smith said. "The values, the work ethic. Our show is very popular in the Midwest. Iowa is our number-one market. We've done PBS fundraisers, and they always come out dressed in Red Green attire. Let me show you something."

Smith led me into his office. The computer displayed a cartoon from the Des Moines *Register*: Red in a space suit, captioned "Astronaut Red Green Repairs the Space Shuttle."

There was a knock on the door. The set was ready for Red Green. Back on the hilltop, Smith picked up the books and began lecturing on man's quest for a perpetual motion machine. His jokes were as corny as his props.

"The creation of a perpetual motion machine has been the most baffling mystery the world's great scientists have ever faced. I guess they didn't have to do their own taxes. You look at the famous authors in these physics books: Galileo, Isaac Newton, Dionne Warwick. No, sorry, that's a *psychics* book."

He walked over to the junkpile.

"All you need is stuff you probably have lying around: a gas lawnmower, a downspout, a car alternator, a forty-five-gallon drum, a ceiling fan, a chunk of garden hose and some corn stalks. You're probably saying, 'Jeez, Red, you're using everything but the kitchen sink.'"

He lifted a sink with a dangling drain.

"Well, you're wrong."

The director squeezed off a few frames of Smith struggling with a roll of duct tape. Then there was a long break, while the crew lashed the junkyard castoffs into primitivist rural sculpture.

The "Handyman's Corner" joke is that Red's fix-it schemes never work. Boilers explode. Cars break down. Smith uttered Red's signature line—"So remember, if the women don't find you handsome, they should at least find you handy"—and pulled the lawnmower cord. The engine didn't catch. He adjusted the choke. Still nothing. He pulled and pulled and pulled, feigning exhaustion, until the director yelled "Cut!"

★ ★ ★

Hamilton is also the birthplace of Tim Hortons, the Third Coast's favorite doughnut stand. Whenever I was hungry in southern Ontario, whenever my sweet tooth ached, I went to Tim Hortons. I ate muffins there in the morning, egg salad sandwiches at noon, and Boston cream bismarcks before bed. I drank morning orange juice and evening tea, I snacked on "Timbits"—bags of donut holes—and calmed my stomach with vegetable soup.

Canada has more doughnut shops per capita than any country on Earth. Tim Hortons was founded in the 1970s by a Maple Leafs defenseman looking to make money in the off season. It is now on every city block, highway exit, and suburban strip mall in the country. It has been suggested that Tim Hortons is to Canada what McDonald's is to America. Not even close. McDonald's has to compete with Burger King and Wendy's. Dunkin' Donuts and Krispy Kreme have not dared to poke their noses above the border. On the other hand, Tim Hortons has infiltrated New York, Ohio, and Michigan, a doughnut imperialism running against the cultural tide on this continent. The Third Coast is a winter country. Its people prefer hearty sinkers to the spun-sugar confections of Krispy Kreme.

I have never seen a franchise that dominates its native landscape the way Tim Hortons has overrun Canada. Mathematicians at the University of Waterloo are trying to determine whether it's possible to plot a route across Ontario that does not pass a Tim Hortons. This is considered more challenging than the four-color problem, and whoever solves it will probably win the Fields Medal, the world's top mathematics prize.

No matter how many Tim Hortons they build, there is *always* a line inside. Once, I was trapped in a ten-deep queue with a soccer mom from Niagara-on-the-Lake.

"Oh, I must come here three times a day," she said. "There's always one of these on the way to where I'm going."

The Canadian appetite for doughnuts is bottomless. Tim Hortons could build a continuous counter from Halifax, Nova Scotia, to Victoria, British Columbia—which I believe is the company's ultimate goal, spelled out in a secret business plan, locked in a safe in Toronto—and you'd still have to wait five minutes for a cup of coffee.

18

The New Canadians

ONTARIO—TORONTO

The dancer seemed to have absorbed every race on Earth into her shuddering body. Her skin was Darjeeling tea, lightened with two thimbles of English cream. When her cheeks caught a shaft of August sun, they glistened with the golden-tan warmth of equatorial peoples. The sun, too, illuminated the auburn undertone of her starling-black hair, which was straightened to spread into a mane as she bounced to the soca music filling every chest like a second heartbeat, but still springy enough to uncoil down her bare back, to drop vines over the gilded paint that followed the curve of her eyebrows. She wore a white bikini, accented with serpents of gold braid. Egyptian armbands encircled her biceps, and beads dangled from her waist, leaping whenever she humped her hips or flung an arm.

I thought Toronto was the unsexiest city in North America (OK, second—no one can take that title from Washington, D.C.) until I went to Caribana. My idea of a parade is a brass-heavy high school marching band, a stout politician in a convertible, and Shriners

A Caribana dancer.

hunched on go-karts. At Caribana, the vanguard marcher was a bare-chested man in blue harem pants, harnessed to a fan of twenty-foot tall peacock wings. He was followed by a chorus of Aztec warriors flying turquoise banners. Their women wore triangular headdresses, like Teletubby antennae.

Ludacris pinned Caribana on his party map in "Pimpin' All Over the World": "I used to think that it was way too cold / Till I went to Canada and saw beautiful hoes / Now I hit the Caribana every year in Toronto." Billy Dee Williams, more of a gent, comes to the parade because the dancers are "some of the most beautiful women I've ever seen." Or so he said in the program I found at the parade grounds.

★ ★ ★

After that first, turquoise band, only the colors changed—the colors of the outfits, the colors of the skins. The spectrum of flesh deepened from dun Latina to the dark earth of West Africa, although once in a while, you would see a Scots-Irish woman, damply florid under the harsh, pale sun, looking like a changeling inserted into the line.

The marshals were lax—this was a party, a Caribbean party—so I squeezed through a gap in the police fence to take photographs. I got a shot of an oncoming gorgon, lewdly flicking its tongue at the crowd. (BOOMP! BOOMP! BOOMP! BOOMP! These images are not complete without the sound of soca pounding from flagbed trucks). A stocky Trinidadian couple dry-hump dancing (BOOMP-BOOMP-BOOMP-BOOMP). A quintet of ghostly men in red masks, carrying swords and dragging bed pans (BOOMP! BOOMP! BOOMP! BOOMP!). A death's head float, wearing an Abe Lincoln hat. A bald-headed man covered in silver glitter (BOOMP! BOOMP! BOOMP! BOOMP!). And then I saw the woman I described at the beginning of this chapter. She grasped the air with an outstretched hand. She jiggled her pierced belly. A red whistle, the Caribana noise-maker sold everywhere, balanced on the lower lip of her half-opened mouth. There was something about dancing in front of a million people that made her less self-conscious, not more. I snapped a dozen photos then packed my camera in its bag and left. Caribana still had hours to go, but they were hot afternoon dog hours, and there was no way the parade could get any better. Anyway, the festival would continue the following day, on Olympic Island, in Lake Ontario.

★ ★ ★

I got directions to Queen's Quay from the Scottish ticket-taker in the subway station. "You wanna teck the streetcars," he said. "The five-tayn, to Union Stee-shun. Tale the driver you wanna git off at the ferry dock."

The Queen's Quay Ferry Terminal was thronged with holidayers, a tide of immigrant families pressing toward the ticket booths, eager for a bench on a boat to the islands. This was Civic Day, the August holiday, and all Toronto was in a hurry to have fun.

Chicago, the Third Coast's other great-city-by-the-lake, declared its beaches "forever free and clear," but Toronto built right up to the waterline. Harbourfront Park is a squared-off patch of grass hidden behind office towers. There is no sand—only a rusty, corrugated wall, buffered by tires. The Eastern Beaches are in a swanky neighborhood far from downtown. If the masses want to enjoy chilly Lake Ontario, they head to the islands.

Once I hit the dock on Olympic Island, I hurried through a children's amusement park, hoping to guide myself by the sound of soca. I didn't hear any. I walked the length of the island before discovering a tiny amphitheater and a thousand or so West Indians sitting in folding chairs. The skin show for the white folks was over. This looked like a community picnic. Up on stage was a steel drum band. They were obviously from Trinidad—one member was black, the other four Indian. When the last aluminum note had rung from the kettles, a man in a sunglasses walked slowly to the microphone, moving with the deliberate confidence of an island grandee. His paunch was just substantial enough to lift the buttons on his burgundy camp shirt—

he swelled forward like a Victorian banker. Of course, he did not speak without an introduction: "Lennox Farrell," heralded a lesser personage on stage. "Director of the Toronto Caribana Committee."

Here was someone to meet. I fidgeted through his very proper address—"What you see here in Canada, this is a new face. Give a round of applause to Caribana, a beautiful festival in a city by the lake." Then I raced back behind the stage, yanking a business card from my wallet. Lennox Farrell was in the VIP pen, behind a snow fence, but he accepted my card, and stepped out of the gate, his grandson trailing him.

"Come, Ishmael," he said. "Let's get you some water." He turned to me. "Come, let's walk this way." As Ishmael drank from a fountain, Lennox began his story.

"When I first came to Toronto," he said, "their idea of a parade was a few people in sashes and a drum."

This was in 1969, when the biggest celebration in town was the sober Orange Order parade, cousin to the Protestant marches in Northern Ireland. Back then, the city was still known as "Toronto the Good," for its British rectitude.

"Toronto used to be a very Anglicized city," Lennox said. "We made it into a Caribana city. Initially, there was resistance. Toronto wasn't used to street festivals. The police couldn't understand what these guys were doing. You weren't supposed to have fun in the street. You were supposed to have fun at home, and even then, it was not wholly legal."

By the mid-1980s, the city fathers began to notice the crowds— and the money they were spending. Now the program included a photo of the mayor, wearing his chain of office.

"The greatest impact is not even economic, it's social," Lennox argued. "You take a look at the audience today, it's multiracial, multicultural. Caribana is the face of the New Canada. This is how it was in Trinidad. I grew up in a village where we had to work out a whole range of accommodations. I grew up in a village where there were Christians, Hindus, Baptists, Muslims. Everybody went to everybody else's feast. I helped make the Hindu feast. Religion wasn't a barrier to relationships, it was a bridge."

The New Canada was a better Canada for Lennox Farrell. As a young immigrant, he had worked in a dreary door handle factory. The police pulled him out of a subway car because he looked like a rape suspect. Now he was retired from a thirty-year career as a teacher of geography, English, and biology. Wherever he walked on the Caribana grounds, someone stopped to shake his hand.

"You need me?" he asked a supplicant.

"Call me if you need anything," he told another.

"Once, I was pulled over nine times in one year," he told me. "Now, the police call me 'Mr. Farrell.'"

★ ★ ★

I sank into Toronto as though it were a soft bed. I had just spent the hottest week of the summer crossing southern Ontario, sleeping in my tent, trying to strike up conversations with reticent small-town Ontarians. My body was exhausted, my brain felt grated, and I was homesick for urban life. Although most at ease when enclosed by city limits, I had not been in a metropolis since leaving Chicago, nearly two months before. Toronto held me for nine days, twice as long as I spent anywhere else on the Third Coast. Were it not for the immigration laws, and a contract requiring me to finish the journey, I might be there still.

I hid out in a Victorian guest house near Spadina and Bloor, at the crossroads of the Annex, the funky off-campus ghetto attached to the University of Toronto. Bloor Street is an all-night boulevard. In the evenings, the outdoor beer gardens are crowded with drinkers and scholars. On the sidewalks, it is no surprise to see a Trinidadian man holding hands with a Vietnamese girl, but neither is it shocking to encounter a pair of thirty-year-old men walking their adopted daughter.

One evening, I discovered a used bookstore that stayed open until midnight. As a U of T haunt, it was a dumping ground for last semester's CanLit syllabus. I built a pile of Timothy Findley, Alice Munro, Margaret Atwood, and Robertson Davies, all avatars of Southern Ontario Gothic.

"I like to read about wherever I'm visiting," I explained.

"Are you from another country, trying to learn about Canada by reading novels?"

Was I from another country? Was he trying not to insult me, by accusing me of Americanness? In Europe, I knew, it was considered impolite to ask a flat-accented traveler, "Are you American or Canadian?" lest you offend the Canadian. Toronto has been called the most American and the most anti-American city in Canada. There's a thin line between imitation and disgust, and it's not likely to be any thinner than at the country's leading university.

"I'm from the U.S." Say it loud.

"You know," the clerk pontificated, "that's old-school Canadian literature."

"What's the new school?"

"Jane Urquhart. Michael Ondaatje."

I returned to the fiction section, where I found *The Underpainter* by Jane Urquhart. The first sentence was about the North Shore of Lake Superior.

"You know the customers," I said, paying.

"It's been said that Canada is the best parts of the United States," the clerk declared.

"I'm not sure about the best," I responded. "The least objectionable, maybe. I'll give you that."

"Kurt Vonnegut once wrote that the only things America invented were baseball and jazz."

"Kurt Vonnegut is a misanthrope. Don't forget rock and roll. We invented that, too."

"True."

"And say what you want about America. If it weren't for us, there would be nothing good on TV."

"That's your specialty."

"Or at the movies."

"Or on the radio," he conceded.

That one always got them.

★ ★ ★

Homesickness drew me to Jane and Finch, the neighborhood everyone in Toronto wanted to avoid. I first read about it in the Toronto *Star*. A modern dance revue called Dusk Dances was congratulating itself for risking a trip to this remote, semicolonial souk of Jamaicans, Somalis, Italians, Trinidadians, Pakistanis, Grenadians, Chinese, and any other Third World expat who had fled a tropical despot for the chilly safety of Canada. Their refugee papers qualified them for the Canadian starter kit: a berth in a public housing high-rise. Jane-and-Finchers spoke over one hundred languages, making it Canada's most polyglot outpost. But was it the Third Coast's? Back in Chicago, my alderman made the same claim for the Rogers Park neighborhood, which is also on the northern edge of the city, and contains, in a single block, a Korean discount mall, a Belizean barber shop, a Romanian kosher butcher, and a jingling fleet of Mexican *elotero* carts. To me, Rogers Park's diversity represents America as it ought to be. It would comfort me to see the same experiment reproduced in Canada. I had been away seven weeks. I wouldn't be back for another seven. Jane and Finch was the closest thing to home I was going to find in this foreign country. Maybe it was the closest thing in the world.

The Dusk Dances were on Monday. Over the weekend, Jane and Finch made the papers again and again. Only now, it was front-page news. Toronto was suffering its most violent summer ever. Through mid-August, thirty-two people had been shot to death. For a large American city, that would be a cease-fire. For a large

Canadian city, it was a scandalous crime wave. "CITY OF GUNS," the *Toronto Sun* trumpeted after two young Somali men were murdered outside a nightclub. In American papers, inner-city slayings are boiled down to the bones of news briefs, but the Canadian press was still capable of above-the-fold outrage over the killings of poor blacks.

That weekend, a four-year-old boy was shot in the legs, the collateral damage of a drive-by shooting in Jane and Finch. "TINY GUN VICTIM LAST STRAW," the *Sun* thundered. Canada's bubble of safety against the world's violence—against American violence— was collapsing. The mayor blamed weapons smuggled across the border. The chief of police announced a crackdown on gangs. Mothers marched down Jane Street in prayer.

In Jane and Finch, I was expecting to see Johnny Too Bads in beehive rasta caps, dingy apartment blocks with caged walkways and smoke burns around broken windows. To my disappointment, it didn't look like a slum at all. The apartment blocks were clean white monuments. Ranch houses looked out on barbered greensward parks. The neighborhood's center of commerce was the Yorkgate Mall. Inside, rap music from the Foxx hip-hop boutique battled for sonic space with the Bollywood soundtrack of Krazy Sam. Somali women in blue wimples walked with stilt-like gaits, past old Indian men whose canes were capped by bony hands.

★ ★ ★

The young Australian-Canadian woman who'd brought Dusk Dances to Jane and Finch carried a clipboard, a radio, and the attitude that she was doing the natives a favor.

"We decided to take it to a new audience," she said. "To a community that's underserved. People would *never* pay twenty-five dollars to go to a dance troupe, but if they're out walking their dog, they're part of the dance audience. It fits in from a multicultural point of view, because it's pay-what-you-can."

"This is a very multicultural area, isn't it?" I observed. "I've noticed a lot of immigrants here."

In Canada, it's not nice to call someone an immigrant. Toronto the Good hasn't disappeared. Its puritanism has been replaced by political correctness.

"We prefer the term 'New Canadians,'" the woman said. "'Immigrant' is a term that might be seized on by conservatives to suggest they don't belong here."

A moment later, I made another faux pas.

"If this is the roughest neighborhood in Toronto," I said, "then Toronto is in good shape."

"He's from Chicago," an assistant stage-whispered. "They have *gangsters* there."

No, we're not going to live down Al Capone.

★ ★ ★

The Dusk Dances did a fair job of representing Canada, New and Old. A Grenadian drum circle pounded out the overture. For the finale, an Ojibway girl from Manitoulin Island skipped through a hoop. The acts in between were modern art made flesh: three women in green vests dangled from a tree while a man in sunglasses played a mouth organ; identical blondes in taffeta prom dresses danced with the traffic on Driftwood Avenue. After it was over, I met an Old Canadian. Wanda MacNevin, a native of Prince Edward Island, had come to Jane and Finch when she was twenty, a mother of two with an ex-con husband who beat her, burned her, and tried to turn her out as a prostitute. When the police locked him up, she had nowhere to go but a housing project. Now her children were grown. She was remarried to a Vietnam War draft resister from Albany, New York, but had stuck with the neighborhood for thirty-five years, running a program for "teen mums" at the community center. She invited me to visit before I left Toronto.

"We are probably the most diverse neighborhood in Canada," Wanda boasted. "Possibly the world."

That's exactly what we say in Rogers Park.

★ ★ ★

The Jane/Finch Community Centre is a few good-enough-for-government-work rooms on the bottom floor of a Metro Housing apartment building. Wanda took me on a tour.

"This building is half Somali," Wanda said, showing me an empty one-bedroom apartment with oatmeal-colored walls. "We have a fair number of Tamil and Sri Lankan people coming in. Where you've got social housing, you've got great diversity."

"What would you think," I asked, "of trying to start a sister-neighborhood relationship between Jane and Finch and Rogers Park? We're the most diverse neighborhood in the United States. You're the most diverse neighborhood in Canada. I think we have a lot of the same issues. We've got a gang problem in Rogers Park. You seem to have managed diversity better than we have, but I guess that's Canada."

Wanda beamed.

"That sounds like an excellent idea," she said. "I'll talk to my councilor about it."

"And I'll talk to my alderman."

Wanda handed me a sheaf of census sheets—the largest ethnic group was actually the Italians, who held the City Council and Parliamentary seats. Then she introduced me to Byron, a second-generation West Indian who ran the center's youth program. I asked him about the gangs. I'd heard there were two rival factions—G-Side, who lived on Gosford Avenue, and D-Side, from Driftwood avenue.

"They're both Jamaican gangs," he said. "They're fighting over turf. It's got nothing to do with drugs. It's all machismo."

The kids in Jane and Finch were dazzled by the styles of inner-city America, Byron said. For a while, the gangs had called themselves the Bloods and the Crips. Now they wore Duke basketball jerseys and New York Yankees baseball caps. Anything American had street cred. They idolized the rapper 50 Cent, because his body was full of bullets from gang shoot-outs. Byron himself was wearing a green Puma pullover with yellow piping—the Jamaican colors.

Jane and Finch's teenagers relished the street cred of living near Toronto's most notorious corner. They gossiped about the latest shooting the way kids in suburban Mississauga might talk about college plans. Taking a bullet was a five-star status symbol.

"There's a local kid who just got shot. He's in the hospital. When he comes out, he can play it one of two ways—he can say 'Don't do this!' or he can say 'Look how tough I am.'"

Byron shook his head.

"When I was younger," he said, "There was fighting and knifing, and then it calmed down for awhile. Now it's come back, with guns."

★ ★ ★

The most celebrated chronicler of twenty-first-century Jane and Finch is not a writer, but a webmaster: Paul Nguyen, a twenty-six-year-old Vietnamese Canadian who maintains jane-finch.com. The site is a community bulletin board with clips from the ever-curious media and films of neighborhood picnics. But what really draw the mouse-clicks are the rap videos. There is a phone number on the site, so I called it from the Jane-Finch Mall, which is anchored by a shoe store with walls of swollen Pumas and Adidas. Paul answered.

"Yeah, I can talk to you," he said. "Just gimme an hour. I gotta take a shower. I'll pick you up in front of the McDonald's."

An hour later, a brand-new, cream-colored Acura rolled up to the curb.

"Are you the author?" asked a voice from under a toadstool-size ball cap.

I slid inside. The leather passenger seat crinkled under my weight.

"This isn't mine," Paul assured me. An Acura wasn't good for his image as the spokesman for inner-city youth. "I'm not making any money off this site."

We drove to a strip mall, parked in front of Wali's Discount Mart, and walked up a set of stairs to the sort of narrow hallway where noir detectives kept their offices. There was a karate dojo, a business that wired money to the West Indies, and, in the smallest room of all, the headquarters of jane-finch.com.

"The guy who owns the karate studio lets me use it," Paul said. It doubled as the dojo's storage locker. On the walls were a Japanese flag and china-faced Kabuki masks. On Paul was a baggy T-shirt advertising AsianAdvantage.com. He slid behind his computer. I told Paul his site wasn't popular at the community center. He seemed flattered.

"We reach the kids," he said. His voice had the slight quality you often hear in young Asians. It whispered through the consonants. "They don't have no reach. That's why they're pissed at us. Most of the kids, they go straight for the videos, the rap music. People criticize us for violent videos, but we've got to stay hip with the kids. If I had put flowers up there, I would have been out of business long ago."

Paul showed me his most notorious video, "You Got Beef." In it, a Vietnamese gang beats up two black kids who stole a basketball from one of their friends.

"You want beef?" their leader raps. "We right here / There won't be no more peace / It's all about Vietnamese."

Then he starts rapping in the Old Country tongue.

Life in a tough neighborhood is all about rep, and being Vietnamese isn't as hard-core as being Jamaican. Paul once asked his little brother what he wanted to be when he grew up. "I want to be black," the kid had said. "You Got Beef" flipped the stereotypes of the violent black and the nerdy Asian.

"People say, 'You're inciting racism,'" Paul complained. "But I show it to black guys all the time. They say, 'Holy shit, that's fucking wicked.' Asians like it, 'cause they have a rap here. The only people who don't like it are older people or white people."

Paul shot the videos himself, filming rappers he heard about at parties, or on the Internet. The kids from Jane and Finch didn't have much, but they could pull off a thug persona better than their suburban peers.

Paul had learned to use the Jane and Finch mystique to his advantage. At his downtown high school, none of his classmates believed he was from the neighborhood, so he invited a black friend for show-and-tell. They were impressed. Now he was a regular voice of Jane and Finch on CBC. He'd just been quoted in the *Globe and Mail*. ("I made an offhand comment to the reporter that my girlfriend was afraid of the neighborhood, and that became the lead.") Some residents resented the sensationalism, but Paul saw it as good publicity for the site.

"You Got Beef" had been screened at a Vietnamese American film festival in California. Now Paul was working on a feature about Vietnamese Canadian gangsters. The Jane and Finch angle, he figured, could win it a spot at the Toronto Film Festival.

"I want to make it like a Vietnamese *Boyz n the Hood*," he declared. "We need our own movie. We want to get power."

The phone rang. It was Paul's partner, Mark Simms, the black kid he'd brought to school.

"Yeah, what's up?" Paul asked. "Oh, shit, where are you? Yeah, we're gonna have a meeting tonight."

And then Toronto's inner-city rap mogul was back in the Acura, trying to hustle his way to Hollywood.

19

For Queen and Canada

ONTARIO—PRINCE EDWARD COUNTY, ADOLPHUSTOWN, KINGSTON

Prince Edward County is an asterisk-shaped island punctuating the Lake Ontario shoreline. I drove across it on the Loyalist Highway, which is marked by the silhouettes of a colonial soldier and his bonneted wife, posed before a giant crown. The highway was dedicated by Queen Elizabeth II in 1984, two hundred years after the first settlers arrived here, seeking to continue their lives as subjects of her great-great-great-great-grandfather, George III. During the American Revolution, a "loyalist" was a colonist faithful to the crown. The victorious rebels drove them from their farms, and when they fled across Lake Ontario, this was the nearest landfall. The loyalists became the basic stock of English-speaking Canada. Their ancestors are keenly British: in Wellington, a convenience store on the town square sells the *Weekly Telegraph*, the local baseball team is called the Dukes, and the Women's Institute holds programs titled "Discuss Our Loyalist Roots."

I met my first Loyalists at the Prince Edward County Archives, where senior citizens were combing through genealogical records,

Loyalist Heritage Centre, Adolphustown.

looking for a dead sponsor to second their membership. When I walked into the record room, every gray head stared.

"You want to know about the United Empire Loyalists?" a sixty-ish man said. "The best place to go is Adolphustown. There's an old preserved house there, the Allison House. They have the Loyalist Culture Centre."

The United Empire Loyalists sounds like a fusty organization, a losing-team counterpart to the Daughters of the American Revolution. It has its own flag—a Union Jack without the red diagonal St. Patrick's cross—and its own seal, a pale squire's hand and a red Native's arm, raising a banner. It even has a Latin motto: *Ducit Amor*

Patriae, "Patriotism Leads Me." Prince Edward County is the real New England. Every region has its temporal obsessions: in the Far West, they are building the machines of the twenty-first century; in the Midwest, we pine for the twentieth, when there was a factory pay-check in every pocket; in the South, it's the Lost Cause of the nine-teenth. Here, it is the eighteenth.

I took the ferry across smooth, sheltered Adolphus Reach, to a shore that was Northern in its greenness. Not two miles from the dock was Allison House, its long, severe Victorian face looking over the Loyalist Highway. The dwelling's tall, narrow windows, its peaked doorway arch, its pinch-shouldered roof—all suggest temperance, piety, prudence, frugality, and reverence for the Crown. In the park-ing lot, three men were securing a wooden boat to a trailer. I walked over to investigate.

"This is a bateau," said the largest and loudest of the trio. "We're going to use it in a War of 1812 reenactment this weekend in Sackets Harbor, New York."

David Smith, the trio's leader, was that rare subarctic bird, the jin-goistic Canadian. He and his mates belonged to the Canadian Fencibles, military nostalgists who dress like toy soldiers. This whole trip, I'd been trying to see a War of 1812 reenactment.

The War of 1812 began as a dispute over the British Navy's kid-napping American sailors. Yankee war hawks quickly realized it was a chance to bring Canada, which was still a British colony, into the Republic. In the timeless language of American military adventures, a general promised to liberate Canadians "from tyranny and oppres-sion" and restore them "to the dignified station of freemen."

If Americans know anything about that war, they know the burn-ing of the White House, "The Star-Spangled Banner," and the Battle of New Orleans. But most of the action took place on the Great Lakes: The Battle of Lake Erie, where Oliver Hazard "Don't Give Up the Ship" Perry defeated a British squadron, declaring, "We have met the enemy, and they are ours," thus coining two deathless phrases in a single encounter; Detroit, surrendered by a panicked general, making it the only American city ever captured by a foreign army; Queenston Heights, on the Niagara Frontier, where Isaac Brock—the savior of Canada—fell and is commemorated by a 185-foot column. The Americans burned Toronto, then known as York. The British retaliated by storming Sackets Harbor, New York. The War of 1812 was the only war fought on the Lakes, and I've always thought the United States would have been better off winning that one and losing the Civil War. That would have united the Great Lakes under one flag, and allowed the South to fulfill its destiny as a Cotton Republic, an Anglo-Saxon Argentina. Or, as a historian once noted, if the British had won, Detroit, Cleveland, and Chicago might have become Canadian cities. Either result would have created a true Freshwater Nation.

So these were guys I wanted to hang out with. I walked back to Allison House with Dave and his comrades, Brandt Zetterberg and Jon Wannamaker. Jon had reddish hair and skin so florid his face wore a permanent blush. In this part of Ontario, the people looked more Anglo-Saxon than the English. We sat down in a Chippendale dining room, under a portrait of George III, all of us looking out of time in T-shirts and shorts.

I threw out a question: Did Canada win the War of 1812? Dave nearly jumped off his chair to catch it.

"Oh, withote a dote!" he shouted. "With-ote a dote! In most of the engagements, the Americans outnumbered the British and Canadians three or four to one, and we still kicked your asses."

"But what did you win? Nobody gained any territory."

"It defines the border that we live on," Dave retorted. "It's one of the single most defining events in our country. It ensured Canada would be an independent society. Otherwise, we'd be part of the United States, and George Bush would be our president."

"Actually," I pointed out, "he wouldn't be anyone's president."

"Well, you'd be surprised. Some people from this area . . ."

I had no doubt Prince Edward County was Tory country. But Ontario's electoral votes would have defeated Bush.

"You're right about that," Dave conceded. "We were for Kerry, because he had a Loyalist ancestor who went to Halifax. When Canada did not support Bush in going to Iraq, more people were upset about not supporting the Commonwealth than anything else."

Dave referred to himself as a "loyal American"—loyal to the Crown. When the Queen dedicated the Loyalist Highway, he joined the throng in the streets of Kingston. He'd once sworn to ask for asylum with his British sovereign if Ontario became a state. When I mentioned that Quebecers weren't monarchists, Dave made a sneering reference to their license plate motto, *Je me souviens*—"I Remember."

"Yeah, they remember they got their butts kicked."

The Queen made Canada distinct from the United States. This close to the border, the locals were anxious about their Canadianness.

"In North America, what makes us different from the people across the lake is that quirk," Dave said. "When we confederated in 1867, the great threat was that once the Union Army was done, Lincoln was going to turn on Canada. A lot of Americans thought it was their destiny to possess all of North America."

The Fencibles drove away with their bateaux, and I crossed the road to Alban's UEL Memorial Church. Its graveyard is filled with tumbledown markers blown backward by centuries of Lake Ontario winds. Most have been scoured to blankness, but one engraving was still sharp enough to read: "William Buttan Who Died October 1843, AE 84 Yrs. also of Margaret His Wife who died February 1844 AE 80 Yrs. They came here as UE Loyalists in 1783. Fear God Honour the King."

Dave Smith would have agreed with that motto. The War of 1812 had been over for 190 years, but he was ready for the next American invasion.

★ ★ ★

"Well, God *bless* you!" Mrs. Marlene McCracken crooned. Even over the telephone, I could hear she was the type of woman who conducted her conversations the way Leonard Bernstein had the New York Philharmonic, swinging lustily at the air for emphasis. Mrs. McCracken was president of Kingston's branch of the Monarchist League, and she'd be *delighted* to see me. Most of the members were cottaging this time of year, but she could introduce me to Mrs. Davy, who was very big in the UEL, and Mrs. Stafford, a devoted monarchist from Napanee.

The Monarchist League was founded in 1970, to resist Prime Minister Pierre Trudeau's efforts to remove the Queen from Canadian life. Trudeau succeeded in replacing "God Save the Queen" with "O Canada" before hockey games, but thanks to the Monarchist League, the Queen's profile is still on coins and stamps, and New Canadians still swear their allegiance to Her Majesty.

When I rang the doorbell of Mrs. McCracken's suburban home, she greeted me in a blue dress, pinned with a broach bearing a photo of Her Majesty, Elizabeth II, by the Grace of God, Queen of Canada. It was over her left breast, near the heart. Mrs. McCracken had decorated the house with images of her lifelong idol. Mounted in the foyer was the latest official Canadian portrait, from the governor general's office.

"I had a chap in from the Masonic Lodge and he wanted a new picture," Mrs. McCracken said, gesturing at the Karsh. "That was the one he had!"

On the table, she'd set out a plate commemorating the Golden Jubilee. Beside it was a book, *Happy and Glorious*.

"Have you seen the new book that's out?" she asked excitedly. Mrs. McCracken had contributed a story about her first encounter with the Queen. In 1973, young Marlene was a page at the Library of Parliament, in Ottawa. When the Queen visited to unveil a plaque, Marlene was starstruck: "I was ready to curtsy, but when Her Majesty arrived in front of me I froze, my knees locked, and I looked like a deer caught in car headlights. May Her Gracious Majesty grant me humble forgiveness for not showing the respect our Queen deserved."

Mrs. McCracken had only locked eyes with the Queen, but she remembered every detail of the glance.

"She looks right at you. Of the hundreds of people she's met in her lifetime, you never get the feeling you're just another one. She's a very intuitive woman, I believe."

Mrs. Davy and Mrs. Stafford arrived. I closed the book, and the party went outside to the deck, where Mrs. McCracken set out maple cheese and crackers.

While we sipped iced tea, Mrs. McCracken described the Queen's virtues. Mrs. McCracken was married on July 17, 1976— the only day the entire royal family was in Canada, to watch Princess Anne ride in the Montreal Olympics. That morning, she was flustered because she didn't know how to do her nails. So she copied the Queen's manicure. Ever since, that's how she's done her nails. They were a ladylike length—not pared to the quick, but buffed flat along the tips. They would not open envelopes. The Queen has people for that.

"I think she's been a tremendous role model for young women today," Mrs. McCracken said. "She is very knowledgeable. She knows what's going on. She knows the whole world. She's traveled to so many countries, and she's met every U.S. president since Harry Truman. And the fact that she was given her duty, and she had no choice. Every other position, you are voted into. For me, I could give up teaching to raise my children, because it's my duty. My whole life has been, 'If the Queen can do it, I can do it.'"

Now Mrs. McCracken was working on her next-door neighbors. They were from Vietnam, but they were monarchist material.

"They're very well read," Mrs. McCracken said. "They see the Queen's intelligence."

★ ★ ★

Kingston is the only Old World city on the Third Coast, belonging as much to the Saint Lawrence River as it does to the Great Lakes.

Kingston calls itself the Limestone City, because its quarries built the gloomy, pillared City Hall with the four-eyed cupola announcing the time in each direction. On Princess Street, modern bookstores and Internet cafes live inside Georgian brick shells that were built for taverns or liveries. The shutters are peeling; the tuckpointing flakes.

The Great Lakes come to an end here, flowing into the Saint Lawrence under the walls of Fort Henry, which was built during the War of 1812 to defend the route to Lower Canada. Directly south is Wolfe Island, the first and the largest of the Thousand Islands, sitting like a stopper at the mouth of Lake Ontario.

20

The Burned-Over District

NEW YORK—SACKETS HARBOR, NEW HAVEN, OSWEGO

The tramp ferry to New York runs every half-hour. It looks like a metal-shop project, assembled from boatyard scraps. The deck is shaped like a soap dish, while the cabin resembles the pilot house of a harbor tug. When I reached the cul-de-sac at the end of Wolfe Island, the ferry was full, so I stood on the asphalt dock and watched it shuttle the five hundred yards to the United States, flying both the Stars and Stripes and the Maple Leaf. Twenty minutes later, the ferry returned. It holds only a dozen cars. The crew arranged them like pieces of a block puzzle—some facing south, some facing west. A sailor waved me on board, and I parked at right angles to a van.

If you want to avoid a border hassle, cross on a ferry. The customs station at Cape Vincent is the size of a photo booth. It was manned by a pair of Homeland Security officers whose short-sleeve uniforms and Sunday ease made them look like park rangers selling tickets to the three-and-a-half-million-square-mile preserve they guarded. The pedestrians gaggled to the window first. Once they'd been cleared, I rolled forward, with my passport snapped open. The gray-haired senior officer recited the admissions quiz by rote.

"Citizenship?"

"United States."

"How long have you been in Canada?"

"Since July 7."

The officer had more questions.

"Do you have any beef?"

"No."

"Any alcohol, tobacco, firearms, fireworks?"

No, no, no, no.

"OK, go ahead." He called to his young adjutant. "He's done!"

The United States and Canada boast the longest undefended frontier in the world. Here, it was true. There aren't enough German shepherds and cigarette boats to cover all 5,522 miles. And life in a Saint Lawrence river village can turn the most gung-ho border patrol trainee into a genial constable.

A right turn would have taken me to the Tibbetts Point Lighthouse, the Pillar of Hercules at the eastern end of the Great Lakes. But I was in a hurry to reach Sackets Harbor before the Canadian Fencibles broke camp.

I only just made it. The bateau had been hitched to Dave Smith's GMC, and he was loading a wooden box, labeled CPL. SMITH CANADIAN, into its bed. The vessel had appeared on the front page of that morning's *Watertown Daily Times*, carrying a cargo of redcoats.

"The boat got banged up a little bit," Dave said, showing me chalky scuff streaks, where the bow had ground against the same rocks that defended Sackets Harbor in 1813, when it was a strategic target for the British Empire. The shipyard of the United States Lake Ontario fleet, Sackets Harbor was garrisoned with four thousand soldiers—three times the number of villagers who lived here now—and had launched the raid that burned Toronto. At the Battle of Sackett's Harbor, U.S. regulars and local militia repulsed 840 British marines. The battlefield was preserved as a greensward, bordered by a low brick wall, and overseen by elms whose grandparents had sheltered American infantrymen.

Dave ducked into a white canvas tent, and came out with a folding cot. He was in mufti now: a pair of shorts, and unfastened hiking sandals that flapped against his blushing insteps.

"I slept on this," he said. "Some guys think this is cheating. They sleep on mattress ticking stuffed with straw."

"Have you ever read *Confederates in the Attic?*" I asked. "The Civil War reenactors have a term for guys who aren't a hundred percent authentic. They call 'em 'farbs.'"

"I've heard that," Dave said. "We've also got a term for people who carry it too far. We call them 'thread counters.'"

Ashes smoldered in the fire pit. Wood smoke clung to the damp lake air. It was an autumn smell, although this was mid-August. The afternoon's drill had been called on account of rain. Black powder rifles won't fire in wet weather.

I told Dave I'd received an e-mail from another unit, the Incorporated Militia of Upper Canada. They were offering to dress me up and put me on the firing line at a reenactment. He looked alarmed.

"You don't want to line up with those guys! They don't use flash guards."

"What are flash guards?"

"Look. Stand over here." He seized me by the shoulders and turned me toward the tent. Stepping beside me, he raised his arms, pantomiming a rifle.

"When the guy to your right fires his rifle, you're exposed to his firing pan. If you've got a flash guard"—he lifted his palm, like a mail flag—"then you're protected. If you don't have a flash guard, you could get powder burns on your face."

I promised Dave I'd be careful, but this was my last chance to join a reenactment. Powder burns I could live with. Authors don't have to look pretty. As the Fencibles piled up their support poles, their tents collapsed like grounded balloons. The reenactment was over, so I took a walk through Sackets Harbor, which could be the setting for one of

Richard Russo's small-town New York novels. It is one of those Eastern villages that feels entirely self-contained—isolated from the highway, enclosed by a range of hills, sheltered by trees that have grown and aged alongside the weathered frame houses. Beside the old battlefield is a gray limestone building housing the local museum. At the end of the lone commercial street, past the art galleries and sandwich shops, is a Presbyterian Church. It was three o'clock in the afternoon, but music oozed from the sanctuary, faintly, as through an open window. The rain was returning, so I stepped through the heavy doors, sat down among the elderly parishioners, and listened to the jazz combo on the altar.

★ ★ ★

A tent is more restful than a Super 8—inside that nylon cabin, there's no cable TV, no cut-rate Jell-O mattress, no polyester sheets. Just the coziness of the sleeping bag, and reading by lamplight, until the book tumbles from your hand. That is, as long as you have an air mattress. Mine had sprung a slow leak in Ontario. At first, I wallowed in my sleep, as though lying on a waterbed. By the time I reached New York, it would no longer support my weight. At a state park east of Oswego, I awoke with a sore hipbone pressing into the dirt. That morning, I drove to the nearest Home Depot.

"We don't sell them," said a clerk in an orange vest. "You might try Wal-Mart."

Wal-Mart. I'd read an article about Wal-Mart in *Macleans*, the Canadian newsmagazine.

"Thousands of consumers," it declared, "would sooner go barefoot than buy shoes there."

I was one of those customers, and this was my chance to prove it. That night, I decided, I would sleep on the hard ground because I wasn't going to buy an air mattress from Wal-Mart.

Sam Walton founded his retail chain in rural Arkansas, and his company has attempted to impose small-town Southern values on the rest of North America. Wal-Mart is *Norma Rae* in reverse: instead of the New York liberal converting Carolina millworkers to unionism, the Arkie tycoon is forcing New Yorkers to work for nine dollars an hour, with no health care. I was dismayed to see one in Western New York, because this region is the cradle of Great Lakes liberalism. It was settled by dispossessed farm boys from Vermont and Massachusetts, who crossed the Adirondacks, bringing along their beliefs in equality, education, and solving disputes without guns.

In the early nineteenth century, Western New York was known as the Burned-Over District, for its Evangelistic fervors. The celibate Shakers had their biggest following in this region, but it was also home to the Oneida Community, early New Age advocates of free love. Charles Grandison Finney, the proto–Billy Graham who became president of Oberlin College, held his first revival in Rochester.

A laboratory of social progress, the Burned-Over District was the forcing ground of abolitionism, women's suffrage, and temperance. The Underground Railroad spirited slaves onto Canadian-bound packets at Buffalo. Rochester was the hometown of Susan B. Anthony. Elizabeth Cady Stanton held the first women's rights convention in Seneca Falls. In every valley, on every narrow lake, was a liberal arts college with its roots in self-improving Methodism or Presbyterianism: Cornell, Colgate, Hamilton, Syracuse, Wells, Hobart and William Smith, Cazenovia.

You can see this world reproduced in Michigan, Wisconsin, Minnesota, Northern Illinois, and the Western Reserve of Ohio, where the next generations of Yankees migrated, following the Erie Canal and the Great Lakes, spreading the values of Western New York to the Old Northwest. They brought with them the names of their hometowns: Genesee and Lansing went to Michigan, Oswego and Geneva to Illinois, Medina and Sandusky to Ohio, Waterloo to Iowa. And they founded more colleges: not just Oberlin, but Kalamazoo, Macalester, Knox.

And in this sacred country, which had done so much to enlighten America, there was now a Wal-Mart, one of the triumvirate of institutions, along with NASCAR and the Republican Party, that has been making such headway in restoring the South's antebellum dominance over the nation.

I drove back to my campsite, prepared for a bumpy night. On the way, I passed a sign: "DEMPSTER CAMPGROUND. CAMP MEETING 7 P.M." This had to be a pageant from the days of the Burned-Over District. Thrilled, I pulled over to the side of the road. Dempster Campground looked like the set of a frightening summer-camp movie. Graying cottages, showing the neglect of the second home, stood at sullen parade rest along a pebbled lane. The dank presence of Lake Ontario cooled the evening. At road's end was an old white barn, its side panels propped open like awnings. Inside, the dark walls had been stained by a century of damp summers. The dim chancel was illuminated by a glowing cross, with an honor of guard of furled flags, one for the United States, one for the Methodist Church. Behind the Roland organ was this banner, writ in felt: "Jesus Is The Rock of My Salvation. His Church Is Built on A Firm Foundation. He Welcomes Me Unto His Banquet Table. He Lifts Me Up to His Heavenly Places."

In the faint light, I could just read a framed newspaper clipping. This was the camp meeting's 131st year. It had been named for John Dempster, a Methodist circuit rider who'd helped found the Garrett Evangelical Seminary in Evanston, Illinois (where he has a street named after him). Yankee New York has no firmer foothold in the Midwest than Evanston: the Women's Christian Temperance Union is headquartered there.

An iron bell called the worshipers inside. I sat down on a wooden stadium chair. All around me, campers chatted in the stretched vowels and snapped consonants of the Upper Midwest: "I couldn't get Maahm to come tonight," a woman said.

"Oh, Gaahd. What was her excuse ta-day?"

It was an evening of hymns—old-timey songs from library-worn copies of the Cokesbury Worship Hymnal.

"Well, let's start with 'The Church in the Wildwood,'" said a smiling preacher with a stooped neck and a smooth, pink head.

The organist pressed a synthetic overture from his Roland, and we stood to sing exactly as mainline Protestants should: tonelessly. Ecstatic abandon is for Baptists. Church is about fellowship, not showing off. It's rude to wail like Barbra Streisand, even if you've got her chops. You'll just make your neighbor feel self-conscious about his humble, half-octave range. Better to be brothers and sisters in mediocrity.

After we mumbled through "His Eye Is on the Sparrow," "This Is the Day the Lord Has Made," "Blest Be the Tie," and "Away in a Manger," a maternal young woman appeared on the altar. Her left arm was elbow-deep in a puppet. It wore a frilly pink dress and blond Shirley Temple curls.

"Today, we're going to tell a parable."

The puppet's half-moon jaws clapped open and shut. Its ventriloquist squeezed a squeaky voice from the top of her palate: "Is that two bulls with horns?"

The adults laughed with polite restraint. The children stared at the puppet. The ventriloquist told the story of the Prodigal Son.

"He was sorry," she concluded, "and he asked his dad to forgive him. Do you know someone who forgives us?"

She looked over the gathered children. A boy's hand shot up.

"God," he said—always the safe Sunday School answer.

"God is the bestest in the *whole* world," the puppet simpered.

"Yes he is," the ventiloquist agreed. "I know a song about that: 'He's Got the Whole World in His Hands.' Do you know that? Can you sing it with me?"

Maybe this wasn't the fire-and-brimstone Methodism that had inspired "The Battle Hymn of the Republic," but to me, a child of the 1970s, introduced to Christianity at vacation Bible school during the heyday of *Godspell* and *Jesus Christ Superstar*, it was old-time religion. Then, our weekly bulletins were illustrated with drawings of a long-haired Savior leading lambs and children through meadows. On Saturday mornings, we watched *Davey and Goliath*, an animatronic cartoon about a button-eyed Lutheran boy and his dull-witted, kind-hearted dog.

The sleek-headed pastor reappeared.

"It is likely that more than one of you has a son or daughter who's gone off, rejecting the values the parents have taught them, embracing a lifestyle that breaks the parents' heart. I ask you: have you ever given up on that child? I say to you tonight, the love of the Father is constant. If God can forgive the adulterer, the murderer, and the man who denied Jesus to save his own skin, what have we done that's so all-fired awful he can't forgive us? I want you to turn to your neighbor and say, 'Child of God, come home.'"

After the service, I was steered toward Tom Hooper, a retired pastor from the nearby hamlet of Mexico. He'd been coming to the camp meeting for decades. We walked across the campground to the nightly ice cream social, where sundaes were a dollar fifty.

"Almost everything in the religious realm in America had some seeding here," Tom told me. "Port Byron is the home of Brigham Young. A little bit east of us is Palmyra, where the Angel Moroni showed the tablets to Joseph Smith. It all had its roots in the religious experience of New England. The people were tremendously isolated, and they felt the need for other humans. The camp meetings used to bring out thousands. There was a national camp meeting in Geneva. The theory was this was called the Burned-Over District because these waves of religious enthusiasm rose and declined, and in so many forms, that it finally hardened the people, and they became harder and harder to reach."

Tom's colleagues were surprised that the camp meeting was still going, after 131 years. It was kind of old hat, he acknowledged. There hadn't been more than fifty people in the barn that night. Many were second- or third-generation cottagers. Certainly not the kind of crowd you'd see in a megachurch, or even at the tent revivals thrown by the Christian Alliance, a Pentecostal congregation down the road in Fulton. The Methodists of the Burned-Over District had gotten civilized, and their fire had guttered out.

"What you find around here these days is almost a repeat of what you saw when the Methodist Church was developing," Tom said.

"Today, the religious activism is the domain of fundamentalist church-es. Now they are becoming some of our larger churches. Their real growth is reaching the socially dispossessed, the same growth as the Methodists, Congregationalists, and Presbyterians made here. But as the churches became respectable, they shut out the lower class. If you went to that meeting, you might see a more . . . vigorous expression."

He lectured excitedly about the Burned-Over District's glory days, but beneath the words, I could feel a sigh. *He* still believed in crusading Methodism, *he* still loved upstate New York, but modern Americans found both too cold.

"We used to be the most progressive when it came to social con-cerns," he said, his voice rising with fussy pulpit fury. His church expected its ministers to be professors, not demagogues, so he could only crank it so far. "I'm one of those who say it's time for us to speak out. I was opposed to the Vietnam War. I'm opposed to this one. I think it's terribly evil what we've done. It was built on a lie. It's terri-ble to see boys coming back with no limbs. I stopped flying my flag because of it."

"You shouldn't do that," I said. "I'm against the war, but I have a flag sticker in the back window of my car. The flag belongs to every-one in America. It's not just for right-wingers. Make it stand for what you want it to stand for."

"Well, yes," he said. "I think you're right about that. I think you've taught me a good lesson. I'm going to put my flag back up."

I told Tom I'd be heading west after this, along the Lake Ontario shore. I've always considered New York the most complete state in the union: spanning the East and the Middle West, it touches the ocean at one end, the Great Lakes at the other. New York City is the world's greatest metropolis, but the Adirondacks are still wilderness. Buffalo and Albany are minor-league cities here, but they would dominate at least half the other states. New York is one of the original thirteen colonies, but its age alone does not make it historic. Connecticut is equally old, but no one would call it a seven-layer slice of America. More Americans have lived in New York than in any other state, and they have left monuments in all its valleys and villages. Baseball was invented in Cooperstown. Franklin Delano Roosevelt lived and died at Hyde Park. Walt Whitman, the first thoroughly American author, wrote his earliest poems in Brooklyn. *It's a Wonderful Life*, the greatest movie about small-town America, took place in Bedford Falls, a fictional village near Elmira. As the centers of American culture have shifted to places like Nashville, Atlanta, and Los Angeles, "New York" has come to mean a place at odds with heartland values. But when al Qa'eda attacked America, it chose New York as its target, and three thousand New Yorkers took the bullet for three hundred million Americans.

I wasn't quite so effusive there at Dempster Campground, but Tom appreciated my point.

"I think this is a good part of the country to live in," he said. "A lot of people have moved away, though. Syracuse, they're starting a new program to keep their young people. Rochester is having trouble. Their main industries are Kodak and Xerox. Buffalo is struggling. A lot of our friends go south for the winter, but I'm not interested in that. I don't mind a little snow."

21

The Irony of Buffalo

NEW YORK—BUFFALO; PENNSYLVANIA—ERIE

I was eating pancakes at a family restaurant in Olcott, grazing through the *Buffalo News*, when I read about the REO Speedwagon–Styx double bill. That night. At the Erie County Fair. I paid my bill, hurried to the car, and drove to the nearest public library, where I logged onto ticketmaster.com. *I had to be there.*

Arena rock is the Third Coast's greatest contribution to popular music. REO Speedwagon formed at the University of Illinois, but they named themselves after a truck built in Lansing, and we loved them from their hungry bar-band days to their nostalgia act dotage. I saw them in 1982, at Jenison Field House, with one of my burnout friends from the high school cross-country team. They were at the stratospheric pinnacle of rock heroism, but still sporting enough to play donkey basketball for charity at the local high school. That year was the low point for the Rust Belt's factories, but our music had never been more popular. Styx, from Chicago, came out with their goofy Japanese techno-opera, *Mr. Roboto*. Cheap Trick, from Rockford,

Illinois, was part of the cassette jumble in the glove compartment of every peach-fuzz stoner's Firebird, right on top of *Intensities in Ten Cities*, by the Motor City Madman, Ted Nugent. This new cable channel, MTV, played videos by April Wine, Triumph, and Rush, three Ontario bands who'd honed their chops in Junior A hockey arenas. Bob Seger filled Cobo Hall for five-night stands. Yeah, Journey was the biggest act around, but they'd stolen our sound, and wasn't their biggest hit about a kid "born and raised in south Detroit"? (There's no such place, but thanks for thinking of us.)

REO Speedwagon last hit number one in 1985, with "I Can't Fight This Feeling," the most mathematically perfect power ballad ever recorded. Then they became as embarrassing a relic of 1980s adolescence as leg warmers, returning to the public eye only for their obligatory *Behind the Music* special. Lansing never hid the old LPs in the basement. In the mid-1990s, REO Speedwagon returned to play the Michigan Festival, and drew forty thousand people, the biggest crowd in the event's history.

Ticketmaster wasn't taking orders the day of the event. Frantic, I called the fairgrounds box office. The infield was sold out, but I could have a grandstand seat for thirty-five dollars.

"You're going to have to pay separately to get into the fair, though."

I paid. This was a cultural happening. When REO and Styx play at a county fair five miles from Lake Erie, you don't worry about money.

★ ★ ★

In line for the grandstand, I stood behind a couple in matching Journey T-shirts. I thought immediately of the Great White fire, in Rhode Island. All its victims were thirty-three years old. If these bleachers collapsed tonight, would I be mourned alongside hundreds of other early-middle-aged rock fans with petrified musical tastes? I worried less when I sat down behind a squad of fourteen-year-old girls, and a gray-mustachioed man introducing his son to arena rock.

A disc jockey bounded onto the stage.

"How many of you were here for the 2003 REO-Styx concert?" His pep rally tone made me feel, even more, that I'd wandered back to high school. "A little rainy that night, too. All I want to say is if there's a group of people ready to ride the storm out, it's *this group.*"

We cheered ourselves for still partying on a Friday night, after all these years. Eight thousand of us weren't enough to generate the Coliseum Roar. "Whoo-hoos" and wolf whistles pierced the static.

"97 Rock is going to carry all the Bills games this year. They're gonna win tomorrow night, right?"

Yeah! This crowd was gonna rock. The Bills were gonna win. Buffalo was *still* in its prime, and so were we.

Back in the day, Kevin Cronin, the lead singer of REO Speedwagon, had worn his dark locks in a Louis XIV perm. The county fair stage lit up like Shea Stadium, and Cronin—or the Cronin-size action figure under the sunlamps—jogged out under a head of platinum blonde hair, worn in a housewife's wash-and-wear bob. His voice, though, was a marvel of preservation. After thirty years, he had learned to imitate himself perfectly. As he sang "Don't Let It Go," biting down hard on his Midwestern *r*s, he sounded *exactly* like *REO: The Hits*, on my Klipsch speakers. Beside me, a woman in a pink tube top jumped up on the bleacher bench and started dancing, her open-toed shoes flashing metallic toenails.

During the next song, she whipped devil horns toward the stage.

"You take it on the run, baby, 'cause that's the way you want it, baby . . . "

Woozily, she bumped me, gripping my shoulders for support.

"I'm sorry," she said. "This is my old high school band."

"Mine, too. I saw them in East Lansing, Michigan, in 1982."

"I've seen them every year since I was *five.*"

In her purse, she found a milky bundle of plastic wrap and unspooled it, revealing the prize at the core: a hunk of marijuana. It looked like a flop from a bonsai cow. She broke off a chip, stuffed it in a pipe, and lit.

"Smoke?" she offered.

"No, thanks."

"Do you mind?"

"No. It's part of going to a concert."

After the band crash-landed "Keep Pushin' On," Cronin told us how glad he was to be in Rochester.

"It is good to be back here. We got friends around here in Rochester. Y'all come to see us in limousines. That's the kind of people we like."

The guitarist stepped across the stage and murmured in Cronin's ear.

"I *thought* I was in Buffalo," he said. "Last night I was in Rochester, now I'm in Buffalo."

Then he reminisced about REO Speedwagon's golden age. He couldn't have been more than fifty-five, but already he was George Burns spinning vaudeville stories.

"There was a time when all the stars were aligned perfectly for us, and that was 1985, when we had the number one record in the country."

"Eighty-five," the woman in the tube top moaned. "We're all gettin' *old*. Hey, you want some beer?"

She handed me her frothing cup. I drank. It was cold and astringent.

REO Speedwagon ran through its hits like an old hi-fi piling 45s on a turntable: "Keep On Lovin' You," "Roll With the Changes," "Take It on the Run." My neighbor danced so wildly she fell out of her slipper. While she slid it back on, she gripped my shoulder, for balance.

"You know I'm going to abuse you before the night is over," she promised.

In three and a half months, that was as close as I got to a date.

"Let's have a shout out to the hardworking mothers!" Cronin shouted.

"*Wooooo!*" She raised her fist in salute.

Of course, they ended with "Ridin' the Storm Out." As I tell my hipster friends, you can talk all you want about Ani DiFranco's lyrics, but when REO hits that organ solo, *you're gonna be dancing.*

★ ★ ★

From downtown Buffalo, I called Mitch Gerber, Buffalonian in exile. Mitch was my editor at *Washingtonian* magazine, where I worked during the three months I lived on the East Coast. During the job interview, he'd told me he was from Buffalo. When he appeared on *Jeopardy!*, he was introduced as "a magazine editor originally from Buffalo, New York." The day the *Buffalo Courier-Express* ceased publication, forcing him to choose between journalism and Buffalo, was one of the most agonizing of his life. He chose journalism, but he was raising his son "as a Buffalonian," with a Bills jacket and annual trips to Ralph Wilson Stadium. It was said of Petrarch and Laura that they must always be apart, so they would always be in love. That's how it was with Mitch and Buffalo.

"Where are you?" he asked breathlessly.

"I'm sitting at the corner of Church and Main, right by two hot dog carts."

"You're in Shelton Square," he said. "That's where the streetcars used to turn around. There used to be a restaurant called Foodie's there. There was also a burlesque club. My grandfather had a drugstore, and he sold makeup to the strippers."

"I'm running into a lot of 'used-to-bes' around here."

I'd already heard that Buffalo used to be the eighth largest city in the United States, and used to have the most millionaires.

"Well, that's upstate New York," he said.

"I want to know what life is like today in Buffalo."

"I'm not interested in that. My vision of Buffalo is forever preserved in amber in 1962."

"Maybe that's when Buffalo peaked."

"I hung on until 1982," he said. "I didn't want to leave. I would have stayed there forever."

★ ★ ★

Buffalo is the mother of Great Lakes cities. The immigrants who settled Cleveland, Detroit, Chicago, and Milwaukee had to pass through Buffalo to get there, and they copied its layout of balkanized ethnic villages, ordered around Gothic churches and neighborhood taps. Buffalo pioneered the Rust Belt death cycle: it began its decline in the late 1950s, when the Welland Canal and the Saint Lawrence Seaway gave ships an end run around the Erie Canal.

I was standing in the middle of an old-growth downtown. Buffalo's aspirations seem to have ended in the era of brick and stone. In one or two places, you can see glass towers glistening through gaps in the masonry—but these seem like photos of an imaginary future Buffalo, interlaid among the real model.

A few blocks away, the McKinley Monument Square orbits a martial obelisk. The square is dominated by City Hall, twenty-eight stories tall, with art deco fluting climbing the entire height. The stone is stamped with classical friezes to industry, commerce, power, and art. Buffalo's two U.S. presidents pose in front, their girths cast in bronze. Millard Fillmore signed the Fugitive Slave Act, which his hometown defiantly ignored by sneaking slaves across the Niagara River. Grover Cleveland, a.k.a. "the Beast of Buffalo," was the nineteenth century's Bill Clinton: as regally rotund as the Prince of Wales, he fathered an illegitimate child, married a twenty-one-year-old woman in the White House, and is reputed to have relieved himself out his office window.

Buffalo has half as many people as it did in 1950, but really, it's the city's own fault. A Buffalonian invented the device that shifted America's population from the Third Coast to the Sun Belt. In 1902, Willis Carrier was a twenty-five-year-old engineer at Buffalo Forge, a manufacturer of heaters and blowers. A company salesman asked

Grover Cleveland statue.

Carrier if he could help a client with a heat problem: the Sackett-Wilhelms Lithographic Company of Brooklyn, which printed the humor magazine *Judge*, found that its paper expanded and contracted as the temperature changed, causing colors to overlap. Could Carrier come up with a device to regulate heat and humidity in the summer months? Carrier devised a system that circulated cold water through a heating coil. He called it the "Buffalo Air Washer and Humidifier." We know it as air conditioning.

As Carrier's official biography puts it, "A place like Houston could only be tolerable with air conditioning." Florida was once a marginally habitable peninsula of humid swamps and hard-packed beaches. Since the invention of air conditioning, its population has increased fifteen-fold. Carrier started his own company, locating the factory in Syracuse. It became the biggest blue-collar employer in town. At one time, Carrier employed sixty-two-hundred workers. But then Carrier closed its centrifugal chiller factory . . . and moved the jobs to North Carolina. Four years later, it shut down the container refrigeration plant and the compressor plant . . . and moved the jobs to Georgia.

★ ★ ★

The motel was right beside a toll booth on the New York State Thruway, and right across the street from Dickie's Donuts. I ate breakfast at the counter every morning. Outside was a picnic table under a white tent. A conspiracy of old men sipped coffee there, looking like a euchre club without the cards. One morning, I was sitting a stool away from a pouchy old man in a U.S. Merchant Marine cap. Pins hung from the crown like fishing lures: a U.S. flag, a propeller, a campaign ribbon from Gulf War I. He had a cup of coffee. I had a bismarck and a *Buffalo News*.

"That guy pitched a heck of a game for the Yankees last night," he said, gesturing at my paper. "Who's pitching tonight?"

"Hasek," a voice called from a back booth. Dominik Hasek was the goalie who'd led the Buffalo Sabres to a Stanley Cup final.

"I told you to stop talking," the waitress shot back.

"Well, that'll be a shutout."

I looked in my paper.

"It's Leiter," I told the veteran.

"Leiter. Oh, no."

"Well, the Yankees have got all the old guys. That's what Steinbrenner does. He signs veteran free agents. He tries to buy the pennant."

"Their farm system has been shot for the last forty years, ever since Steinbrenner took over," he groused. "But I'll tell ya, he's not a bad guy. He does a lot of stuff for people he never gets credit for."

I mentioned I was headed for Cleveland, Steinbrenner's home-town.

"Wasn't he head of the American Steamship Company?" I asked.

"Oh, no. That's here in Buffalo. I used to work on their boats. I was an engineer."

That's when I noticed his hands. An anchor was tattooed over his left thumb. Ink ages like copper, so it had turned green, and blurred. As had the chain links drawn around his wrists.

"I was ten years in the Navy, then thirty years in the Merchant Marines," he said. "I started out on the Lakes, but then I went to deep water. I could see where it was going with the Lakes. There used to be four, five ships docked out there, all the time. Now you hardly see anything. A guy I worked for told me, 'Bob, go into deep water!' I used to work with iron ore in Duluth before the mines figured out it was cheaper to ship taconite pellets. That stuff was a mess. I didn't mind, because I was in the engine room, but the guys who had to work with it hated it. They couldn't get it out of their clothes, especially when it rained."

Bob had sailed five months at a stretch, earning a day off for every two on ship.

"Once I switched to deep water, I'd come home for three months. I worked nine months out of the year."

"Didn't your wife mind?"

"She married me when I was still on the Lakes. And her father was a sailor."

After Saddam Hussein invaded Kuwait, Bob was called out of retirement to ferry tanks from Germany to Saudi Arabia.

"That's how I got this ribbon," he said, pointing at his cap.

It was 10:30, but Bob was still lingering over his coffee. He had a lot of company. Every few minutes, another crony pushed through the door and pumped him on the shoulder.

"Hi, Will," he'd greet them. "Hey, Jim."

He turned back to me.

"You know what you should do," he said. "You should just go into the office of one of those shipping companies in Chicago and ask them to get you on a boat."

It sounded like a good idea, but at that moment I was interested in getting on another boat. According to the *News*, the *Faire Jeanne*, a tall ship, was in port from Ottawa.

Buffalo's waterfront is overarched by highways on stilts. Billboards for personal injury lawyers mark the exits like milestones. I drove this skyway three times before I found the chute that carried me to the river. A humid, misty rain beaded my windshield. By the time I found the *Faire Jeanne*, the boat rides had been canceled for the afternoon. But a picnic was under way. A lake wind had swept out the sky, so the early evening was blue and brilliant. A sailor poured me a cup of wine. He was ruddy and hearty and wanted to be a big-shot host.

"Are you gonna be here on Monday?"

"I'm staying in Buffalo until Tuesday."

"You come down to the marina on Monday, and I'll take you for a boat ride down the Buffalo River."

★ ★ ★

Monday was gray, but it was a dozen shades of gray. Not even the cinematographer of *Citizen Kane* could match the black-and-white artistry on display over Buffalo that morning. Lake Erie had boiled up a piebald quilt of clouds, with patches of lint, static, bruise, gruel, and black powder smoke. On the Third Coast, cloudy days are as common as clear. Anyone who wakes up on a colorless morning longing for the sun ought to study the sky more closely. There is great variety in clouds. Their shelter is comforting. Who would want to live in the desert, where the sun is a lidless eye? You'd have to squint all the time.

I was early at the dock, and I waited fifteen minutes before a boat sidled up to the jetty. I dipped my toe onto the idling vessel, then jumped aboard. The boat slid around in a half circle, gouged a frothing J on the water, and roared upstream, its wake bubbling like ginger ale. Right away my nose caught a sweetish kettle-corn odor.

"What's that?" I asked the pilot. His name was Mark. He wore a University of Buffalo cap and a beard turning transparent white.

"That's the Cheerios," Mark said.

The General Mills plant fills millions of boxes every year. Over the weekend, I'd seen a freighter emptying itself into an elevator, which had been built when Buffalo was the granary of the East, the last stop for oats from Duluth. As the river uncoiled, I saw another grain elevator, rising ten stories above the bank. It was tagged with graffiti. A rusting skeleton showed through its flaking concrete walls.

Every bend of the Buffalo River revealed another empty elevator, bearing the faded logo of a brewery: Schmitt's, Cook's, Carling, Fred Kuck Malting. The gray cylinders were tombstones for Buffalo beers.

"Don't these look like castles?" Mark marveled. "They just go on as far as the eye can see. Down in Youngstown, Ohio, they took a grain elevator and made a shopping mall out of it. I keep threatening to paint them white and start a drive-in movie theater."

The sky was packed with fleece. On shore, four men emerged from a doorway in the bottom of a tower. Further on, boys dipped lines into the water, angling for fish too toxic to eat. We were not far from Times Beach. A heron swept across the surface on dragonfly wings. The trip felt peaceful and eerie at the same time, like a visit to an abandoned city in a dystopian science-fiction movie.

"Why doesn't anybody use these anymore?" I asked Mark.

"They haven't used them for decades," Mark said. "Nineteen-twenties-ish, the whole industry, because of trains, became obsolete."

"So why aren't they torn down?"

"The cost of tearing them down would be frightening."

And nobody wants the land. Other old cities are building condos and shopping malls on their rivers. Buffalo still thought of its river as a damp industrial access road. Who'd want to live on that?

"There's very few things that Buffalo has done perfectly," Mark said. "They have perfectly separated the citizens from the waterfront. You cannot take public transportation to the waterfront. Buffalo is the last city of its size I've seen to re-gentrify. They keep moving further and further out."

★ ★ ★

It was my last afternoon in Buffalo, and I was hungry. I had just finished a two-hour walking tour of downtown Buffalo, where I'd seen the spider hole where runaway slaves hid on their last nights in America, before crossing the Niagara River to Ontario. It's in a basement bathroom of Michigan Street Baptist Church, and no doubt it had concealed the ancestors of some of the Emancipation Day picnickers I'd met in Owen Sound.

In search of an authentic Buffalo lunch, I drove to a tavern on the bottom floor of a brick house near the Buffalo State campus. I'd been there the afternoon before. The barmaid had turned away from *Judge Joe Brown* just long enough to rasp, "We don't serve food on Mondays." So I went back on Tuesday. A hunched pair of beer drinkers twisted on their stools to stare. Through an open door, I could see shoes and coats on a landing—signs of the family life upstairs.

"Do you have a menu today?" I asked.

This time the barmaid just swiveled her hand slowly. Chicago taverns are like that too. "We don't want nobody nobody sent" is how they put it.

So that's how I ended up as the only mid-afternoon diner at Santasiero's, on Niagara Street. I skipped past the Italian dishes and ordered roast beef on weck. Beef on weck is the tastiest local delicacy on the Third Coast. The sandwich set in front of me consisted of tissues of rare roast beef, still soggy from the oven, packed between a Kaiser roll studded with pretzel salt and caraway seeds. I lifted the lid and squeezed a sleeve of horseradish sauce over the meat. Beef on weck entertains all the nerves on a tongue. Every mouthful is sweet, salty, and pungent.

The sandwich was popularized by German breweries looking for a food to parch their customers. "Weck" is an abbreviation of *Kümmelwecken*, the German word for "caraway seed roll."

Unlike the chicken wing, beef on weck never made it out of Buffalo. Buffalo Wild Wings, the restaurant chain, originally called itself BW3. The third "W" stood for "weck." But it was dropped from the menu. A pity. They got rid of the wrong item.

★ ★ ★

The tail of the New York State Thruway curves along the eastern shore of Lake Erie before expiring at the Pennsylvania line. Pennsylvania has less lakefront property than any other state—forty miles. Its only port is Erie, which built the fleet that Oliver Hazard Perry commanded in the War of 1812. He sailed out of Presque Isle Bay, which is sheltered by a curving spit of land that is a mirror image of Long Point, on the Canadian side. Perry's flagship, the *USS Niagara*, is on display here, but modern Erie shuns its maritime origins. The city lies on high ground, and has no tall buildings, so Lake Erie is always visible—a baby-blue moon, always about to sink below the horizon. But all the action has shifted away from the water, toward the highway.

It was time to buy a new air mattress. Big Lots on 12th Street, a franchised-out boulevard drawn parallel to the shoreline, looked like a cruise ship, in art deco black-and-white. It didn't sell air mattresses. I had to go to Target, at the meeting of I-79 and I-90. The junction is eight miles from the water, but it is Erie's commercial hub. It has also gathered the Best Buy, the Lone Star Steakhouse, and the Microtel. I spent most of my twenties trying to get away from graveyards of ambition like this. The city's sourest, most cloud-oppressed natives call it "Dreary Erie," and the local newspaper runs one of the saddest features I've ever read: "They Started in Erie."

Instead of visiting the *Niagara*, which lies at anchor at the Maritime Museum, I went to a baseball game. The Detroit Tigers have minor-league teams all over the Third Coast: the AAA Mud Hens in Toledo, the AA SeaWolves in Erie, the A Tigers in Oneonta, New York. The ladder to Comerica Park follows the Great Lakes.

Jerry Uht Park, where the SeaWolves played the Akron Aeros that night, is across the street from a tire store. The scoreboard was missing chunks of lights. It was too late in the season to replace them, so the SeaWolves logo looked like a BB gun target. The outfield wall was papered with ads for Smith's, "Erie's Hometown Hot Dog." Six dollars bought me a seat behind home plate—and right in front of a Bronx chorus that heckled every miscue on the field. This was the bush leagues, so they had plenty to talk about.

In the first inning, the home team's shortstop shied away from a darting grounder, but still managed to glove it. He whirled and pegged the ball into a crowd of box seat holders, who frantically ducked for cover.

"Nice play, you idiot!" The fan had a megaphone in his throat. "That's why you play in Erie!"

The shortstop scuffed around the infield, looking abashed. Detroit grew further away with every error.

In the bottom of the inning, the SeaWolves scored when the Akron center fielder dove for a skimming fly ball. It skipped off the grass like a pebble. The right fielder tried to pick it up, but it burned his hand. Erie took a 4–0 lead, but that didn't satisfy the bloodlust in the stands.

"Oh, beautiful," one of the chorus called when Akron's left fielder walloped a slider over the fence. "Haven't seen a run like that since Marilyn Monroe. *Come on, kid!*"

Late in the game, an Akron reliever threw a wild pitch, rushed to home plate, and wrenched his knee trying to tag the runner from third. He was carried off the field in a John Deere cart.

"I hope he broke his neck," I heard.

Erie won 14–5, even though its shortstop once again overthrew first base, threatening the team's insurance rates.

22

Ethnic Jazz

Eddie Mugavero was a homesick New Jersey songwriter driving down a Nashville freeway when he saw this bumper sticker: "I'd Rather Be Killing Yankees." Where Eddie was from, no one ever thought about the differences between the North and the South. But now that the biggest difference of all was being shoved through his windshield, a lyric popped into his head: "We won the war, but we don't brag." A couplet followed: "And we salute just one flag." Eddie went home and built a song around it: "That's What I Like About the North" is a tribute to "pierogies, hoagies, pretzel carts, cheesesteaks, clambakes, Reggie bars / Camden Yards and Fenway Park," and everything else he missed about the states on the other side of the Mason-Dixon line. It was a takeoff on "That's What I Like About the South," the western swing/proto-rap novelty hit by Bob Wills and His Texas Playboys. Mugavero played it at Wolfy's, a downtown Nashville joint where his band, BadaBing BadaBoom, had a house gig. The tourists and the Yankee transplants loved it, but some of the Tennessee boys scowled at that line about the war. More than once, Eddie was met in the parking lot by rednecks who threatened to kick his little Italian ass.

"That's What I Like About the North" became BadaBing BadaBoom's most popular number, and it caught the ear of Lynn Marie Rink, a Cleveland polka doll who'd also moved to Nashville. LynnMarie, as she is known on record, added an accordion and an oompah bass, and changed a few of Mugavero's Jersey shout-outs. "Hoboken, the Home of Frankie" became "Collinwood was the home of Frankie"—that's accordion god Frank Yankovic, son of Cleveland's Slavic East Side. LynnMarie's version became an enormous hit on Cleveland's morning radio shows, the most requested song ever on WGAR. You can buy a copy of "That's What I Like About the North" at the National Cleveland-Style Polka Hall of Fame in Euclid. The song's celebration of Northern culture so matches the theme of this book that when I got to Cleveland, I had to find its source.

The hall of fame's president is Cecilia "Cilka" Dolgan. Cecilia is the baby boom LynnMarie, a polka princess who tried to hit the pop charts. Her old record sleeves are framed on the museum's walls. On *Cecilia Sings in Polkatown U.S.A.*, her hair is spun into a black bouffant, like a palace guard's hat. The story of her career is the story of white ethnic music, which dominated the radio from World War II until the advent of Elvis Presley and the Beatles. She told it in the museum office, on the Saturday morning I visited.

"Cleveland, Youngstown to Pittsburgh is called the Polka Belt," Cecilia explained. Her closely bunched features were heavier than on those old covers, but they also looked kinder. "Anywhere between those three cities, you can probably find a place that plays polka. There are polka radio shows. In Cleveland, we have Tony Petkovsek, every Saturday from noon to two."

When Cecilia was growing up, the TV show *Polka Varieties* was syndicated across the Third Coast—Cleveland, Detroit, Chicago, any industrial city with a Slavic working class. Her parents were from

Slovenia, so there were regular polka parties in their Collinwood home.

"My father could play the button accordion just enough to be the life of the party, not enough to play professionally," Cecilia remembered.

Slovenian polkas, which are slower than the Polish and German hops, are descended from the Viennese waltzes once popular throughout the Austro-Hungarian Empire. The immigrants bought their accordions to America, and played those smooth three-steps at weddings and dances. The bands added guitars, then banjos, then fiddles, making American music out of European folk songs. When the soldiers came home from World War II, they crowded the polka dances at the Slovenian National Home, on St. Clair Street. Polka was happy music for a happy era when victorious Americans were working good factory jobs, getting married, and starting families. From 1948 to 1954, it went far beyond Frank Yankovic and the "Blue Skirt Waltz." The polka was "essential popular music," Cecilia said. Doris Day and Arthur Godfrey recorded polkas, while Bob Hope wrote about the "polka craze" in his newspaper column. Cecilia's father taught his children the accordion, forcing them to sit on the floor and listen when Slovenian music came on the radio.

"In 1955, when rock and roll took over, up until that time, they had polka dances at the homes. They were out by the time I went to high school. The teenagers wanted their musical identity, and polka was their parents'. It still remained very prominent at weddings and taverns, but the radio shows were just on weekends."

Cecilia had a nightingale's voice. After high school, she sang with the Cleveland Symphony Orchestra, and in honor of her heritage, she pursued a polka career. By the late 1960s, though, the music had a terrible image problem. It wasn't just the sound of the World War II generation. It was the sound of a way of life America had abandoned. The Old Neighborhoods were emptying into suburbia. Their sacred institutions—Catholic churches, hard-hat unions, American Legion halls, bowling alleys—were not just out of fashion. They were seen as reactionary. Polka was derided as musical kitsch. As a bumper sticker put it: "Play an Accordion, Go to Jail." Cecilia still seemed embarrassed by Columbia Records' attempt to make her sound hip. With a flat expression, she opened a jewel case of *Cecilia and the Second Generation*, and set the CD into a tray. The first cut was a Slovenian polka, sung in English, with Herb Alpert horns and a disco beat. The second was a waltz, backed by *Shaft*-style wakka-wakka guitars.

"This came out thirty-two years ago," Cecilia said. "They said it was ahead of its time. It's still ahead of its time. It isn't like we didn't try."

Cecilia shrugged.

"Brave Combo and LynnMarie are trying to play crossover polka now. I think LynnMarie is more country. People in Cleveland prefer the traditional style, and that's the truth."

Cleveland had a twelve-year-old accordion prodigy named Anthony Cilkar, but Cecilia's own children refused to listen to the music.

"I made them sing in my children's choir for fourteen years," she said, with the same "I tried" expression she used while explaining the disco/polka fusion. "My daughter likes country, and my son likes 311. I don't know what that is . . . alternative?"

On the way out, I met Cecilia's brother, Joe Valencic. Polka's square reputation, he told me, dances bosom-to-bosom with Cleveland's.

"Cleveland is a city of 'white socks communities,'" he said. It's the butt of comedians—"I just flew in from Cleveland, and boy are my arms tired!"—because "there's a rule that anything with a *k* sound is funny." Even the locals keep their heritage at an ironic distance.

"I remember at Oldies Night at Kent State, they would play one polka song, and everybody got up and danced," Joe said. "If you'd played a second polka, it wouldn't have worked. The novelty would have been gone."

★ ★ ★

Outside the West Side Market, graffiti taggers sprayed red mist onto blank canvases. Break-dancers spun like gymnasts. Hucksters peddled African gowns. A woman in gypsy dress read tarot cards. Nearby, the Great Lakes Brewing Company sells Burning River, "A Handcrafted Pale Ale from Cleveland, Ohio." Along with the Rock and Roll Hall of Fame, which Cleveland landed by stuffing the ballot box in a *USA Today* survey, the West Side is supposed to represent Cleveland's new-found hipness.

This is all wrong. Cleveland is not cool. Cleveland can never be cool. Think of Cleveland's greatest entertainers: Drew Carey wears thick horn-rimmed glasses and a Marine buzz cut. Fred Willard has played so many cluelessly gregarious suburban dads that you can't film a tasteless summer comedy without writing him a cameo. Fellow Clevelander Martin Mull put Willard's talent to use in *The History of White People in America*. Cartoonist Harvey Pekar—record collector, file clerk, irritable bachelor schlump—knew "From off the streets of Cleveland!" would clash perfectly with *American Splendor*, the title of his comic book. Their uncoolness made them stars. Cleveland needs to embrace that quality. Uncoolness is so much a part of Cleveland's character that the city is cooler when it's uncool than when it tries to be Brooklyn or San Francisco.

This might be Cleveland's moment, too. In America's hippest urban neighborhoods there's nothing cooler than looking uncool. From coast to coast, alienated, countercultural twenty-three-year-olds have raided Cleveland's closet for Penguin sport shirts, Jack Nicklaus golf slacks, chunky glasses, and granny skirts (preferably worn with sneakers). They think bowling and Pabst Blue Ribbon beer make a great night out. Cleveland's thrift stores and alleys could become major tourist attractions. But Cleveland isn't cool enough to pick up on that. Instead, it flogs the Rock and Roll Hall of Fame. Rock and roll isn't even cool anymore. Rock and roll is the music of baby boomer dads. It's the soundtrack to *investment ads*. Memphis was the logical winner of that *USA Today* poll, but I've come to agree that the Rock and Roll Hall of Fame belongs in Cleveland. Only Cleveland would think putting rock music in a museum is cool. That's why you should go to the polka hall of fame instead. It's up front about being uncool. Which makes it so much cooler.

The real Cleveland is on display *inside* the West Side Market. The inventiveness of Cleveland's Slavic butchers far surpasses the Germans of Wisconsin. The refrigerated glass cases contained enough flayed tissue for a veterinary college: tasso, jowl bacon, beef smokies, Slovenian sausage, knockwurst, old-fashioned wieners, ham spread souse, pigs' feet, beer bratwurst, beef tongue, and back fat. Bratwurst sandwiches were on sale for $2.50 a plate—$3.00 with sauerkraut. Animals had been diced, jellied, liquefied, and skinned. A gutted pig flapped on a sheet of butcher paper. The heaping guts flushed in fleshy tints as varied as humanity's: pink, red, brown, and every mottled shade in between. In the diversity of meat was the diversity of Cleveland, at least of its white ethnic population. You could see it on the names of the stalls: Wercek's Meats, Brenck and Kindt, Kluth Meats, Edw. Bedstaber and Son, Lavarsay Dohar, Magyar Kolbász. The broken Hapsburg Empire has reassembled itself, right here in the West Side Market.

★ ★ ★

Before moving to Cleveland, my stepbrother Greg lived in a suburb of Chicago. He vastly prefers the charms of a depopulated Rust Belt city.

"Everything's a notch below Chicago," Greg explained. "The Cleveland Opera isn't as good as the Chicago Lyric Opera, but it's twice as easy to get to. One nice thing about living here is that we've got a symphony and an art museum and a zoo, whereas, if the city was just starting out, we might not have those things. Cleveland was full of millionaires, and they're still here. Charlotte doesn't have all that. They might get it, eventually, but we've got it now. Also, because the city isn't so big, I don't have to share it with as many people."

Cleveland has lost half its people, but that means 500,000 cars on freeways built for a million. The commute is a breeze.

As any local will tell you, Slavic Village, on the South Side of Cleveland, has "changed" since the days when everyone's last name ended in "-ich" or "-ski." Perhaps, but it changes back the last weekend of every August during the Slavic Harvest Fest, as Poles migrate home to "their" neighborhood. Sunday is the day for that. St. Stanislaus, on 65th Street, still holds a 10:00 A.M. Polish Mass. At noon, the festival stage was still occupied by a celebrity kielbasa-tasting contest. Out back, DynaBrass, the band who want to bring back the days of the accordion god, were emptying their U-Haul, laying out an accordion, a fiddle, two trumpets, a bass guitar and a drum kit. They'd driven three-and-a-half hours from Detroit to find a crowd of Poles, but they were willing to travel anywhere on the Third Coast.

"For the Polish stuff we do, it's pretty much Wisconsin, Minnesota, Michigan, Indiana, Chicago, New York," said the trumpeter, Jeff Mleczko. "Buffalo's got a lot of it."

Mleczko had big dreams for polka: just as country music had overcome its *Hee Haw* origins, polka could find an audience beyond "Yosh and Stosh at the pub." Like so many other ethnic totems, polka had been out just long enough to crawl back in again.

"There's a stigma about the word 'polka,'" Jeff said. They might have heard a mom-and-pop band at a wedding. That was music forty years ago. I don't think we can even play 'The Beer Barrel.' We hate that song. People ask for 'In Heaven There Is No Beer,' 'She's Too Fat for Me.' We played at Frankenmuth, and a bunch of college kids, they said, 'This doesn't sound like polka. This is cool.' There is a young undercurrent. We've been trying to foster it."

(There's more of a connection between country and polka than you might imagine. Country is descended from Scotch-Irish fiddle music brought over by migrants to the American South, polka from Polish folk songs. It's Poland's country music, said bass player Curt Majeski, who has visited the old country.

"There's really not a lot of polka music going on over there. They listen to old polka songs set to disco beats. It would be like listening to old-style bluegrass here, or mountain music. It was their mountain music. People from the mountains brought their hillbilly music, and that became polka.")

Once the kielbasa competition yielded to DynaBrass's sound check, Byran Palacz, the twenty-seven-year-old host of *Polish Freight and Music Co.*, lingered by the stage. Byran listened to polka "every single day," but even he considered it a scarlet word.

"When they say 'What kind of radio show do you do?' I say 'ethnic music.' My friend has a band called Ethnic Jazz. That's what he called his band. When girls asked him what kind of band he was in, he said, 'Ethnic jazz.'"

Onstage, DynaBrass had changed into matching tan shirts with scrolled brown embroidery. Paul Goodman, an accordion prodigy who'd won the Michigan State Championship at age sixteen, was buttoning on his instrument, and Jeff was having a "Hello, Cleveland" moment with the crowd, which was sitting on bleachers in the street, queuing at the Bud tent, and gobbling pierogies.

"Since we're in Cleveland," he said, "we're going to do a tribute to the greatest Clevelander—the late, great Frankie Yankovic."

"The Blue Skirt Waltz" was smoother than most of DynaBrass' polk-rock repertoire. But they turned into rowdy Polish roughnecks on "How I'd Love to Be Alone With You." The horns blasted a gale of chords, the rubbery bass bounded across the melody, and the accordion wheezed at one hundred beats per minute. Bryan Palacz grabbed a kinky-haired woman and bounced her over the pavement, three steps at a time, one long, two short. Then came the wedding-party song, "Lucy Down the Aisle."

"Therrre goes Lucy walkin' down the aisle / Arm in arm with Daddy, wearin' a big smile." The trumpets blared like mariachi horns. DynaBrass were serving the Slavic Festival a pierogi stuffed with collard greens and *refritos*. There's nothing more American than that.

During the break, a tipsy contractor confessed to me that his name was Bob Malinski, and he listened to polka.

"Yeah, I listen to polka on the radio pretty much every weekend," he said. "What can I say? I'm a Polack."

He glared at me sharply. The Bud had watered down his good sense.

"That's a closed nomenclature," he added.

OK. It's recorded here in quotes.

The show ended with a song that belonged in a bowling-alley jukebox. "My Hometown" went like this: "Once I had a Polish girl, I loved her all to bits. / Her eyes were blue, her hair was blonde, and she had great big— / If you don't believe it, and you don't think it's true / Then come on down to my hometown, I'll prove it all to you."

In the street, a black kid sparked his upraised lighter. It looked like an ironic gesture, but his friend was dancing intently. Maybe polka is a universal language.

★ ★ ★

The Cuyahoga River is doodled across the flats of Cleveland like an uncoiled hair—all kinks and bends. Its shallow bed is as soft as Jell-O, the ship captains say. The *Calumet* makes the trip upstream almost every week, folding the current aside at one-and-a-half miles an hour. Mule-hauled barges made better time. But there is a salt mine beneath Cleveland, and the *Calumet* was launched in 1927. It is one of the oldest boats on the Lakes. Hauling salt is a freighter's last detail.

I rode out to the *Calumet* with Glen Nekvasil, PR man for the Lake Carriers Association, which is headquartered in the Standard Oil Building, John D. Rockefeller's old headquarters.

"I could do this every day if I wanted to," he grumbled, as we climbed the ladder. "Everybody wants to go on a boat. These aren't cruise ships, you know."

The antique ship seemed to have been built out of rust. Reddish stripes marked its waterlines. Ocher amoebas scabbed the deck. A bitter wind stung my lips with salt: it tasted like the fine grains from a restaurant packet.

The cargo pouring into the holds was headed for Chicago, where it would melt ice on I-94. There the *Calumet* would pick up coal,

The *Calumet*.

swapping it in Green Bay for Cleveland-bound limestone. Thanks to this well-plotted triangulation, the boat almost never "deadheaded," or sailed empty.

The *Calumet* is important because one of its deckhands saved a man's life. It happened on the Cuyahoga River. Once I heard the story, from the ship's captain, I had to meet the sailor. He was on duty, wearing baggy work gloves, and his jeans looked like they'd walked a dozen watches.

"I think they kind of blew it out of proportion," Jeremiah Grockan said. "We were leaving this dock, about 1:00 or 2:00 A.M. Before we got to the first bridge, the bridge operator called and asked if we had all our guys on board, 'cause she saw a guy stumbling around. Mark Wolinsky was calling distances, and he spotted the guy. We told the bridge tender to call 911, and the captain called the Coast Guard."

Three crewmen went down in a work boat. They found a shabby man standing waist deep in the water, eight or nine feet from the bank. He'd been walking on the riprap when he'd lost his footing and tumbled down the concrete shelves.

"His face and his arms were all bloody," Jeremiah said. "He was just kind of standing there, not comprehending anything."

Four policemen stood on the bank, waiting for a diver.

"I guess they don't like river water," Jeremiah figured.

The river didn't bother Jeremiah. He jumped off the boat, wrapped his arms around the man's waist, and held him until a police boat arrived.

"They said he went to the hospital and he lost a lot of blood, but he was fine. He totally would have fallen into the water if we hadn't gotten to him."

"How long have you been sailing?" I asked.

"Six or seven years."

It was easy to lose track of time on a boat. It wasn't measured in days or weeks, but in trips. The *Calumet* had made sixty-five so far that year—only the captain knew the figures, unless crewmembers were notching hash marks on the wall.

"Are you going to keep doing it?"

A pained, weary expression compressed his face.

"I hope not," he moaned. "I started out when I was eighteen. It was great then. I just made money and spent it. Basically, for the first two years, it's interesting. After a few years, it's the same thing over and over. There's a lot of young guys and single guys on the boats. When they get married, they want to spend more time at home."

Jeremiah was from Rogers City, a small port in northeastern Michigan where the only jobs are in the limestone quarry or on the boats. His grandfather was a sailor, so Jeremiah followed him onto the lakes. A sailing town. I wanted to go.

"What do sailors do when they're off the boats?"

Jeremiah snorted. "Drink."

A sailor bar. I definitely wanted to go.

"There's the International Sports Bar. It's owned by a captain for U.S. Steel. You'll meet a lot of sailors there. They all hang out there when they're onshore."

"I'll probably be going through there in a few weeks. Are you going to be up there then?"

"Nah. I don't live in Rogers City anymore. I live in Big Rapids."

That is an inland city, forty miles from Lake Michigan.

"When I'm off the boat, I don't even want to look at the water."

★ ★ ★

Back in the car, Glen had a proposal.

"You know," he said, "if you're writing a book about the Great Lakes, you should take a trip on a boat."

Every Boat Nerd dreams of riding a freighter. There are passenger cabins on every boat, but few people outside the shipping industry sleep in them. (My landlord, a retired salesman for Inland Steel, still had scrapbooks full of Kodachrome-colored snapshots of his trips, in the late 1960s.) I would never have asked for the privilege, but I wasn't going to say no.

"Everybody wants to write about life on a boat," Glen said, peevishly. No one damns the press more than a press agent. "How good the food is, the loneliness, how many guys are divorced. I had a guy who wrote for a newspaper take a trip. He showed me his article, and I thought it was a pretty good balance between the business side and the human-interest side. But then his editor read it and said, hey, why don't you give me more of this stuff about the sailing life. So the story didn't turn out that way. That's why I try to stick to business reporters."

If that was the case, he'd offered a ticket to the wrong writer. But I didn't say anything. I wanted my boat trip.

(Eventually, I took the freighter trip Glen Nekvasil promised me. It happened long after I got off the road, so the story isn't included in this book. You can read it on my Web site, www.tedmcclelland.com.)

23

Black Bottom Blues

MICHIGAN—DETROIT; ONTARIO—WINDSOR

I can't tell you exactly when I crossed into Detroit, but I can tell you when I knew I was in the Third Coast's—and America's—poorest city. I'd driven up from Toledo on the lakeshore pike, through the downriver suburbs of Gibraltar and Trenton. They'd been villages before Detroit drew them into its orbit, and their broad, Coolidge-era main streets were watched by brick storefronts, as deeply brown as old walnut trees. It was that part of evening between the magic hour and dusk. The tarnished light held everything in suspension, like a black-and-white photo. Cars were angled against the sidewalk, but none of them moved. I passed Grosse Ile, anchored in the gap between Michigan and Ontario, where the Detroit River fans out into Lake Erie. Then, somewhere on Jefferson Avenue, the lights went out. The sun had set, and the few streetlamps cast just enough amber haze for a few squares of sidewalk. My tires banged over a badly patched fissure, and when I stopped at a red light, the car beside me edged into the intersection. Detroit is the birthplace of carjacking, and there were no witnesses on this industrial block, beside a Detroit Edison plant.

Detroit may be the last American city with a downtown motel. The Shorecrest Motor Inn is two blocks from the Renaissance Center and directly across the river from Casino Windsor, whose amusement park sign glows like a rising moon. It is also two blocks from a party store that devotes three-quarters of its floor space to cheap wine. As I was checking in, a prospective guest asked if he could rent a room "for two or three hours."

"Noo, I'm sorry," the clerk said crisply. "We don't have hourly rates."

Josie was Canadian. Every day she drove in from Tecumseh, Ontario, to run this motel in the intertidal zone between downtown Detroit and the sprawling ghetto that follows the flat boulevards all the way to 8 Mile Road.

"Do you know how to get to the *J. W. Westcott*?" I asked Josie. "I'm supposed to go there tomorrow. The address they gave me is 'Foot of 24th Street.' I'm not sure where that is."

"Are you going on a boat?"

"I'm going on the *Westcott*."

She thought I was a *sailor*. As I would learn, the *Westcott* didn't just deliver mail to passing ships. It delivered crewmen, too.

"We get a lot of people from the *Westcott* here."

"There's a motel right on the corner of 24th Street," I said. "I saw it coming up Fort. *That* looked like the kind of place you could stay for two or three hours."

Josie smiled and unfolded a map of Detroit.

★ ★ ★

The *J. W. Westcott* is the only floating post office in the United States of America. It even has its own zip code. If you need to send a package to a Great Lakes sailor, address it care of his ship, Marine Post Office, Detroit, MI 48222.

The *Westcott*, a thirty-seven-foot skiff with a chain of tires lashed to the hull, ties up just west of the Ambassador Bridge. When I walked into the cinderblock boat house, on a Friday morning, it was like visiting a fire station. A coffeepot warmed on a hot plate, the TV was playing an action movie at ear-crunching volume, and the house cat, Molly, padded into an office. Sam Buchanan, the 6:00 A.M.–to–2:00 P.M. captain, lounged in a chair, still wearing a life vest from the last run. The day's deliveries were stacked behind him: some lucky crew was getting DirecTV's NFL Sunday Package just in time for football season. There was also a bouquet of balloons. It wouldn't be the *Westcott*'s oddest mission.

"People have called asking for ice cream," Sam said. "We went to Baskin-Robbins and got that ice cream. I called my wife for it. I've had people call for new ranges. One time, we went out and got half a lamb. We've had some hog's heads. We had to go buy a TV for a guy."

George Steinbrenner, who made his fortune in shipbuilding, and whose onboard demands are legendary, asked the *Westcott* for Schweppes ginger ale to serve to guests on one of his freighters. When the boat delivered, he climbed down the ladder to tip each crewmember fifty dollars.

Sam was only thirty-eight, but he'd already spent twenty years on the boat. Growing up in Southwest Detroit, he rode his bicycle down to the river to watch ships, the way other boys watched football. He pestered the *Westcott*'s crew until they hired him as a deckhand, right out of Holy Redeemer High School. Now he spent his off hours piloting a dinner cruise and building model ships, and he knew his boats so well he could identify them at night, by the light patterns. The river was his home. Not so Detroit. He had left for the suburbs.

"I wouldn't move back to Detroit even if you gave me a free house," he said, which is how most whites feel about the city.

The door opened, and Glenn Tanner leaned inside. Tall, gruff, he'd hired on as a deckhand after retiring from the police department.

"I hate to break up this little party," he rumbled, "but we've got a boat coming."

Sam heaved himself up. Darn that alarm. I followed him down to the boat and snapped on a life vest. This was a deadly vessel. In October 2001, after an inexperienced captain guided the *Westcott* too close to the stern of the Norwegian tanker *Sidsel Knudsen*, it capsized and plunged to the river bottom. Two sailors aboard swam to safety. The captain and her deckhand drowned. The boat was dredged up two days later, but didn't sail for the rest of the year.

Out on the river, the *Oglebay-Norton* slid under the Ambassador Bridge. At five miles an hour, its wake was a rippling train. Two weeks before, I'd seen it pouring grain in Buffalo. Now it was headed to Buffalo again, riding low. Sam aimed the *Westcott* straight for its hull. Riding the boat was like standing in a pickup hurtling toward a wall. I balanced on bowed legs as the *Westcott* traced a U, then nuzzled against the ship. The tires squashed and bulged. Sam raced the engine, tuning it to the *Oglebay-Norton*'s pace. Above our heads, a pair of deckhands squatted in the gangway hatch. They lowered a bucket, labeled "MAIL PAIL." Glenn stuffed letters inside. He'd loaded the *Westcott* an hour before, when the *Oglebay-Norton* radioed in. Boxes were arranged on the deck, like building blocks. Glenn seized them with his forklift arms. Paper towels, Windex, napkins, engine parts. Sam stepped out of the pilot house to help. On a calm river, the *Westcott* could run itself.

"Thanks, guys," Glenn called, once the deck was empty. "See you on the rebound."

I looked behind us, and was astonished to see that the bridge had shrunk. We'd been *moving* all that time.

Back on the beach, Sam sat down to a liquid lunch of Spaghetti-Os and Faygo Red Pop, while Glenn showed me the mail room, where every boat had its own cubbyhole. The bookstore sold nautical charts, tide tables, and *Mail by the Pail*, a children's book about the *Westcott*.

Then I met the boss. Jim Hogan was the great-grandson of John Ward Westcott, who'd founded the business in 1881, rowing out to schooners with messages. No one thinks of Detroit as a maritime city, but it's the crossroads of the Great Lakes. Cadillac knew that when he built a fort here in 1701. Almost every ship passes through this narrow vein.

Four generations removed from the founder, Jim had lost the family resemblance, and the passion for the Lakes. John Ward Westcott was a stern, mustachioed captain. His heir was a gentle man with an untrimmed tonsure of reddish hair. He lived in a landlocked suburb, and didn't want his son to inherit this anachronistic business.

"People seem to know about us," he said. "Of course, when we had our accident, there was such an outpouring from the community. This episode in 2001, that was something you always fear, having your boat capsize. I rode the boat in my early days, and I can remember being in some heavy weather, but I never imagined anything like what happened that day. We miss those two. They were probably our newest people on the staff. I'm sure you want to know what happened and why it happened. The Coast Guard has issued its report, and I have my opinions about it, but you can read about it there."

Lunch was over. Sam appeared in the door. For the first time, I noticed his T-shirt: "The Beatings Will Continue . . . Until Morale Improves."

"We got another one coming if you want to go out," he announced.

This time, I also noticed the pirate flag flying from the pilot house. Sam was not afraid of the river.

The *Courtney Burton* had a delivery: a sailor, leaving for his thirty off.

"This one's a pain," Glenn complained, as the *Westcott* chopped across waves and sloughs. "His gangway's half a deck higher than any other ship."

"Where's that wake coming from?" Sam wanted to know.

"Cruise ship."

"Cruise ship? That big? I wouldn't have turned if I knew I was gonna run into a freakin' tsunami."

The vessels mated.

A Jacob's ladder slid through the hatch. Sam leaned on the throttle. A sailor with a Snoopy tattoo on his calf backed down. The man hadn't been on land in a month. He wanted to visit his mother in Detroit before driving home to northern Michigan.

"Do you need a cab or anything?" Sam asked.

"That'd be good."

Sam radioed ashore. When the boat tied up, the cab was waiting. Whatever a sailor needs, the *Westcott* delivers.

★ ★ ★

The Heidelberg Project was a piece of unfinished business in my literary life. When I was twenty-five, I wrote a story about the outdoor urban art garden and its creator, Tyree Guyton. I couldn't sell it, not even to the left-wing broadside that had published my first magazine article, a profile of a crack dealer.

Heidelberg Street is on the southeast side, at the edge of a century-old ghetto that still goes by the name Black Bottom. Once you turn off Jefferson Avenue, you have left modern Detroit for rural poverty. Rotting houses, washed gray by years of Detroit winters, lean against the anchors of their foundations. Vacant lots, chest deep in weeds, conceal chamber orchestras of crickets. If you park long enough beside these silent rectangles of grass and wildflowers, you may see a pheasant skitter into the sky. A tree grows over a house, enclosing it like a hand. A bus, once bound for Rosa Parks Boulevard, sinks into an urban prairie.

You know you've come to Heidelberg Street even before you see the sign. The house on the corner is covered from eaves to porch with stuffed animals: Kermit the Frog, Garfield, and Donald Duck dangle crucified on the rotten wood. On Heidelberg, the scene is even more cartoonish: a house with "OJ" painted on the shingles; a vacant lot of vacuum cleaners; a house, daubed with Twister-board polka dots; an Edsel-era car, with a second skin of pennies; and everywhere, stuffed

Stuffed animal house, Heidelberg Project.

animals, nailed to trees, nailed to telephone poles, piled into an abandoned speedboat. The discards of America, gathered onto a discarded
block. Black Bottom is the poorest neighborhood in the poorest city
in the United States. Whatever the rest of America doesn't want lands
here.

When I'd first met Tyree Guyton, the city had just bulldozed two
of his polka-dotted houses. Now Heidelberg Street is the third most

popular cultural attraction in Detroit, after the art museum and the zoo. By the information booth, which looks like Lucy Van Pelt's 5-cent psychiatry stand, I was accosted by a young man in neatly creased clothes. He handed me a card: "Board of Directors, Heidelberg Project."

"I'm looking for Tyree," I said.

"He's not here," the director said. "He'll be back soon. Why don't you sign our guest book?"

I signed my name beneath those of visitors from Mississippi and Japan. A moment later, a Ford pickup pulled up to the curb. Its bumper declared "LIFE WITHOUT ART IS STUPID." Out stepped a bemused-looking man in a French-mustard turtleneck, stained with paint. He flipped down the gate and pulled out a box containing a trumpet and several alarm bells.

"*That's* Tyree," the director said.

I walked over and introduced myself. His shirt was cut off below the elbows, so I could see the tattoos on his soft inner arms: a red polka dot, and his name, "Tyree," beside a heart.

"I interviewed you way back in '92," I said. "You probably don't remember me, do you?"

Tyree smiled. He didn't.

"You were married to Karen."

"OK." He laughed. "That was a long time ago."

"Anyway, I tried to sell the interview to a magazine, but it didn't work out. Now I'm writing a book, and I want to put the Heidelberg Project in there. It's kind of some unfinished business."

"Well, all right," he said. His voice had a bright, almost fey timbre. When ABC films *Heidelberg Street*, David Alan Grier will play the lead. "But you've got to do two things for me. You've got to buy a poster, and you've got to send me a copy."

I bought a poster. Tyree sat in a chair by the curb, and talked about his Project in phrases that sounded like koans. Or maybe public relations.

"I think the city of Detroit is a hard place to live and be," he said. "The city's been through a lot, with the auto industry. If you can make it here in this city, you can make it anywhere. This is a city of visionaries: Motown, Henry Ford. There's something very magical in this place. It has something to do with the people."

Tyree grew up on Heidelberg, in the 1950s, when a few old Germans remained. His whole family—great-grandparents, grandparents, cousins, uncles—had migrated from Alabama to work at "Ford's." He was twelve in 1967, the year of the Riot, the B.C./A.D. moment in Detroit history. Other cities had riots, but none had the consequences of Detroit's. The whites evacuated by freeway. Since then, the city has lost a million people.

"There was a war in Detroit," Tyree remembered. "You see that street, Mt. Elliott?"

He pointed east, at the main road.

"Can you imagine tanks lined up on the street? Helicopters landing? A guy came out of a store with a case of Seagram's gin. I remember gunshots, pop-pop-pop. Tracer bullets on the street."

When Tyree started the Project, he was thirty-one years old, working on the line at Ford's. It was more activism than art. Crackheads had taken over an empty house. Tyree covered it in polka dots. The attention drove the dealers away. So he painted more houses with polka dots. He draped shoes over telephone wires, hung toilet seats on tree branches. The neighbors thought they were living on the set of *Sanford and Son*.

Tyree stood up, and led me down the sidewalk. Heidelberg Street belonged to him, even though he no longer lived here. Now that he was an internationally known artist, who'd spoken in Sydney and Rome and Prague, he lived in a middle-class neighborhood on the Northwest Side. His cousins lived in the old home. There's a saying about urban life: you can't step into the same street twice. It was true on Heidelberg.

"I'm always out here working and changing things," he said.

We paused in front of a tree. Old shoes drooped from the branches. It was a visual pun on his grandfather's stories of lynchings in the South.

"You know what he saw? He saw souls swaying in the wind."

The only white folks on Heidelberg Street lived at the end of the block, in an orange house. Terry Hopkin, a follower of Tyree's, had moved to Black Bottom to be close to his mentor, and built an annex to the Project, out of masks and truck doors and sunflowers. He was inside, playing electric guitar, but I coaxed him out from behind his gated doorway.

"I met Tyree back in 1986," Terry explained. "I had been encouraged by a therapist to do art, and I was doing found object art. Hanging out with Tyree, I thought, 'Wow, my artwork is art.' Everything out here is found in the city."

For years, Terry felt like a hanger-on. Then he held a show, selling fourteen pieces. Secure that he was an artist in his own right, Terry moved to Heidelberg when a house went up for sale. Tyree seemed proud to have him on the block. He'd pointed out the house where the "Caucasian" lived. A trophy white man proved that art was reuniting the races on Heidelberg Street.

Terry wanted to show me something else. Leading me into the vacant lot next to his house, he pointed at a faint white circle in the grass. A ring of feathers, it defined the fighting pit where a hawk had destroyed a pheasant. That lethal arena seemed to symbolize Black Bottom's return to wilderness, and the fight for survival among those who remained. Terry had witnessed the battle.

"A hawk came by and ate a pheasant," he said. "Chewed his ass up."

Terry shook his head, then went back into his house, where he pulled the grate over the doorway and picked John Lee Hooker chords out of his electric guitar.

"This street is about more than art," Tyree said, before I left. "It's become a cultural center. The Nation of Islam is holding a rally here tomorrow. You should come check it out."

★ ★ ★

I did check out the Nation of Islam rally, but in the meantime, I went to a strip club, and I went to church.

Detroit spends its Saturday nights across the river, in Windsor, Ontario, the Tijuana of the North. In Ontario, nudie bars can serve booze and hire French Canadian strippers. In the interest of research, I checked out the Windsor Ballet.

Of course, I didn't admit this to the customs official. He was a British Canadian.

"Where are you going?" he asked, at the mouth of the tunnel.

"The casino."

"How much money do you have with you?"

I opened my wallet.

"Twenty-seven dollars."

He rolled his eyes, but he let me into Canada.

It must be depressing to live in Windsor. Every night, the world's busiest border crossing is breached by Americans bent on un-American activities. On Chatham Street, Cheetah's advertised the "Only Onstage Shower Shows In Windsor." "Freebird" whanged from the doorway of Fidel's Havana Lounge, where 19-year-olds, legal to drink, fellated Cuban cigars.

I stepped into Jason's dim, curtained vestibule.

"Let me find you a good seat," the bouncer said, leading me upstairs. "You take care of me, and I'll take care of you."

Wow. This was sleazy already. And I hadn't even seen a naked girl.

"I'm OK," I said. "I don't need to be too close to the stage."

The bouncer, sizing me up as a repressed tightwad, offered me a chair near the bathroom. Onstage, an acrobat who'd left her leotard in the Cirque de Soleil dressing room hung from a pole with her feet behind her head.

"Can I get you anything to drink?" It was a hopeful waitress.

"I'll have a cranberry juice."

I felt uptight. Until a stripper offered me a lap dance, I didn't notice my hands were clenched behind my back.

"Are you wearing handcuffs?" she asked.

"Not yet."

Other men were breaking through the fourth wall. One laid his head on the stage, clenching a bill in his teeth. A stripper snapped it up with her cleavage.

I was offered lap dances. I turned down the first two, but the third stripper was persistent. A slender girl in tiny metal glasses and a mini-skirt, she crouched beside my chair.

"I suppose you're going to ask me to dance," I said.

"You are right to the point." She seemed taken aback by my brusqueness. If I didn't want to see a naked woman, why was I at Jason's?

"Well, you're the third one."

"I was going to talk to you," she said. "What's your name?"

Pause.

"Phil."

"Where are you from?"

"Chicago."

"I've heard a lot of nice things about Chicago."

"Where are you from?"

"Montreal." She pronounced it "Mun-treal." All Canadians did.

"Is Muntreal as sleazy as Windsor?"

"I don't know what sleazy is," she said, confused.

"Oh," I said. "You're French. What does sleazy mean? It means, are there many low-down businesses?"

"OK. So are you going to dance with me?"

"No, thanks."

"You're not going to let me twist your arm?"

"It's kind of stuck behind me."

I got out of Jason's with just enough money for tunnel fare and a midnight sandwich. I was the restaurant's only customer, so I told the counter man about my talk with the stripper.

"I don't think they have a word for 'sleazy' in French," he said. "Stuff that we would consider sleazy is totally normal to them. I've gone to Muntreal and seen a married couple sharing a boyfriend."

★ ★ ★

Early one morning, in the fall of 1975, a reporter was walking down Jefferson Avenue when he heard the basso bell of Mariners' Church. For over one hundred years, that bell had tolled for sailors lost on the Great Lakes. The reporter listened, counting every strike of the clappers. Twenty-nine drowned was an extraordinary disaster, the worst since the *Morrell*, nine years before. Pounding on the church's wooden doors, he got the attention of the rector, who told him the *Edmund Fitzgerald* was missing on Lake Superior.

Gordon Lightfoot read about that incident in *Newsweek*, and worked it into his ballad: "In a musty old hall in Detroit they prayed / At the Maritime Sailors' Cathedral / The church bell chimed, and it rang twenty-nine times / For each man on the Edmund Fitzgerald."

In fact, the Mariners' Church is a stone bulwark on the Detroit River, set beside the ramp that swirls into the tunnel to Windsor. The crenellated belfry is marked with a cross in the shape of an anchor, and nautical flags loom over the pews. After the Episcopal service, a stranger can wander the basement, inspecting a model of the *Fitz* and a painting of the *Carl Bradley* in its final storm.

The acting rector, Richard W. Ingalls Jr., is the son of the priest who rang the bell for the *Fitzgerald*. A retired Grosse Pointe lawyer, he is kindly, precise, and obsequious. All good qualities in a pastor, who must be a chief executive to the trustees, and a chaste but hearty headmaster to his congregation. His office was the church's pilot house, with brass anchor bookends, and a clock that chimed the half-hours of the watch.

"This church was founded for the benefit of the sailors on the Great Lakes," Rev. Ingalls explained. "Detroit was a principal port back in those days, and a lot of ships would tie up on the waterfront, and sailors would come up Woodward Avenue. It was for many, many years very popular with the sailors, because they weren't welcomed in the society churches. They had to sit in the paupers' pew. As time went on, and the sailing era gave way to steam, Detroit became less of a destination. The trustees paid the bills by leasing out the lower level to a bank, a post office, a grocery store, a barbershop, a tailor, as downtown decayed. They even maintained an adjacent rooming house that became a flophouse for indigent men. When my father took over in 1965, he would have told you that Mariners' Church was 'dead in the water.' There were only five registered communicants when my father came on board. WWJ wanted to do a live fifteen-minute broadcast from a downtown church. My father agreed, and people started coming that wanted to see what the Mariners' Church was about."

Richard W. Ingalls Sr. established a springtime Blessing of the Fleet. After the *Fitzgerald* sank, he held a Great Lakes Memorial Service, ringing the bell each November.

"Did he ring it twice for the *Westcott*?" I asked.

"He did. And he prayed with the families. The captain who lost his life was a good friend of ours. Her husband puts flowers in our bulletin every year on the anniversary of the accident."

We went upstairs, to the belfry. Just inside the door was a stained-glass window. Among medallions of three ships were these words: "Thanks be to God for all seamen who have given their lives in service on the Great Lakes." A rope hung from a hole in the ceiling.

"Would you like to ring the bell?" Rev. Ingalls asked.

I yanked the cord, and found out I wasn't Quasimodo. The bell clanged like a gong bouncing down a hillside.

"You know, Gordon Lightfoot visited here," Rev. Ingalls said. "He said, 'I made a mistake.' He said, 'Whenever I sing that song from now on, I'll call it a rustic old hall,' and he actually told that story in concert, when he knew we were there."

★ ★ ★

On Heidelberg Street, the stern Fruit of Islam, dressed in bow ties like junior faculty of 1961, were peddling *The Final Call*. The headlines promoted Louis Farrakhan's "Millions More Movement," a ten-year sequel to his Million Man March. So did the hip-hop bards on the outdoor stage.

"The word *black* hung from tongues like brown sap, dripped through lips like loose meat," rapped Darryl, one of the Universal Righteous Poets. "They say there are places in Africa where the soil is so black that anything can grow. That's what I want to be. I wanna be 'How's it goin', brother? What's up, sister?' black. I wanna be Michael Jackson black."

"This guy's cold," nodded a bow-tied gauleiter. "He got a voice."

The Nation of Islam was founded in Detroit, in 1930, when a smooth-haired silk peddler calling himself Fard Muhammad began preaching to Black Bottom about a mad scientist who had bred a race of "blue-eyed devils" from light-skinned blacks. Fard disappeared two years into his mission, but his message was carried on by an acolyte named Elijah Poole, and later by Malcolm X, a reformed street hustler who'd once gone by the handle Detroit Red.

Another poet recited: "Detroit is going through a lot of things right now / What it needs is some love / I still remember when I was a child / Having fun playing in the sun at Belle Isle."

Standing beside the FOI was a campaign volunteer for Kwame Kilpatrick, Detroit's thirty-five-year-old mayor. Kilpatrick, a three-hundred-pound ex-footballer who governed in chalk-striped suits and a diamond earring, had his head on the chopping block. He had leased a twenty-five-thousand-dollar Lincoln Navigator on the city's dime, and traveled with a Caesarian security detail. The ghetto loves a hustler, so Black Bottom was his stronghold. I tried to start a conversation with the volunteer.

"My brother knows your guy," I said. "They went to junior high school together."

The man was unimpressed.

"Oh yeah?" he grunted, turning back to the stage.

It wasn't hostility, just indifference. In Detroit, white people make up one-sixth of the electorate, a negative image of their power nationwide. And they were all voting for the mayor's opponent, a half-black, half-Austrian technocrat named Freman Hendrix. The day before, I'd met a Hendrix volunteer, and even he had dismissed the white vote. The election, he said, was a battle between the bourgeois blacks west of Woodward Avenue, and the ghetto blacks, here on the East Side.

"Having Freman as the white candidate doesn't help," he'd admitted. "There still a fear that the whites will come back and they'll take over the city, they'll take over the water department. People say, 'We stayed. We suffered through the city for forty years. The whites fled. Why should they come in and reap the benefits?' People from around the country know that Detroit represents hope for African Americans. People want Detroit to do well because they want a majority African American city to do well."

But Detroit is hardly a city anymore. The whites have spirited away with most of the department stores, the basketball team, the middle-class jobs, the theaters, and the concert halls, and prevented the blacks from building a train system to chase after them. Detroit can only become a city again by doing what Toronto did: consolidating the old urban core with the suburbs. That will never happen here, though: the whites would complain about sharing tax dollars, and the blacks would complain about sharing power. Detroit and its suburbs will continue to revolve around each other like twinned planets, one black, one white, never touching, but never able to break free into broader orbits.

On the street, I noticed a threadbare man in filthy sneakers, circulating at the edge of the crowd, handing out foam hearts as tiny as Lucky Charms. As he dribbled a helping into my hand, I asked his name.

"Willie Fred Jones," he said. "I been knowing Tyree for the rest of my life. I went to school with his sister. I didn't think this was art when he first started doing it. I thought it was junk. When he started doing his polka dots, I said, 'This is art.' Now I'm his director of something."

Willie Fred lived on Mt. Elliott. He pointed to a cabin with plywood nailed over the windows. It looked abandoned, but Willie Fred and his housemates tapped an electrical line. They ignored the one-thousand-dollar water bill. They didn't have a phone. Willie Fred got around on a bicycle, and hadn't been out of Detroit since he was seventeen. Inner-city life had nearly consumed him. Not even a patchy beard could fill out his whittled cheeks. One of his sons had been murdered, shotgunned while lying on a couch. Another was thirty-five, and already had seven children.

"I been poor all my life," Willie Fred said loudly, his words pouring from an abraded throat. "I wouldn't want a lot of money. I'd be scared someone would steal it. I damn sure wouldn't give it to no bank. It might fail, anything might happen."

"How do you get the money you do live on?"

"I don't do anything but the hustle," he declared. "Pick up garbage, pick up bottles. I used to get six, seven dollars. That'll buy you somethin' to eat, save five dollars, that's enough to pay the rent."

I asked Willie Fred where I could get something to drink.

"There's a gas station on Mack Avenue. You know about Mack, don't you? It's where the prostitutes are. They be out all day, startin' at seven o'clock."

We walked through an alley, past a pyramid of matchstick rubble.

"When was that house torn down?" I asked.

"Two, three days ago."

A teenager greeted us: "How you fellas doing? You enjoying the old Black Bottom? It's different, ain't it?"

Willie Fred pointed out the Citgo on the corner.

"They're all owned by the motherfucking Caledonians," he said. He meant Chaldeans, the Christian Arabs who control Detroit's party stores. "I shouldn't say that. They're just trying to make a living. But we shouldn't have sold our businesses to them."

Inside, the clerk was entombed behind plate glass. I flashed him a bottle of cranberry juice. Willie Fred tried to pay for it, but I talked him into a fifty-fifty split. Back at the Guyton house, he bought me an ice cream cone.

"You should bite off the bottom and suck out the ice cream," he said, presenting me with the cone. "That's the best way to eat it."

I did so while listening to the afternoon's keynote speaker: Professor Griff, the onetime "Minister of Information" for the rap group Public Enemy. Griff had been fired after an anti-Semitic harangue to prisoners, and his bitterness had long outlived the band. He held up a copy of *Time* magazine, with Public Enemy's Chuck D on the cover.

"This is a very, very monumental piece," he said. "The cover of *Time* is for presidents and senators and other white sellouts. Al Sharpton put it better than I ever could. There's a difference between black leaders and leading blacks. Black leaders are out there showing themselves in the community. I'm not seeing that from Chuck D or KRS-One."

Hip-hop artists are in and out of the public ear before the next commercial break. The world had stopped listening to PE a decade ago. Flavor Flav, Chuck D's sidekick, was doing a reality show with Nordic dominatrix Brigitte Nielsen. Griff attacked him for consorting with a white woman.

"Minister Muhammad said the devil would use his woman to destroy us," Griff raged. "I talk all about it on my DVD, *Has Public Enemy Lost Its Flava?*"

The huckster. That's when I stopped listening.

★ ★ ★

I made one more visit to Heidelberg Street. Tyree was sitting on the door of his pickup truck, fixing himself a peanut butter and apple butter sandwich. He invited me to share his lunch.

"Here, you want some water?" he asked, handing me a bottle. "I've also got bananas, fig newtons."

While we were eating, a tiny white woman with kinky, greasy hair walked up to Tyree. She wore dirty white flip-flops. Her teeth looked like Indian corn.

"I've got a bag full of stuffed animals," she said.

"I'll come over after lunch and see what you got," Tyree promised.

"That was Donna," he said, after she left. "She lives over in the crack house on Mt. Elliott."

Then a frail old car paused in the street.

"Tyree!"

The driver opened the back door, pulling out a stuffed lion.

"People bring me things all the time," Tyree said. "Sometimes I'll pay them some money if I can use it. Yesterday, someone brought me a boat. A boat! I said, 'I don't need another boat.'"

"Do you even have to go looking for stuff anymore?"

"Oh, some. I drive around the city all the time. This door over here"—he pointed at a flaking wooden door with a photo of John F. Kennedy nailed to a panel—"I found it up against an abandoned house."

As a PBS art critic pointed out, Tyree is no folk artist. His sculptures are not the naive constructions of a ghetto junk collector. After getting out of the army, he went to art school, where he tried to become an urban Asher Durand, carrying his easel to the few pastoral pockets 1970s Detroit had to offer.

"I used to paint landscapes," he told me. "I'd go out to Belle Isle. My teacher hated landscapes. He was an abstract painter. He'd say, 'You don't need to paint something you can photograph.' Eventually, he came here, and he said, 'I knew you had it in you.'"

Tyree laughed and heaved off the gate. A young couple was lingering in front of his information booth, turning over the brochures. Letting himself in the back door, the artist posed in the window.

"Will you sign my guestbook?"

Their address read "Lapeer," a small town in Michigan's Thumb, but the wife was from China.

"Just yesterday I had a visitor from South Africa who asked me to put together material for a show there," Tyree boasted. Then his conversation turned to the visitors.

"Let me ask you a question," he said. "This may be a little personal. Where did you two meet?"

"On the Internet," said the husband, a chubby computer programmer.

Tyree spun away, clutching his cackling belly. When he'd composed himself, he asked, "Was it love at first sight?"

"It was for me," he said.

"We got to know each other for awhile," she put in.

"Let me ask you another question," Tyree said, his tone sobering. "Do you think the people in this city have the resources to turn this city around on their own, or do they need help from the outside?"

"This is my first time in Detroit," she said. "I've heard people say bad things about it, but it's nice."

"You see," Tyree said. "I think it's going to take all kinds of people. This used to be a German neighborhood. I remember when there were white people living on this street, before the riots. Every house on this block was full."

"The state of Michigan has turned its back on Detroit," the husband apologized, on behalf of all the whites north of 8 Mile.

The wife asked if she could take Tyree's picture inside the booth. He agreed, but only if he could pose with his arm around her.

"You always get something out of it," I ribbed him, as I walked back to the car for my own camera.

"I was trained well."

The husband took a snapshot, and in that composition—a white man photographing a black man and an Asian girl—was the genius of the Heidelberg Project: 300,000 tourists drove by every year. Without Tyree Guyton, Black Bottom would be dying alone.

24

Like 1812 All Over Again

The Walpole-Algonac ferry crosses the St. Clair River fifty miles north of Detroit. Run by the Natives who own Walpole Island on the Canadian side, the vessel is no bigger than an armored personnel carrier. After the gate winched down, I followed a roundabout to a drive-through customs station.

"What is the purpose of your visit?" the officer asked, in a clipped accent one would never have heard a few hundred yards to the west. It was half Scottish, half North American—a voice that belonged beneath a trim officer's moustache.

"I'm on my way to a War of 1812 reenactment in Port Rowan."

"Where is your weapon?"

"They're going to provide one for me."

In fact, my only materiel was a pair of combat boots, purchased at a military surplus store. The Incorporated Militia of Upper Canada, the unit I'd be joining for the weekend to reimagine the Battle of Backus Mills, had promised me a uniform as well.

★ ★ ★

There never was a Battle of Backus Mill. In June 1814, a small force of American marines landed at Port Dover, burned a few houses, and shot a few cows. The marines had been rowing for Long Point: had they found it, they would have tried to burn down Isaac Backus's mill, and the British would have tried to stop them. As a historical what if, it doesn't quite rank with "What if the Spanish Armada had never been swept away?" but it was enough to inspire a reenactment, especially since the mill, and its surrounding woods, have been preserved in their Napoleon-era state.

The parking lot of Backus Mills Conservation Area was full of minivans, but there the twenty-first century ended. Shutting my cell phone into the glove compartment, I rummaged my boots from the trunk, and carried them through the historic village, past a farmhouse that narrowed as it rose to brick chimneys and gables. The grounds were a bazaar of gypsy merchants: women in calico dresses offering clay pipes, pocket watches, brooches, knives, tomahawks, and colonial bric-a-brac. Ontario had a reenactment every fair-weather weekend, and these peddlers followed the circuit, like the crystal and tie-dye vendors outside Grateful Dead shows.

The Incorporated Militia of Upper Canada was encamped at the far end of the grounds, behind a schoolhouse. Paul Kelly was slouched in a camp seat by the fire, holding his coffee cup in a grip he'd practiced during his career as a schoolteacher. In his swashbuckling white blouse and drab gray trousers, he looked like a boatman from a George Caleb Bingham painting.

"We're going to be playing Americans this weekend," he told me. "There weren't enough units from the States, so we agreed to step in. We're now the Incorporated Militia of Upper Connecticut."

Paul handed me a pile of secondhand fatigues and led me to my canvas tent. I stepped inside to become a soldier. The armies of that era were renowned for their foppish dress: pillbox hats, trim waistcoats, fringed epaulets, elevator-button jackets in shoot-at-me crimson and

Incorporated Militia of Upper Canada.

royal blue. Those were for the regulars. We were the militia, a pickup unit that fought in street clothes. Out on that battlefield, we were going to look like a sandlot touch football team taking on the Winnipeg Blue Bombers. My black woolen pants were loose, but I cinched them up with a belt. My muslin shirt sagged on my narrow shoulders. Transformed, I emerged through canvas flaps, and Paul showed me how to wear my roundabout—a waist-length gray jacket—my cross-belt, which drew a white X across my chest, and my haversack, a wool purse. From a jumble of hats, I picked a rounded lid with a turkey feather wagging from the band. It belonged on Natty Bumppo's head; I didn't take it off all weekend. Fully dressed, I looked like a shopkeeper who'd been dragooned from his counter in the middle of figuring accounts, and would drop his musket for a quill at the first loud bang.

At full strength, the Incorporated Militia consisted of two dozen members, including wives and daughters. Once the sun went down, the darkness was blind-black. The moon was a blade. Flashlights and lanterns were prohibited, so we sat around the fire, in a tribal circle. As a stranger and a foreigner, I was treated to Canadian trivia and War of 1812 history, from the other side.

"Did you know," one woman said, "that if you turn a map of Ontario upside down, it looks like an elephant, and Owen Sound is the asshole?"

Yes, absolutely, everyone agreed. That was a well-known fact. Owen Sound was the asshole. (I'd never read the map upside down, but the next time I went to the car, I tried it. If the Niagara Peninsula is the trunk, Windsor the tip of the ear, and the Bruce Peninsula the tail, then Ontario voids itself through Owen Sound.)

Richard Feltoe was the group's historian. A ruddy Englishman, he had emigrated from Sheffield, and joined the unit six weeks later.

"To me, the War of 1812 was Napoleon's retreat from Moscow," he said. "A lot of people in England don't even know it exists. At Waterloo, there were 180,000 men in the field, and England lost 18,000 killed and wounded. In the War of 1812, you were lucky to have 18,000 in the field. It's a lost war. If you ask the Americans, they say 'That's the war we won, because we won the Battle of New Orleans, and we won Baltimore, because that's where we got our national anthem.' If you ask the Canadians, the War of 1812, if it did anything, was to define Canada as a nation."

Will Ward, who'd grown up in Saskatchewan, saw it as a patriotic victory.

"I'm antiwar, but I love history," said Will, a white-haired English teacher. "It was U.S. aggression, taking advantage of Britain's preoccupation with Napoleon. If we hadn't won, we'd be Americans. I've got nothing against Americans, but I'm glad to be Canadian."

As a war that was, essentially, a tie, it doesn't evoke the passions of the American Civil War. No one wants to reverse the outcome of 1812. The reenactors are fewer, and less bellicose.

"An American Civil War event in the states will get twenty or thirty thousand," Richard said. "Here, you're lucky to have three or four hundred. In the American Civil War events, they'll come and check to see if you have the right number of stitches on your boots."

"I've run into Southerners who don't believe the war is over," said a man who'd reenacted south of the border. "They actually make the reenactors march long distances so they'll be too tired to go at each other in the battle. In 1812, the war is fought out on the field, but once you get back here, it doesn't exist."

The next morning, after breakfast and coffee from the campfire pot, I was issued my weapon—a smoothbore musket, with a metal rod for jamming imaginary bullets down the barrel. Paul led me to the green for drill. Drill was the basic training of the nineteenth-century soldier. Since armies fought in formation, a soldier had to become an automaton who marched forward and followed officers' orders, even as the men beside him were shot down. I learned "order arms"—the musket held upright, butt in the grass—and "present arms"—the musket held chest-high, barrel upward. I learned how to transfer my musket from one shoulder to the other, and to pivot on my left heel.

I wasn't taught how to shoot. Since I was a green recruit, my firing pan was covered with a leather sheath.

"When we're in an engagement, just point your musket and pretend to pull the trigger," Will told me. "There. That was two weeks of training in fourteen minutes."

We marched to the American camp, to join a rough-looking militia dressed in buckskins, top hats, berets, slouch hats, leather fringers, calico shirts, moccasins, and Indian sashes. We all looked like the extras from *Easy Rider*.

"How many stars are on the American flag?" Paul asked me.

"Fifty."

"Where's the star for Canada? We repelled the American aggressors."

"That's why you didn't get a star. You didn't want to join the club."

Paul introduced me to a sergeant from another unit.

"He's an *actual* American," Paul boasted.

"Well, I hope you don't embarrass yourself," the sergeant said. "Your president does enough of that."

As a guest in Canada, I could fault the man's manners, but not his politics.

Our first skirmish took place on a dirt road, beside the stream that powered the mill. While we waited in formation, a captain in a burgundy sash smoked a cigarette. Only he knew how the engagement would end—he had choreographed it with his fellow officers.

"We've got to win this, or our great-grandchildren will be singing 'God Save the King,'" a soldier shouted.

Before us, the British redcoats stood in perfect formation, behind an officer in a cocked hat.

"Misbegotten lackeys of a desiccated monarchy," Will shouted.

A bugler blatted a rusty alarm. All around me, men tore open paper cartridges with their teeth, pouring black powder into firing pans.

"Fire!"

Muskets snapped. Sulfurous smoke cast the air a dingy gray. A few heavy bodies rolled in the dirt, moaning and sprawling melodramatically. After several rounds, the referee—a fellow in muttonchops—ordered the British to run off. We were free to burn the mill, but no one had any matches.

As we advanced, a veteran named Gord nudged me, keeping me in line. "Shoulder your musket," he whispered. We walked with shoulders touching, each man supporting the comrade at his side, but I felt as I had when I was a grade-school floor hockey defender, brought off the bench with trepidation, or a softball player relegated to catcher: a burden to the team. The British fell back to a grove beside the pond. We fired another volley, toppling five redcoats. The shout of "Charge!" burst over our heads, and we jogged forward, ululating like savages. Jack, the man to my right, died with gusto, leaving me alone on the flank. He lay in the shade, his top hat tipped on his chest.

I had no awareness of our tactical movements. I knew there were Indians in the woods to my right, but I was concerned only with staying in line. I was no more than my fourteen minutes of training had made me: a private, moving forward.

"Just follow Paul, in front of you," Gord whispered.

I followed Paul until I heard "Kit up!" and "Powder up!"—the signals to put away our weapons. America had triumphed.

"Make way for the liberators!" Will cried, as we marched back to camp. "Make way for the freedom fighters! Make way for the *future!*"

The skirmish was a dress rehearsal for the real show, a full-size battle held that afternoon in front of curiosity seekers from all over Norfolk County. It took place on the green. The British lined up behind a split-rail fence, across a weedy ditch from our position. Even sixty yards away, I couldn't distinguish their facial features. They were a battalion of toy soldiers, fresh from the box. They were the original Red Menace. The nineteenth century's Evil Empire.

We kicked their asses again. On the first volley, I raised my musket as though to shoot, then wheeled to the back of the ranks. We fired, moved forward, fired, moved forward, Gord nudging me constantly. Soon we had captured a bridge, and were routing King George's men across a grove, jogging through our own wafting smoke. But our soldiers were dropping like apples from a torn sack. The referee ordered us to retreat behind a fence, then called "independent fire." In a reenactment, that means "free for all." The British charged the U.S. regulars on our right. As the redcoats bounded forward, their bayonets rippled, slicing the dingy smoke like spears, the tools of more primitive warriors. They were ready to stab, and slash. But a few yards from the fence, they suddenly stopped, held a brief conference, and fell over.

Later, Will explained their demise. The British charge would have been toppled by our well-protected firing line.

"We don't do hand-to-hand for obvious reasons," he said. "I think they were talked to death."

We were 2 and 0. Back in camp, I tried to start a chant of "U-S-A! U-S-A!" No one joined in.

★ ★ ★

In another unit's encampment, an American flag fluttered in front of a tent. A fifteen-star version, just like the banner over Fort McHenry. IMUC had its own flag-bearer, a nine-year-old boy who carried the regimental colors. I asked Paul if I could carry the U.S. flag alongside him in the Sunday battle. There is no one more patriotic than an American abroad.

"You can," Paul said. "But we were going to let you fire your musket today. Gord was going to show you how. But if you want to carry the flag, that's OK. It's your choice."

The flag or the gun. That's not easy for an American, but I chose the gun. Gord had the biggest tent in camp—a sheikh's dwelling he shared with his wife and their two daughters. The women were cooking beneath the awning when I walked up.

"I want to fire my musket," I told Gord.

"All right," he said. "I'll get you a cartouche."

A cartouche is a wooden block with holes drilled for cartridges. The cartridges are sheets of industrial-strength toilet paper, twisted at one end like candy wrappers. Each holds a hundred grams of black powder. You bite off the end, and pour the powder into the flashpan, a trench between stock and barrel. When you pull the trigger, the flint scrapes a steel protrusion, striking a spark that ignites the powder. For show, we also had to shove the ramrod into the barrel. Gord demonstrated, then handed me the musket. After four practice rounds, I was ready for battle.

We prepared for the final showdown with the Redcoats by taking apart a fence and reassembling it as a wedge-shaped rampart, until it bristled with menacing pickets. As we worked, I kept an eye on the Star-Spangled Banner, still flying in the friendly camp. Our flag-bearer was with us, dressed in a white shirt and a slouch hat.

"We could get our little guy to carry the flag," I suggested to Will.

Will had told me he hated America, but not Americans. He didn't hate me, at least. Or that flag. Will walked over to the camp to fetch it. He handed it to the flag-bearer, who took his place behind me. I couldn't stop turning around to check out our colors. Gord was amused.

"It's going to take a week and a half for that grin to leave your face," he laughed.

A soldier's courage must be a sort of fear: a fear of cowardice, of losing face with one's comrades. Why else would a man march toward the firing squad of the enemy line? What's behind must be more frightening than what's ahead. I thought about this as we advanced to meet the British. Drill made a soldier's obedience stronger than the terror of death.

"Make ready," our captain roared, when the lines were twenty yards apart.

We lifted our guns, primed with powder.

"Fire!"

Bang bang bang bang, rippling up and down the line.

"Prime and load!"

For the next fifteen minutes, all I remember is frantically spitting out paper, dumping powder into the flashpan, and jangling my ramrod as I tried to thread it down the muzzle. Gord was beside me the whole time. He had the patience of an old sergeant.

"It's OK," he assured me, when I couldn't load my musket quickly enough. "We'll wait until the next volley."

When Gord saw me struggling to pull the cock back, he switched guns with me. His had a looser spring. It was easier to fire— so easy that my round always went off first—but this caused a new problem. My barrel was heating up. During "make ready," I felt like I was holding a pot of soup, with my fingertips. An oven mitt would have helped, but they're not military issue. I'm sure everyone was suffering as well, but they were veterans. They knew how to handle a glowing muzzle. I wondered whether I would make it through the battle.

Relief came in the form of defeat. After two victories, the United States lost the Sunday matinee. I'm sure that's what the crowd wanted to see.

"Crouch down," Gord whispered. "OK. Now get up. We're going to have to withdraw. Find yourself a spot behind the fence."

Hunched like miners, we hustled back to our redoubt. Our captain parleyed with the British general, and agreed to withdraw.

I had one more test to pass as an imitation soldier: final inspection. I think I earned a D+. I was always half a beat behind at "present arms." At "shoulder arms," my bayonet tilted too far back, waggling in the face of the man behind me. Gord pushed it upright.

"Keep it straight," he urged.

"He's got his head screwed on backwards," someone said.

But Will had the last word.

"Let's have three cheers for our organizer!" he cried.

We acclaimed him in Georgian style: "Hip, hip huzzah! Hip, hip, huzzah! Hip, hip, huzzah!" lifting our caps at every huzzah.

★ ★ ★

I followed Highway 402 into the sunset, stopping at the Sarnia Duty Free, a few feet from the Blue Water Bridge. I had a stack of receipts to cash in for my government sales tax refund. Foreigners don't have to pay. We're not getting the free health care, so why should we? The take was seventy dollars, U.S. I walked around the boutique, searching for a souvenir. The trays of butter tarts, the whiskey in holiday boxes—those wouldn't last until Chicago. I browsed T-shirts printed with maple leaves and cute slogans: "Canadian—An Unarmed American with Health Care." Those weren't right either. I'd spent six weeks in Canada, but I wasn't Canadian. I just had a soft spot for the country—for doughnuts, lunch, and dinner at Tim Hortons; for pockets weighted down with loonies and toonies; for the quizzical northern lilt of the women's voices; for a people traditional enough to swear allegiance to the Queen, but modern enough to choose a Haitian refugee as her representative and polite enough to call her a "New Canadian" rather than an immigrant. For butter tarts and hockey and all the moose I never saw, and for the CBC, a network so considerate it didn't make its comedies funny or its dramas compelling—you shouldn't be forced to laugh or keep watching. The spot was even softer now that I'd spent a weekend camping out with Canadians. When I was making my way up Lake Erie, I'd thought the small-town burghers of southern Ontario were standoffish. But maybe I'd been rude, popping into their villages with no notice. Canadians are as welcoming as anyone else, if you just have the manners to call in advance.

So I bought a baseball cap with the stars and stripes and the maple leaf intertwined. That was exactly how I felt: like an American who'd discovered his Canadian side. Anyone who drives around the Great Lakes would feel the same.

25

The Great Bay Port Fish Sandwich Controversy

MICHIGAN—BAY PORT

The Lower Peninsula of Michigan is shaped like an open hand. Next time you meet a Michigander, ask where he's from. He'll spread out his right palm and point to a spot on that soft map. Detroit is the first knuckle of the thumb, Bay City the webbing, Traverse City the tip of the pinkie. The peninsula-within-a-peninsula between Lake Saint Clair and Saginaw Bay is called the Thumb, a bit of slang that's made its way into nomenclature: there's a Thumb Correctional Facility and a Thumb National Bank & Trust. M-25, the state highway, follows the Thumb's edge like a perfectly cut nail. On the Sunday after Labor Day, it was as little trafficked as a lakeshore road in the Upper Peninsula. The cottage season was over. Gas was three dollars a gallon. And western Lake Huron is the emptiest shore on the Third Coast. Its beaches are hard and pebbly; its mornings are harsh. Michiganders prefer the soft sands and oozing sunsets of their west coast. Northeastern Michigan is the most obscure quarter of the state, maybe of the entire Great Lakes. Nobody talks about it, and nobody visits.

Darkness stopped me in Port Sanilac. The party store was still open, so I stepped past sacks of carrots piled around the door—deer bait—and asked the clerk if Port Sanilac had a motel.

"There's the Bellaire," she said. "I'll call the owner for you."

She dialed quickly—in a town this size, you can use four numbers.

"It's closed, but he says he'll leave a door open for you. Just go into the B&B next door."

The Bellaire was a strip of rooms facing an unlit parking lot. I had to hunt for a room key in the Charles Addams bed-and-breakfast down the road. Its varnished wooden door was ajar, but all the lights were off. Calling into the kitchen, I got an echo and, eventually, an innkeeper. He set down his ticket book between the antique cash register and the peppermint dish, writing by light from the kitchen.

"It's only thirty-five dollars," he said. "The rates go down this late in the season."

This part of Michigan calls itself the Sunrise Side, and that Monday morning shone like the dawn not just of a new week, but of a new world. The sky had been painted a pure blue, and lacquered to keep off clouds. Scales of light glittered sharply on the water—the newborn sun was much more powerful than the mellow ancient who would sink into Lake Michigan that evening. I rounded the curve of the Thumb, past the Pointe aux Barques lighthouse, until I arrived in Bay Port.

★ ★ ★

When you leave M-25 in Bay Port, and drive down the macadam road to the water's edge, you pass a wooden cutout of a mullet dangling a fisherman by his legs. This piece of folk art is titled *Fish Caught the Man*, and it's the logo of the Bay Port Fish Sandwich Festival, which takes place the first weekend in August. I'd missed the festival, but I still wanted a fish sandwich. Only one woman had the recipe: Carolyn Smith, the daughter of Henry Engelhart, founder of the Bay Port Fish Company. According to Thumb legend, the card is locked in a safe deposit box at the Bay Port State Bank. Once a year, Carolyn

Fish Caught the Man sign.

takes it out, memorizes the ingredients, and mixes the batter at a secret location.

The Engleharts no longer own the fish company, but it seemed like the place to start looking for Carolyn. It occupies a building that looks like an airplane hangar. It's a long, gray half-tube, with an aluminum roof, and a wind sock that stiffens to a cone when Saginaw Bay is too rough for fishing vessels.

When I walked into the dim warehouse, lit only by rectangles of sunlight that glowed through the bay doors, I found a woman folding boxes. Connie Williams minded the store while her husband, Tod, fished the bay. Behind the glass display case, prices were markered on a square of cardboard. At $11.95 a pound, perch was the filet mignon of the lake. At $5.99, whitefish was the hamburger: the people's fish.

Connie was a short woman, with a petite chain-smoker's figure and a backyard tan.

"I'm just gettin' these ready for the next whitefish catch," she said, in a barbed Lower Michigan accent that cut through her words like a steel drill. "Everybody wants whitefish. We ship a lot to Chicago. Right now, we're shipping a lot to Jewish markets for Rosh Ahana and Yom Kipper. We're shipping a lot of white buffalo, too. Normally, I don't want those, because they're carp and they're bony. But they use 'em as filler for gefilte fish during Rosh Ahana and Yom Kipper. They're supposed to be whitefish, but they put in filler. That's why they're rich. They're Jewish."

When Connie and Tod bought the fish company in the 1970s, they also served carloads of blacks who drove up from Flint for buffalo, catfish, and crappie, the humble species they'd eaten down South.

"We had to hand out numbers. Now they have too much money, or they're on welfare and can't afford it. I still see a few of the die-hards."

As Connie described the tastes of her ethnic customers, two men appeared at the far end of the room.

"You got any fish guts for bear bait?" the larger one called. "We're goin' huntin' in the western UP."

"How much ya need?" Connie asked.

"Four buckets. But I don't want it till Friday."

"OK. I'll freeze the guts for you."

Finally, I got Carolyn's phone numbers. She had two, one for Bay Port, another for Lansing, where she'd worked many years for the state government. Apparently, Smith and her husband were the local eccentrics. Elderly and childless, they lived alone in a big old house, and carried on a tradition their neighbors thought archaic. Sure, the Fish Sandwich Festival was good for Bay Port, Connie said. But Carolyn insisted on mullet sandwiches, and that messy batter, because that was how her father had done it.

"This year they started doing a lot better because they added whitefish," Connie said. "I think they sold over eighty-eight hundred sandwiches. People liked having a choice. And we used a mix for some of the sandwiches. We're trying to get away from her liquid batter. It takes twenty-five to thirty people to stir, and it draws flies."

I stepped out into the parking lot and called Carolyn on my cell phone.

"We just got back from Lansing," Carolyn said when she answered. "We'll be home tonight. Come in through the side door."

The Smiths didn't get many visitors. Their house was nearly hidden by foliage. I walked past a roadside stand, long boarded up, then shuttled through a maze of bowers that lay across my path like layers of green smoke. Finally, I saw Carolyn, standing in the yard with a flashlight. A brown-haired woman, petite as a wren, she wore a housedress, and a pair of laceless sneakers. Like the bird she resembled, her movements were bright and fussy.

"It's not easy to find, is it?"

The kitchen was even more disordered. A garbage bag sagged with files. In the corner, a secretary supported toppling towers of old books. The Smiths lived like professors who need the scent of yellowing paper as much as fresh air. Carolyn cleared a space on the table and set down a scrapbook, fringed with clippings.

"This is my semi-Bible," she said.

It contained everything ever written about Henry Englehart and his fish sandwiches. Carolyn was his heiress, his culinary executor, and she told his legend with the intensity of a biographer relating a lifetime's research.

"My father lived until he was ninety-one," she said. "He was never hospitalized. He had no heart problems. We ate fish every day.

We ate freshwater mullet, herring, perch, whitefish—everything, everything, *everything.*"

Whenever he posed for a photograph, Henry dressed in a tie patterned with fish. At fish conventions, he wore a T-shirt: "I Speak Two Languages, English and Fish." Henry, his daughter related, learned the fish sandwich recipe from a mysterious short order cook who served Bay Port Fish at his diner in Indiana. In 1949, the man took a bus trip to the Thumb and revealed every ingredient to the Engelharts. In exchange, they promised to guard the recipe until their graves, and beyond.

"We're under legal constraints," Carolyn explained. "We have to keep it in the family for one hundred years. You know those ninety-nine-year leases? Nobody knows the recipe but me and my sister. I have a niece I'm going to pass it on to."

Carolyn's mother built a fish sandwich stand in front of the house, selling the treat for twenty-five cents. The stand opened for business each spring when the ice melted on Saginaw Bay, and didn't close until the sugar beet harvest ended, in the fall. At first, the Engelharts used herring, but when that fish disappeared from Lake Huron, they switched to mullet.

The Bay Port sandwich didn't become famous until 1978, when Henry sold the fish company to the Williamses. After a lifetime of working from sunrise to midnight, he was stranded in idleness, so he agreed to chair a fundraiser for the Chamber of Commerce. But even that wasn't work enough, so day after day, he wrote to newspapers, magazines, and TV shows, plugging his hometown's Fish Sandwich Festival. New York editors love Americana. The fruits of his PR blitz were pasted in the scrapbook.

"We were on *20/20, Midwest Living,*" Carolyn said. "He just sat at his typewriter twenty hours a day."

"You know," I told Carolyn, because it was late, and she was eyeing the trash bag of fish sandwich files, "I'm going to have to try a fish sandwich."

She paused, stopped short.

"Well, OK," she said, in a flustered tone. "Let's see—I've got something going in the afternoon, but if you come by around four, we can go over to the fish company and get what we need."

★ ★ ★

Carolyn stood in front of the display case, inspecting herring, catfish, smoked chub, trout, smoked whitefish, salmon, whitefish, perch, and a pat of salmon spread.

An Original Bay Port Fish Sandwich should include mullet, she said, but that fish has become as scarce as herring.

"This summer, I made sandwiches at the Great Lakes Folk Festival in East Lansing, and I had to use whitefish," Carolyn tutted. "I told them, 'Yes, I could get you enough mullet, but you'd have to rob a bank.'"

Connie Williams waited for Carolyn's order, looking bemused, then impatient, by the old woman's nattering. Connie's husband was hanging around the shed that afternoon: the bay was too rough for his dory.

Carolyn decided on two whitefish fillets, and opened a change purse to pay.

"Now I'm going to make it for you with the batter *and* the breading," she said. "The breading is very salty. For anyone with kidney problems, it's not a good thing, but I want you to taste it so you can draw your own conclusions."

Connie's face squinched in distaste. I recalled our earlier conversation.

"It looks like you don't like the batter," I said.

"Nooo. It doesn't have any salt, any spices."

"That masks the taste," Carolyn said firmly.

"Well, let's find out." I shifted a foot toward the door. As we walked toward the car, I looked back to see Connie slumping her shoulders in exasperation.

The kitchen was the least cluttered room in the Smith house. At the counter, Carolyn dumped three cups of flour into a bowl of cornmeal mix. The batter was already prepared—a thin, yellowish broth, like strained egg yolks.

"Lou!" she called to her husband. "Do we have more oil in the basement?"

"What kind?"

"Peanut oil."

Lou appeared at the head of the stairs, holding a bottle of corn oil. Distressed, Carolyn unscrewed the top. Whitefish, corn oil. This was not a Bay Port fish sandwich.

"I don't have any peanut oil because I wasn't prepared," she said. "If you'd called me ahead of time, I'd have had peanut oil."

Carolyn dusted a fillet with cornmeal, dragged another through the batter, and dropped them side by side into a sizzling pan.

"I wish we had fresh, fresh fish off the boat," she lamented. But September was too stormy for a daily haul. "These are a few days old."

The sandwich was devised as a one-handed meal, so the Earl of Sandwich could eat and play cards at the same time. Henry Engelhart wanted his sandwiches to command full manual attention. The fish, he declared, should overlap the bun on both ends. His motto was, "The sandwich so big it takes two hands to eat one."

Carolyn handed me the sandwich. It was a loaf, a football, a torpedo of bread and fish. I took a bite. It was tasteless, airless. The second sandwich, with the breading, was just as bland. What had I expected? Fish sandwiches were out of season. Looking for a Bay Port Fish Sandwich in September was like trying to find good apple cider in February. If I wanted the real thing—mullet, fried in peanut oil— I would have to return for the festival. But even then I might be too late. I asked Carolyn how she felt about the campaign to do away with her secret batter.

"There's no point in worrying," she said. "If it happens, it happens. But then they won't have the original fish sandwich."

Reader, get one while you can.

26

What Do You Do with a Drunken Sailor?

MICHIGAN—ROGERS CITY

Rounding Saginaw Bay, I crossed the mythical Bay City–Muskegon line, a backslash across the Lower Peninsula, dividing the forests of northern Michigan from the rich farms of the south. You can see it on a soil map. Above is loose sand where only hardy evergreens can get a roothold. Beyond Tawas, the leafy trees become rarer by the mile. As I followed a flat, empty, two-lane road through the pines, I knew I was back in the North Country.

Rogers City, the hometown of Jeremiah Grockan and so many other sailors, is as dependent on its lake as any community on the Third Coast. In fact, you could dynamite the roads that link Rogers City to the rest of Michigan, and it would still thrive. This is still a port, a place where people live as close to the water as they can get without building sampans.

The limestone quarry made Rogers City a maritime town. Its owners built a fleet to carry the rock around the Great Lakes, and sailors still call this destination "Calcite." On Quarry View Road, the southern approach to Rogers City, there's a metal viewing platform. Stand on it and look to your right, away from Lake Huron, and you'll see a desert scene. All the greenery has been shaved away. Picks, shovels, and bulldozers have dug through millions of years of rock to uncover a barren, colorless valley: the plateaus between slopes are sprinkled with crumbly stone. This is earth, stripped to white bone.

★ ★ ★

When I walked into the International Sports Bar out of the hard blue late summer afternoon, the room was in a lull between late lunch and happy hour. The barkeep, a potbellied man whose reading glasses rested on his paunch, was stocking a cooler. The keno screen was flashing numbers no one had bet on. And two old men were sitting at the end of the bar, trying to make their Miller High Lifes last until suppertime.

Approaching the bar, I introduced myself.

"I heard about this place from a guy named Jeremiah Grockan, in Cleveland," I told the barkeep. "I met him when I visited the *Calumet*. He said a lot of sailors come here."

"Jeremiah Grockan," he returned, in a wary, nasal drawl. "Yeaaaah. He comes in here."

It's always awkward invading a small-town tavern. Here, every face that came through the door belonged to a Rogers City local or a Great Lakes sailor, right off the boat. So I was twice a stranger.

"I'm writing a book on the Great Lakes, and I'd like to talk to some sailors," I said.

"You wanna talk to some *sailors*?" the barkeep repeated. He gazed at the old men. "This guy sailed for forty years. Talk to him. Hey, Art!"

I don't know if there's a freshwater term for "old salt," but if there is, Art Gapczynski fits it. Eighty years had snatched off most of his hair, so he made do with a ball cap cocked on his scalp. Art's son Mike, the captain of the *Arthur M. Anderson*, owned the International. Art just drank here. We each ordered a beer—there was an hour or two to kill yet—and Art told me sea stories. He'd been born and raised in Rogers City, but the boats took him away before he was old enough to vote, drink, or marry.

"As a kid, during the war, I worked on the fish tugs, and I always looked at them big ships," he said. "When I was in the ninth grade, they were looking for sailors. They came by the school."

Art went to St. Ignace for his sailing card, and the Michigan Limestone Company, which owned the calcite boats, put him to work as a porter. Some guys last a month on the Lakes. Art was the opposite: that was as long as he could stay on land. In ten years, he was a head chef.

"I coulda had a job with my father-in-law," he said. "He was an electrician. He offered me bulldozers, building I-75. I didn't want to get off the lake. I worked in the quarry nine days. I got tired of eatin' dust. When I started sailing, there was no vacations. We started fittin' out March 15, we didn't get back till December 15. When I was home, I had housework. I had ten children. The most I could take was thirty days. I loved that life. It was a good life."

His son Mike was the same. Mike was a "hawspipe": he'd worked his way up from deckhand to captain. In Rogers City, that's upperclass. The captains are the only guys in town pulling down six figures. While Mike sailed, his wife Pam ran the kitchen.

It took an hour for Art to reach the bottom of his beer can, and the end of his career—he was, he said proudly, the patriarch of a family with 282 years on the Lakes. Another son was captain of the *John G. Munson*. A grandson was a deckhand. When Art was finished, Pam dealt out snapshots of her husband's boat.

"He's supposed to be in about 8:30 tomorrow," she said. "My sister tells me I have the best of both worlds, because my husband's never home."

There were eight boats coming in that weekend. Pam kept track of all the shipping schedules. If I hung around, there would be plenty of sailors in and out. So I ate supper at the bar, and sure enough, around seven, the crew of the Canadian freighter *Algorail* began filling the stools. The first to sit down was Alex Mackenzie. Alex had twenty-nine hours left on a three-month tour, and he was in such a hurry to close the gap between his mouth and a glass of beer that he'd called a taxi from the dock. Right away, he ordered a tall stein and began tippling. Alex was getting off at Windsor, the following midnight, and he couldn't wait to sit at home in Niagara Falls with a refrigerator full of Molson.

"When I get off the boat, I just want to be by myself for a few days," he said. "When you're on the boat, you're surrounded by people 24-7. If you've got a roommate, you've got no privacy."

"What about your wife?" I asked.

"Oh, I had two of those. Now I've got Irene. She's my good friend. I've got my place, she's got her place, and it all works out great."

Since I'd been in Ontario the weekend before, refighting the War of 1812, I traded Alex a loonie and a toonie for two American dollars. I fed them to the jukebox, punching in Bob Seger and Kid Rock, two generations of long-haired Michigan rock 'n' rollers. I couldn't step into an Up North bar without playing Seger. Alex followed, playing Eric Clapton's "Bell Bottom Blues" and the Beatles' "Long and Winding Road."

"I know my music," he said. "I just got that new John Hiatt album. You like him? He's a *poet*."

We talked about music, and then we talked politics. A Yank and a Canuck can't go ten minutes without discussing the vast differences between the closest neighbors on Earth.

"You know," Alex said, "not everyone is born with the same amount of brains, so you've gotta have laws to make sure the smart guys don't take advantage of the people who aren't so smart. Here in the States, it's dog eat dog."

"But one of the reasons you're able to have all those social programs is that we're paying the freight to defend this continent," I pointed out.

Alex couldn't dispute that. But he could shift the blame south.

"Fair enough," he said, ducking his head for emphasis. "Fair enough. But no one's making you do that."

Kurt Friedrich, the *Algorail's* electrician, came in from the library across the street, where he'd been checking his e-mail. Kurt kept a bicycle on board for trips into town, and he'd leaned it up against the International. No one was going to steal it in Rogers City.

"Rogers City is one of the friendliest towns for sailors," he said. "In the big cities, like Chicago or Milwaukee, sailors get absorbed. The best sailor bars are in small places, like Ashtabula or Conneaut."

A bald, broad-faced German, Kurt had been sailing since 1978, when a shipping company executive picked him up as he was thumbing a ride from Thunder Bay to Duluth, and offered him a job right there in the car. Kurt lived on the other side of the lake, but as a European, he didn't understand the U.S.-Canadian rivalry. He couldn't see much difference between the Anglo nations.

"This whole Great Lakes," he said, "the language is the same, it's the same people. Ontario, Michigan. I don't know why there's a border. It's just a nuisance."

The last to arrive were Gilbert and Wanda. They'd walked the mile-and-a-half from the dock. Both were in their twenties, and both spoke about the boats with the disillusionment of young sailors who hadn't resigned themselves to life on the Lakes.

"I can last two more years," moaned Wanda, who worked the galley. She was sipping a screwdriver through a straw. "You see the same ports *over* and *over* again."

"That's why I'm switching to deep water," Gilbert said. "I'm going back to school."

They went off to shoot pool, at one of the tables beneath the Big Ten banners. Kurt turned to watch until they were out of earshot.

"A lot of people say they are going to quit, but they stay because of the money," he said. "I had a friend who quit sailing. Once he was back on land, he decided that being on the boats was a waste of life."

Right then, I felt I belonged in the International Sports Bar, sailor or no. It was September 15. I'd been traveling around the Great Lakes for three months—as long as my trip was supposed to have lasted. I should have been home in Chicago that very night. Instead, I was sitting on a barstool hundreds of miles away, looking for conversation and companionship with strangers.

The *Algorail* was sailing at midnight. At 11:00, I offered the crew a ride back to the ship. On the way, we stopped for a final beer at Greka's, a scruffy bar in a gray frame house on a back block.

"I wish I could take you down to our ship," Kurt said. "It used to be so easy, but since September 11, there's so much security."

Then Kurt hopped on his bike, and I drove toward the lights of the ship. Suspended above the water, they formed a fallen constellation. On my way back into town, I passed Kurt. He was pedaling lazily.

"Send me some pictures from the ship!" I shouted.

"Yes!" he said. "You have my e-mail. Keep in touch!"

★ ★ ★

The *Anderson* docked in Rogers City around noon the next day. When I went to the International for lunch, its owner was standing behind the bar.

"Are you Mike?" I asked.

"Captain Mike," he corrected.

Even on the beach, Mike Gapczynski insisted on his rank. Captain Mike showed me a picture of his bar's predecessor, the old International Hotel, an inn and tavern built in 1887. When it burned 110 years later, Mike and Pam rebuilt it as a twenty-first-century sports bar. (I'd heard a complaint about that in Greka's: "The International used to be better before it burned down, but then they made it all *nice*.") Sailors came in because they could cash a check, borrow a twenty, or catch a ride to the dock if they failed to coordinate their drinking with their boat's departure.

"We even helped a sailor who got thrown in the slammer," Captain Mike said. "I bought his bus ticket to Duluth, so he could meet his boat. I got him something to eat, I gave him a blanket."

The captain had an errand to run—time on land was always short—so he left me with Rodney Halterman, a thirty-year sailor.

"There's a bar like this in every port on the Great Lakes," Rodney told me. "The Flatiron Café in Cleveland, Mugshots in Toledo, the Brass Rail in Superior. I could go around the Great Lakes and borrow a hundred dollars in any of the towns I go to. I always see people I know. It's like I got a lot of hometowns."

Rodney's real hometown was Haslett, a suburb of Lansing, my hometown. When I told him that, he asked if I'd ever heard of Kuerbitz Drive.

"I used to *live* on Kuerbitz Drive," I said. "When I was in kindergarten."

"Did you know a Lynn Cummings?"

"Yes! She was the neighborhood hippie. She went to Woodstock. She had a mean dog who always wore a muzzle."

"Yeah, well she's my wife. She was a hermit when I met her. She was living in a cabin in the UP. It works great. We're both pretty independent. I won't see her the whole time from July 15 to January 1. I'm working six months straight."

There was one degree of separation between us. In a portside bar, that's close enough for a long afternoon chat.

★ ★ ★

On my last night in Rogers City, the moon was full. After pitching my tent in the state park, I walked through the trees toward the beach, to watch the lunar dawn. Only once before, on a mountain in southern New Mexico, have I seen moonlight so dissipate darkness. When I emerged from the woods, I squinted to stare at that bright silver eye. My body cast a spindly shadow on the sand. The water glittered like satin turned in the sun. Far down the shore, the lamps of Rogers City were an orange-and-white star map. I couldn't tell whether a ship was loading at Calcite: a native might have noticed that alteration in the pattern of lights. The moon glow was an endless dusk that would last until sunrise. This beach was a planet lit by a weak sun, a place where only raccoons, owls, and other night creatures could see clearly.

In the morning, I went back for the sunrise. The moon was perched above the ragged tree line, opposite the sun, preparing to withdraw for its brilliant successor. I'd found the most remote beach on the Third Coast. Not even the North Shore of Superior is a dark spot on so many travelers' maps.

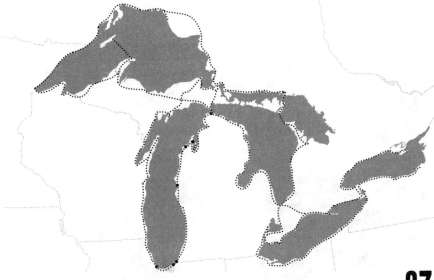

27

My Home Lake

MICHIGAN—MACKINAW CITY, SUTTONS BAY, GLEN ARBOR,
LUDINGTON, NEW BUFFALO; INDIANA—MICHIGAN CITY

As the Lower Peninsula narrowed to a point, I began passing light-houses. Michigan has more than any state. These northern beacons had been built to guide ships through the Straits of Mackinac. They are hardly needed, now that freighters are steered by computers, and the Coast Guard can mount automated lamps on piers. But their brick towers are monuments, reminders that Michiganders are a maritime people. Europe has castles. Michigan has lighthouses, and whenever the federal government abandons one, local history buffs adopt it as a home-improvement project.

The Forty Mile Point Lighthouse is just north of the state park, on Hammond Bay. Forty Mile Point is just that far from both Alpena and Mackinaw City. The tower looks to have been modeled on the guardhouse at Alcatraz: at the top of a white pillar with slit-like windows, a searchlight glows. The roof is surrounded by a railing where sharpshooters might pose. On the beach are the remains of a ship the lighthouse couldn't save: the *Joseph S. Fay*, which ran aground in 1905.

Forty Mile Point Lighthouse.

Nothing is left but an empty shoeprint of blackened slats, a Hiroshima shadow, cast on the sand. Forty Mile Point is a lovely place to rot.

The Front Range Light, in Cheboygan, is much more cheerful, looking like a sided, shingled home whose owner decided that adding a lighthouse to the kitchen would boost his property values. For five dollars, you can tour the digs that the Taft Administration built for the keepers. For even more money, you can buy lighthouse keychains, lighthouse mats, lighthouse mugs, or a lighthouse puzzle, illustrating all the bright spots on Michigan's coasts.

★ ★ ★

I reached Mackinaw City on the third Sunday in September. The Season was long over. The motels, which house ferry-riders who can't afford the Island, were nearly empty. I found a room in an old house by the waterfront. To get my key, I crossed the street to the Mackinaw Bakery. It's the home of the $2.50 Big Mac donut, which is big enough to save a baby from drowning. The floury baker had eaten too many. Her apron was full, like a sail. Her face glowed like a pie from the oven.

"It's fifty a night in the summer," she said, "but this time a year, I'll give it to you for forty."

My room was a five-minute walk from the iconic vista of the state of Michigan, maybe the entire Third Coast: the Old Mackinac Point Lighthouse, with the Bridge in the background. If I'd owned a better camera, it might be on the cover of this book. With the Brooklyn and the Golden Gate, the Mackinac forms a triumvirate of great American bridges. Two hundred-foot towers, the same buff color as the Senate walls, heave a five-mile-long road from Mackinaw City to St. Ignace, in the Upper Peninsula. The green span arches its back above the water like a serpent. The support cables cross the Straits in oscillating waves. Because it opened a wilderness, the Mackinac is even more impressive than its urban rivals. It did not replace the ferry across the Straits until November 1, 1957. That was just in time for deer season, which was causing twelve-mile backups, all the way to Cheboygan, as Detroit shoprats headed for their Upper Peninsula camps.

I would cross the bridge tomorrow. That afternoon, I visited the lighthouse. The guide was dressed in the uniform of the long-defunct United States Lighthouse Service: flat cap, trim blue jacket, just like a railroad conductor. Our tour group included a couple from Nebraska, drawn by the romance of Mackinac. We filed up a corkscrew stairway, crouching to avoid a blow from the landing, and popped up in a stuffy, octagonal chamber, where the lamp was encased in glass, like a precious crystal. It was not lit. The ships don't need it, now that they can set their course by the lights on the bridge. Out a grainy window, I saw the green dome of the island, and the long white block of the Hotel. The Bridge, the Island, the Hotel. At Mackinac they don't need first names. On my first visit to the Straits, I'd been full of questions. Now I simply listened to the spiel. The guide said there was a man in Mackinaw City—lived up the street in a house with an anchor in the yard—who'd grown up in this lighthouse. I wrote down the name: Richard Campbell.

Then, our guide revealed his real identity: he was a retired history teacher at St. Ignace High School.

"So you must know Jim Boynton," I said.

"Oh, gosh, of course. You know Jim?"

"I stayed with him on the island, back in June. He really runs that parish."

"He sure does. I remember I assigned his class to write a paper taking one side of an issue or another. And he wrote one in favor of smoking! He wasn't really in favor of it. He just wanted to see if he could make the case. He was one of the smartest students I ever had."

I ended the afternoon in a tavern, watching the Lions lose to the Bears. Regrettably, I was seated beside a pest unavoidable in any Lake Michigan resort, from New Buffalo to Mackinac: the FIP. FIP is the Michigander's polite acronym for "Fucking Illinois Person," the wealthy Chicagoan who builds a two-million-dollar cottage, then bans deer hunting and snowmobiling on his land. You can usually trap a FIP by placing a *New York Times* in the local party store, or opening a wine tasting room. This FIP was venting his urban tastes by banging the bar when the Bears (a) scored a touchdown, or (b) intercepted a pass. When the Lions fell behind 21–6, I knew their season was over, and so was my drinking.

★ ★ ★

I called Richard Campbell from outside a Laundromat in St. Ignace. I'd needed some excuse to cross the Bridge. This was the same place I'd washed my clothes after leaving Mackinac Island. That made St. Ignace one of three cities I visited twice—Sault Ste. Marie and Windsor were the others—and it made St. Ignace Laundromat the only coin laundry.

"Oh, they told you about me down at the lighthouse, huh?" Richard said, obviously tickled to hear from a writer so early on a Monday morning. He had a story few could tell anymore: a lighthouse childhood. "You come by about two o'clock. I'll be home then."

★ ★ ★

As I vaulted up the approach ramp for the trip back to the Lower Peninsula, I set the trip meter on my odometer. It couldn't be five miles. Five miles would be my daily run, cast in concrete and steel. Five miles is all the hot dogs eaten at the Super Bowl, laid end to end.

Making that leap across the straits, you understand why Big Mac is called a suspension bridge: it suspends you in midair, over blue wings of water spreading away from the narrows. On a windy day in 1989, a Yugo was blown over the railing. Now, Bridge Authority employees will drive the cars of timid motorists. My Neon wasn't much bigger, but it held the white line, and when it came back to Earth, I had driven exactly five miles.

★ ★ ★

Richard Campbell claimed seventy-two years, and a quadroon of Indian blood, but only the latter was obvious, in the ribbon of black hair running down his back. His basement living room, which looked out on the straits, was decorated with trophies from boats that had passed through that nautical door: an axe from the *Cedarville*, lost on Lake Michigan in 1965; a life ring from the ferry *Straits of Mackinac*, put out of business by the Bridge. Richard had lived his life on the water, but he hadn't started at Mackinaw City. He'd started on Huron Island, a rock in Lake Superior so tiny and remote it's not even illustrated on the state map.

As a wounded veteran of World War I, Richard's father, John, was eligible for a lighthouse keeper's job. But that didn't mean he got to choose the lighthouse. Rookies had to take the hardship posts. The only way to make the fourteen-mile trip to Huron Island was to hop a boat in Skanee, a UP fishing village. It had to be a small boat. Huron Island had no marina: visiting vessels were cranked up the dock.

John Campbell and his fellow keepers had to endure this isolation for the entire shipping season, from March to December. Richard

Old Mackinac Point Lighthouse.

spent the cold months at school in L'Anse, but in the summers, he and his three sisters joined the castaway society of Huron Island.

"It was just a big outcropping," he described it. "Being kids, mostly what we did was run around exploring the island. There were a few rabbits, and a lot of caves. We did a lot of swimming in the cold Lake Superior water. We did a lot of fishing. There was no running water, so whenever anyone went down to the boathouse, you carried a bucket of water back with you, for cooking."

He also helped his father with the lighthouse work. The flashing light had to be covered each morning, to keep away dust motes. The house had to be painted, and when anyone spied a Coast Guard inspector, approaching from Skanee, there were frantic episodes of cleaning.

Richard saw a movie once a year. He never drank a chocolate malt. His only books were a chest of musty volumes dropped off annually by the Lighthouse Service's rotating library. One summer, the family's solitude was relieved by a WPA band, which took a fish tug to the island, set up a picnic, and gave a concert. This was in the 1940s, at a United States government installation.

But as a lighthouse boy, Richard learned to fish, and sail, and dive (a skill he'd later use to build the Bridge). He also learned how to be alone. His father, who was half Native American, dealt with the solitude by drinking, like so many other keepers. Richard withdrew into himself. For the rest of his life, he was "a loner to the people," he said. He'd been eager to invite me to his house, and he was telling his story genially, but "I don't belong to any organization," he said. "The only thing I do is volunteer fire department and ambulance service."

When Richard was a teenager, his father was promoted to the Old Mackinac Point Light. The family was thrilled. Living on the mainland, in the middle of Mackinaw City, meant fresh food, running water, walking to school—and togetherness, year-round. They still led an odd home life. Their kitchen was right beside the fog signal, so on damp mornings, "we'd be sitting there talking, and the horn would blow. We would stop talking. It was part of life. People who came to visit couldn't get used to it. They couldn't sleep. It would rattle the dishes and the windows."

When the Bridge opened, Richard's father closed the lighthouse, shipping the equipment to Detroit and moving to Frankfort, on Lake Michigan, which had a lighthouse that still needed tending. Richard stayed on in Mackinaw City, working on the ferries, then for the Bridge Authority. He revisited Huron Island in 1991. The noble stone lighthouse was still standing, but it was powered by a solar generator, maintained by Coasties who visited in a helicopter.

On a table in Richard's basement were albums of black-and-white snapshots from the island, and books whose authors had interviewed him: *Reliving Lighthouse Memories*, *Lighthouse Families*, *Lighthouses of Northern Michigan*. Loner or no, he loves talking to writers, because who else grew up in a lighthouse? The last Great Lakes keeper is retired. Who else can correct the romantic notions of the preservationists, who imagine lighthouse life as a Thoreauvian sojourn?

"I never understand," he said. "People have lighthouse pictures and lighthouse T-shirts. They want to visit every lighthouse on the Great Lakes. But I don't think you could ever find people to live there nowadays. Occasionally, during the war, they'd send out Coast Guard crews, and they couldn't take it."

★ ★ ★

That night, the lake was seething, suffering a storm it could not digest. All day, it had rained, and now, from my room, I could hear surf blasting against the shore. It sounded like a gale, sieved through branches of shuddering leaves. This was the overture to the ship-tossing blows of autumn. Donning a slicker, I walked down to a waterfront park. The gray waves raced up a concrete breakwall, shattering into thousands of droplets that sizzled on the sidewalk. It looked like a painting of a Japanese tsunami.

Dawn wiped the sky clean, but the lake was still unsettled. I had a ticket for a lighthouse cruise, but when I lined up at the dock, a porter appeared with bad news.

"The trip is canceled," she announced. "The water's too rough. It's going to be like this all day."

★ ★ ★

The beach in Wilderness State Park, five miles west of the Bridge, is the upper right-hand corner of Lake Michigan. I was back on my home lake, and it felt almost like home itself, even though I was still sleeping in a tent. On the other side of those surging waters was Chicago. There is a border down the middle of every Great Lake, but the lakes don't divide us, they unite us. In Chicago, I went to sleep every night to the sound of Lake Michigan's surf, just as I did here.

Chicagoans have very little in common with the people who populate the prairies of Illinois. They're citizens of the Third Coast. While the city's middle class vacations in Wisconsin, its upper class summers in Michigan. I'd thought that meant southwest Michigan, where the mayor has a cottage. But really, Harbor County is too close to the hordes. In the northern Lower Peninsula, a Gulfstream hop from O'Hare, I discovered a class of vacationer I'd never imagined. Harbor Springs has a men's store on *Esquire*'s Top 100. It was pushing 50-percent-off shorts, in Palm Beach colors. In Petoskey, I checked

my e-mail in the reading hall of a library as big as a brand-new suburban high school. Cottagers pay double property taxes, so the Rust
Belt has a silver buckle here. Driving through Charlevoix, worrying
lest the bluffs collapse under their monumental white houses, I felt I
was drawing close to some enormous source of wealth, a pot of gold
whose power to gentrify small-town Michigan became stronger with
each passing village. Rounding Grand Traverse Bay at Traverse City
and heading up the little finger of the Leelanau Peninsula, I finally
found it, on St. Joseph's Avenue in Suttons Bay.

★ ★ ★

The cable guy sat down at the bar of the Lucky Duck. He ordered a
Philly cheese with fries. The cable guy brought HBO and the Food
Network to Suttons Bay and the entire Leelanau Peninsula, but he
couldn't afford to live there. He lived in Interlochen, twenty miles
away.

"I call this place Little Detroit," he grumbled. "Land is, like, a
hundred thousand dollars an acre here."

Sipping resentfully at his Coca-Cola—"if I weren't workin', I'd
have something stronger"—he glared at the antiwar ad that had inter-
rupted a CNN hurricane watch.

"You know," he ruminated. "I totally disagree with that ad. My
brother just got back from Iraq, and he's proud of what he did there."

When the cable guy rolled off his stool and went back to work, he
took most of Leelanau County's rural character with him. The bartender
swept away his ketchup-stained basket and scoured the formica with a
wet rag. He'd come up here to sling drinks from Grosse Pointe, where
"kids get BMWs on their sixteenth birthdays." But his real ambition was
to make it as a car salesman in Chicago. He'd turned down a job at a
Mercedes dealership there. "Biggest mistake of my career"—but had
another interview, next month.

Like the Hamptons, the Leelanau is in the country, but it is most
definitely not of the country. I'd first read about the peninsula in *Letters*

from the Leelanau, a book of essays by Kathleen Stocking. A local girl, she's the daughter of Pierce Stocking, who built a scenic drive along the Sleeping Bear Dunes. In the 1960s she went away to the University of Michigan, and then to New York City, but returned home to marry an Odawa man and raise children. It was a good move for a writer. By making her world smaller, Stocking saw more than she could have in a city of millions. At that time, Leelanau was populated by a mix of old-timers and artistic cranks fleeing the big city. Stocking was a bit of both, so she was just as comfortable with the village woodcutter as with novelist Jim Harrison, who lived on the peninsula for many years. Her subjects—a retarded man's birthday, an old fart's coffee club—could have been the stuff of twee newspaper features, but Stocking brought to each a lifetime of observation. After waking to thousands of summer dawns, she could write: "A damp coolness permeated the half-light in my bedroom; outside under the centuries-old maple trees there were pooled dark green lozenges of night." Leelanau County sounded like Brigadoon. It was the little finger of Michigan, another peninsula on a peninsula, a place apart from our gray, factory-stained state.

Before arriving in Leelanau, I'd written Stocking a postcard. Her number was in the phone book, but it didn't seem proper to call a reclusive Northern writer. She might be at her desk, looking out the window at a loon. A few days later, I received a cryptic e-mail, titled "Maybe." "Don't interview writers," Stocking wrote me. "Interview farmers, fisherman, mechanics. Know the names of trees, birds, wildflowers." I replied that I'd interviewed several fishermen, so she agreed to a 7:00 A.M. breakfast at Kejara's Bridge, Lake Leelanau's eco-hippie cafe. Was she trying to put me off? Did she like to build a sense of intrigue before a public appearance? I would find out the next morning.

In the meantime, I poked around Suttons Bay. Across the street from the Lucky Duck is Bahle's, né O.C. Bahle Clothing and Dry Goods, founded 1876. The store has evolved to survive Leelanau's upper-class invasion. For its first hundred years, Bahle's sold overalls to fruit pickers, calico to housewives, black suits to deacons.

Working the sales floor was Mr. Bahle's great-granddaugher Lois, who was dressed as smartly as a real-estate agent, and had learned the poised posture as well. "We sold Hanes underwear," she explained. "That was the high end. We put it in a drawer for the summer when the migrant workers came to pick fruit, because they wanted a cheaper brand of underwear."

Then Lois's brother Karl came home from college with a business degree and shocked the family by ordering half-a-dozen camel-hair coats.

"We sold all six," Lois said, "and my father's next question was 'Can you get more?'"

Karl got more. The money still passed across an old wooden counter, but the washing machines and the rolls of homespun cloth were gone, replaced by Robert Talbot ties. Instead of closing to an end-of-an-era eulogy in the local paper, Bahle's had lived to become the second-oldest family department store in Michigan.

"You go with the flow," Lois said. "I'm just glad my great-grand-father didn't stop before he got to Suttons Bay."

★ ★ ★

The days were still warm in northern Michigan, but the mornings were chilly, and dark. Kathleen Stocking arrived at Kejara's Bridge swaddled in a puffy parka. She was a short woman—shorter than I'd imagined from her author photo. Inside that coat, she looked busy and small. She sat down, and stared at me across the syrup dispenser.

"Take off your hat," she said. "I want to see your eyes."

Those were not the first words Kathleen Stocking spoke to me. But they were the first I remember. I removed the U.S.-Canada cap I'd bought in Sarnia, setting it beside my water glass, self-consciously smoothing my bedhead cowlicks. For thirteen and a half weeks, I had been the observer. Now I was being observed, by a tiny sixty-year-old author whose perceptions were much deeper than my own. I had traveled nine thousand miles, and I knew a little about every place in the Third Coast. She rarely left her native county, but she knew every tree and dune. Now she wanted to know about its latest visitor.

"One of the reasons I was reluctant to meet you was that after I wrote that book, for five years I was like the Chamber of Commerce. Whenever someone wanted to buy land in Leelanau they called me." Then, as intently as a schoolgirl poet, she said, "Tell me about your journey." The diner table brought us as close as opposing chess players.

I told her about the Boat Nerds, and the *Ziemia Łódzka*, about fishing with Harley Toftey and camping with Moses Beaver, about the Emancipation Day picnic, the accordionists of Cleveland, and the Heidelberg Project of Detroit. By the time the vegan pancakes and the tofu scramble arrived, I had taken her on the entire Circle Tour, right up to this restaurant.

"Where did you stay?" she wanted to know.

"At campgrounds. In motels."

"I wrote a book about islands called *Lake Country*," she said. "I slept in my car. I slept at campsites. One night, for some reason, I was in Escanaba, and I had seven dollars, and I was too tired to drive home. I asked if I could sleep in the police station, and they say, 'No way.' It was a time when homeless men were sleeping in Wal-Marts, and so on, and so I slept in my car."

I'd bought a copy of *Lake Country* in Harbor Springs, read it in Traverse City, and had it in the car, ready for her autograph. Since writing that book, she'd taught at a local college, lost that job, and now worked with the homeless. There would be no more books, she said. She no longer had time to write. *Letters from the Leelanau* and *Lake Country* had been products of "luck."

"I got a Michigan Emerging Artists grant, and I was a writer-in-residence for $20,000 a year. Overall, I got $300,000. My first book sold ten thousand copies, and it was reviewed in *The New York Times*. My second book sold almost as many copies. My publisher, University of Michigan, got ten dollars for every copy, and I got seventy cents. I should have self-published."

"Would you be interested in the book I'm writing?" I asked.

"I don't think so," she said, not dismissively, but ruefully. "I'm not interested in Midwestern sense-of-place stories."

"But that's what *you* write," I protested.

"That's what I *wrote*. I'm interested in social issues now. We're living an unsustainable life in this country, with terrible government greed. Whenever a child dies in Darfur, all of us are diminished."

Kathleen Stocking's literary career was a grim topic, so I switched the discussion to Leelanau County. She had grown up right here, in Lake Leelanau. Her parents were well-situated old-line WASPs, the descendants of colonists who'd arrived in New England in the 1630s, and moved west until they'd settled in this cul-de-sac. Even in a community divided between townies and resorters, "we never considered ourselves less than. There was always culture in our house."

Abruptly, she turned the conversation toward me again.

"Where did you summer?"

I was impressed with her timing—only Barbara Walters could spring more quickly—but I laughed at the question. In my family, summer is a noun, not a verb. We were descended—or ascended, as we liked to think—from Georgia crackers who'd made their living by preaching, grist milling, and real-estate speculation. We had culture— our bookshelves were so full that we piled volumes on the carpet— but unlike many of our Michigan-born neighbors, my parents never bought a cottage. My mother was proud of that. "We're not like one of those families with a big boat in the driveway," she'd boasted, as though that frivolous purchase would threaten our real goal: education. As for my father, his idea of the outdoors is a golf course. Lansing is eighty-five miles from a beach, and in my entire childhood, I remember seeing Lake Michigan once, on a weekend trip to Ludington. It was like being English and never visiting the sea. Perhaps that's why I'd wanted to see every corner of the Great Lakes. I was claiming my birthright as a Michigander.

"We never summered," I answered. "I summered in the backyard."

Had I given off an upper-class vibe? Did she think I was one of the resorters who had bedeviled her childhood?

"The children of the locals had jobs," she said. "The children of the resorters had lessons—tennis lessons. If you were good-looking or charismatic, you could snag a rich resorter. Some people would start hanging around the boats when they were teenagers. I knew a few girls who married rich resorters, and it was disastrous. They were like heroines in a Thomas Hardy or a Theodore Dreiser novel. A lot of local people learned skills in carpentry or plumbing and made a good living working for the resorters."

It had been a strange interview. Two writers, going one-on-one, neutralize each other's skills. I had forgotten to ask obvious questions: Where was she working with the homeless? What had her father done for a living? The Stockings were obviously not "less than," because they'd followed paths trodden only by people unworried about money, or status. Pierce Stocking had been an environmentalist, his daughter a writer. Her daughters, who were half-Odawa, had finally moved all the way west, to California.

"My daughters don't want to live here," Kathleen said. "They're very happy in San Francisco. One of my daughters is married to a Tanzanian, and they wouldn't want to live here, because there are no black people."

I paid the bill, then ran out to the car to fetch *Lake Country*, for a signature. The inscription covered the entire title page: "To Ted McClelland, with best wishes for your next book and many more. Kathleen Stocking." Ms. Stocking, if you're reading this after all, I'm wishing you the same.

★ ★ ★

It was a perfect autumn afternoon. Down in East Lansing, the Michigan State Spartans were winning a football game, 52–7. Up in Glen Arbor, I was walking the streets, kicking brittle leaves. They had fallen from the blushing Ents that shaded the village. If Suttons Bay is pretentious, Glen Arbor is pretentiously unpretentious, like the Lands' End catalogue. Its most notable institution, Cherry Republic, sells cherry salsa, cherry burgers, cherry chutney, cherry soda, chocolate-covered cherries, cherry jam, and cherry ice cream, and celebrates its Ben-and-Jerry's quirkiness with pit-spitting contests and the sign "Cherry Republic customs: Declare All Bananas."

At the Leelanau County Museum, I met Laura Quackenbush, who had graduated from my old high school in 1967 and moved Up North fifteen years later "because I had a wooden boat. There aren't too many other wooden boat enthusiasts, so we formed a community here. There are a lot of us here of a certain age, people who came of age in the '60s. Living on a peninsula gives you a strong sense of identity. You know where your boundaries are. There's nothing fuzzy along the edges. I think of Leelanau as feminine. There's a pink glow in the sky from the lake."

The Sleeping Bear Dunes are Leelanau's most feminine feature. Lake and sand are female: they change shape constantly, like a woman maturing, giving birth, and aging. The Natives must have recognized those female qualities: The dunes take their name from a legend about a mother bear who led two cubs across the lake, in flight from a forest fire. The cubs drowned, but the mother waited in the dunes for their return. To console her, the Great Spirit raised their bodies, transforming them into North and South Manitou Islands.

The easternmost dune, which faces a parking lot, is a hundred feet tall, and was speckled with children who climbed it on hands and knees, then rolled down in mummy poses. As I climbed its shifting stairs, I saw another reason the dunes are womanly: this was the loveliest scene in the Third Coast. A white dairy barn rests on the saddlebacked hill that separates Lake Michigan from quicksilver-smooth Glen Lake. The grass in this damp country is a piney green. Far away, over the water, I saw the hazy backs of the Manitous, as insubstantial as smoke.

Hiking toward the beach, I passed through a wilderness of sand. It supports a thin crop of brittle grass and wildflowers. I checked each plant off my laminated brochure: thistle, aster, basswood, dune grass. The overcast sky was rippled like the lake on one of its gray evenings. I was descending my fourth dune, or maybe my fifth, when I encountered a hiker headed inland.

"How much farther to the lake?" I asked him.

"You're almost there."

I was almost there for the next half hour. The crests of each dune are crimped, and on every peak, I expected to see the lake. Instead, I saw another barren depression. It was like marching through the Badlands. When I finally glimpsed the water, it filled the ragged bowl of the crest ahead of me. But then, the more I walked, the less water I saw. I was descending toward the shore, so each peak gave away a narrower slice.

Once I heard the white noise of surf in my left ear, I knew I *was* almost there. But Lake Michigan still took me by surprise. I stepped through a gap in the dune grass, and there it was, as green as jade. This was the hardest-won beach of my life. Right then, I was too tired to walk back, so I lay down on the sand, using the Sleeping Bear Dunes as my pillow.

★ ★ ★

It was the *SS Badger*'s shoulder season. In the summer months, the car ferry runs twice a day between Ludington, Michigan, and Manitowoc, Wisconsin. But in September, the lake is rougher, and the vacationers have gone home, so the *Badger* makes one trip only. In a few more weeks, it would lay up in Ludington's harbor, beside its sister ship, the *SS Spartan*, which hasn't sailed since 1971.

The *Badger* is the last coal-fired ship on the Great Lakes. As it took on a cargo of cars, its tilted stack coughed blackly into the cool morning. I'd been planning this trip since June, when I'd picked up a schedule in Manitowoc. Now I was less than a week from home. The circle was almost closed, but the *Badger* would take me on a detour back to the beginning.

From the parking lot, the ship looked like a building afloat. The cars climbed an on-ramp. I raced up the steps to the passenger deck, which is known as the Steel Beach. In the summer, during night runs, passengers camp out in sleeping bags to see the constellations. Even now, in this flag-snapping weather, jacketed tourists sat on the deck chairs, reddening in the fresh air.

If you want to feel the power of the Great Lakes, you have to sail in the autumn. The waves beneath our hull were six feet high, enough to toss a 410-foot boat, and its passengers' stomachs. Everyone was issued wristbands with metal buttons pressing against the medial nerve, an acupressure point. Still, a woman from North Dakota looked as sickly as the paint on a police station wall. All over the ship, there were blue paper buckets, the type stacked behind concession counters. I didn't smell popcorn, though. Finally, I asked a crew member. "Oh," she said, "those are vomit buckets."

After a few hours of note-taking, I was queasy. Retreating to my cabin, I lay down on the bunk. It was like resting on the belly of— this is not a cliche coming—a sleeping giant. The lake was breathing, exhaling every few seconds. My bed rose and subsided.

The *Badger*'s PR specialist took me to the pilot house. The captain wasn't happy to have a visitor on this rough crossing. When a spume of water splashed through the window, he yanked it shut irritably.

"There's no way these are three-foot waves," he grumbled, and then, without taking his eyes off the pewter sky, he told me, "There's an old sailor saying: 'The best cure for seasickness is lying under a tree.'"

The engine room crew was less agitated. You couldn't even see the waves down there. Bill Kulk, the engineer, stood at the bottom of a narrow, stainless-steel stairway, tending the boiler as Mike Mulligan tended his steam shovel. A coal engine may be a Steam Age relic, but Bill was proud to keep it burning. The *Badger* began its life as a railroad ferry, he explained. Railroads carried plenty of coal, "so you got free fuel, delivered free. That's a pretty good argument. And coal's looking pretty good these days, as expensive as diesel is."

Now the coal arrived in dump trucks—sixty tons a day, enough to fuel one lap of the lake. Below the engine room was the ship's own Hades—the furnace, where the coal was burned. It was inhabited by only two men—the coal passers, who stoked the fire and shoveled away the ash. Their lamplit, subaquatic chamber was as dark as the Kentucky caves where their coal had been mined. Rodney, the senior passer, had been working the furnace for thirty-five years. He liked it down there, Bill said, but he wasn't much of a talker. He might not have much to say.

He didn't, but his partner did. Lonnie Dietz slipped off his fire-proof glove, shook my hand, and handed me three chunks of coal, as a souvenir. The job hadn't turned him into a Morlock. It was darn good to get a visit from upstairs. Lonnie pointed at a vent in the oven-thick metal. Inside, the fire was bright orange, the last stop on the spectrum before white. It seethed at two thousand degrees. The furnace had been lit in April, and would burn until the last voyage was over.

"It gets up to a hunnerd'n'ten degrees in August," Lonnie boasted. Satan was never prouder of his inferno. "You've got to drink a half-gallon of water every four-hour shift. You lose weight. You sweat drastically."

Lonnie didn't mind the heat. Both his parents had worked the *Badger*, his father as a deckhand, his mother as a housekeeper. He wanted work it, too, even if that meant shoveling coal. The ship was the pride of Ludington, his hometown.

"This is World War II material," Lonnie said. "Built in 1953. It's a nice old boat. It's nice to be part of it."

By the time the ship reached Wisconsin, we'd sailed away from the eastering clouds. A chambermaid stood on the Steel Beach, her face lifted to the sun, the lake wind puffing her hair. On the car deck, drivers in *SS Badger* sweaters eased off a truck carrying a giant yellow backhoe. Like parking valets, they raced back and forth, from mini-van to pickup to sedan. As the convoy moved down the ramp, I stepped ashore to call the medical researcher who was subletting my apartment.

"I'll be back in Chicago this week," I told him.

The ferry crosses Lake Michigan at its narrowest point. If you think of the lake as a foot, with the big toe digging into Indiana, this is the instep. Even so, it's a four-hour trip each way—shorter than the nine-hour drive through Chicago, but still a whole afternoon to kill. I watched *Remember the Titans* in the passengers' lounge, then went outside to watch the docking. On deck, I ran into Lonnie. At first, I didn't recognize him. His shift was over, so he'd scrubbed the coal dust from his pink face. Most of the crew lived on the boat, but he was from Ludington, so he could sleep in his own bed, now that the night runs were over. Once the season ended, life would be even better.

"I ice fish, hunt, collect unemployment," he said. "I'm on a men's league bowling team."

Slowed to a knot, the *Badger* drifted between the breakwalls, past the pier-end lighthouse. When the gangway opened, Lonnie Dietz stepped on shore, cradling his lunch cooler under his arm. He was home.

★ ★ ★

A team of surfers brought me back to Chicago. Back in Duluth, I'd seen a documentary called *Unsalted: Surfing the Great Lakes*. The climactic scene took place at Minnesota Point, in January, with California surf dudes in double wetsuits riding twenty-eight-foot Lake Superior waves. The Duluthians went nuts.

Unsalted's director, Vince Deur, lives in Grand Haven, Michigan. After the show, I told him I'd be coming through in September. That's surf season on Lake Michigan: the water is churning, but it's not yet cold. Now that I'd made it, Vince was in Los Angeles, promoting the movie. So he e-mailed me the number of Chris Matteson, one of his surf buddies. On a Wednesday night, I called.

"Yeah, we're going out tomorrow, if the weather's right," Chris told me. "We'll be checking the buoy reports up and down the coast first thing. Give me your cell, and I'll give you a call when we pick a spot."

At 8:00 A.M., my phone rang.

"We're going to South Haven," Chris reported.

South Haven is fifty miles down the shore. I was halfway there when my phone rang again.

"Change of plans," Chris reported. "There's no waves at South Haven. We're gonna try New Buffalo," which was fifty miles more, right on the Michigan-Indiana line. "There's a storm from the north, collecting at the bottom of the lake."

The surfers were gathered by the pier. They had already changed into their wetsuits. Ryan, the test surfer, was carrying his board over a breakwall.

"Man, I wish we'd known you were coming sooner," Chris said. "We would have gotten you a wetsuit and a board."

"I'll just take pictures," I said, opening my camera. "And I'll take notes. You can tell me about surfing in Lake Michigan."

"I started windsurfing when I was fourteen," he began. "A lot of times, the wind would die down, and we'd ride the waves, for something to do."

Since then, a surf scene has grown up in southwest Michigan. The Third Coast Surf Shop opened in New Buffalo, an author calling himself P. L. Strazz wrote a guidebook, *Surfing the Great Lakes*, and Vince filmed his movie. Now Chris was the operator on a phone bank that lit up every fall. In September and October, most of his cell phone minutes were consumed by calls beginning, "Where's the waves?"

Ryan paddled back to shore, with bad news. The waves were too choppy. You couldn't catch a good, long swell.

"Well, let's try Michigan City," Chris suggested.

That was over the border. Surfing Indiana sounds as ludicrous as a cattle drive across Delaware, but I followed the caravan south, to a coal-fired power plant. There, Chris and his friends finally found their waves. Next to the plant's Devil's Tower smokestack was a little har-